MARC BOLAN
1947-1977
A CHRONOLOGY

This edition published in 2002 by Helter Skelter Publishing
Denmark Street, London WC2H 8LL

Copyright 2002 © Cliff McLenehan
The right of Cliff McLenehan to be identified as author of this work has been asserted by him
in accordance with Section 77 of the Copyright, Design and Patents Act, 1988

First published in Germany by Zinc Alloy Gmbh

All rights reserved
Typesetting and design by Richard Prochazka, Bolzanova, 6a, 618 00, Brno, Czech Republic
with additional work by Caroline Walker
Printed in Great Britain by The Bath Press, Bath

A CIP record for this book is available from the British Library

ISBN 1-900924-42-0

MARC BOLAN
1947–1977
A CHRONOLOGY

Helter
Skelter

Publishing

Contents

Introduction

Since the first edition of this book came out as a privately published hardback in 1999, a considerable amount of new information regarding Marc Bolan's career has become extant. This includes information on recording sessions, television appearances as well as concerts. As I write this new introduction, the 25th anniversary of Bolan's tragic death is drawing increasingly closer. Now seems an appropriate time to make this new information more generally available. It also affords me the opportunity of correcting errors which appeared in the first edition of the book, as well as giving me the chance to re-write passages with which, in retrospect, I wasn't particularly happy with.

If you're coming in a little late and are unaware of the existence of the first edition (and hopefully there are a few thousand of you), I'd like to take the opportunity to restate some of what I wrote three years ago. The book represents a comprehensive attempt to chronicle the career of Marc Bolan. It's not the first, however. The credit for that must go to Dave Williams who, back in 1985 or 1986, included a live date chronology in his privately published book 'The Motivator'. I remember seeing the book at Nikki Sudden's place in 1986 and being suitably impressed. Have to be honest Dave, I didn't buy a copy. I just wrote out the information. Belated apologies.

What I didn't realise at the time was that Dave had made some serious errors in his research, including duplicating autumn 1970 concert dates in that of 1968. These errors were then compounded by a couple of unscrupulous apples (work it out friends), who used his work, uncredited, passing it off as their own. What's important though, is that Dave Williams did this work. I think every Bolan fan owes him some gratitude for this for being the one who started the ball rolling.

My interest in doing this project was further stimulated on the same visit to Nikki's place. I was reading a Fairport Convention fanzine which contained an article about the group's BBC sessions. After reading the article, I realised it was possible to obtain the same information about Marc Bolan's radio sessions with Tyrannosaurus and T. Rex. I had made an attempt in 1979 to find out about the sessions by contacting BBC producer Tony Wilson. He informed me that it wasn't possible, but at least they played a selection of sessions on Tommy Vance's Friday night rock show on Radio One.

A few weeks after the visit to Nikki's, I found myself at the BBC Written Archive Centre in Caversham, near Reading in England, where I spent two days combing through their microfilms, coming away, not only with details of the radio sessions, but also of the many T. Rex BBC television appearances. The method of research wasn't foolproof however. I was working from a list of contract dates which had been given to me. In the process, some were obviously missed.

Anyway, I'd like to thank the staff at BBC Written Archive Centre for their assistance, particularly John, whose surname I've regrettably forgotten. This research subsequently formed the basis of articles that I wrote for Record Collector magazine in England.

From that point the project just seemed to explode. In the beginning I was content to add to Dave's core information; tweaking it a bit here and there. However, having realised that there was a serious problem with his chronology, I ditched everything and started again. I went back to the sources of Dave's original data - the British weekly music press. I spent hours carefully checking old issues of the Melody Maker, Sounds, New Musical Express et al, scouring the news sections and live ad pages, re-reading interviews, record and concert reviews, all in an attempt to try and piece together a chronology of what actually happened, and where and when. In addition to the British music press, I also spent a great deal of time looking at newspapers and magazines from North America, Europe and Australia. The Japanese press defeated me, however.

Most of the work was done at the following libraries: National Sound Archive, Kensington, London; The British Newspaper Library, Colindale, London; The British Library, Bloomsbury, London. I'd like to thank the staff at these institutions for the (unwitting) assistance they gave me.

Rereading the press was an education in itself. Memories of half remembered interviews were stirred. As was the spitefulness of the British music press, something I had largely forgotten about in the wake of Bolan's posthumous rehabilitation. To be honest, I could have done without that. When Bolan made his initial commercial breakthrough in 1971 the British music press were generally favourably disposed towards him. Indeed, he was very much championed by journalists such as Chris Welch and Nick Logan. Unfortunately, somewhere along the line, there was a change in mood. The knives came out and these were viciously wielded. One or two journalists (the aforementioned Chris Welch, Geoff Barton of Sounds and Rosalind Russell) stuck by Marc. The majority, a bunch of disaffected pseudo-radical hippies, took the opportunity to settle old scores.

True, Bolan was no angel and he often deliberately baited the press with a series of provocative statements. However, a large amount of the material written about Bolan and T. Rex which surfaced in print, couldn't, under any liberal definition of the word, be described as criticism. It was abuse, plain and simple. With the onset of punk and a new generation of music critics (Paul Morley et al), the press began to take a more measured view of Marc and his music. The venom that had been prevalent from mid-1972 to early 1976 largely dissipated. I've tried to give a feeling of this by including extracts from contemporary record and concert reviews.

The following British music newspapers proved to be invaluable sources: Disc (And Music Echo), Melody Maker, Music Now, New Musical Express, Record Mirror and Sounds. Other magazines and newspapers which were consulted include the following: Abendzeitung München, Beat Instrumental, Berlingske Tdende, Best, Billboard, Bravo, Calgary Herald, Chicago Tribune, Edmonton Journal, Frankfurter Allgemeiner Zeitung, Frankfurter Rundschau, Gandalf's Garden, General-Anzeiger Wuppertal, The Globe and Mail Winnipeg, Hamburger Abendblatt, Information (Copenhagen), International Times, Leatherhead Advertiser And Country Post, Los Angeles Times, Mannheimer Morgen, Music Now, New York Times, Nürnberger Nachrichten, Nürnberger Zeitung, Radio Times, Record Collector, Rheinische Post, Rock et Folk, Rolling Stone, Saarbrücken Zeitung, San Francisco Chronicle, Svenska Dagbladet, Tageszeitung München, Time Out, The Toronto Star, Trouser Press, TV Times, Univibes, Vancouver Sun, Washington Post, Westdeutsche Allgemeiner Zeitung, Winnipeg Free Press.

Several T. Rex fanzines also proved to be invaluable sources. I would especially like to credit Cosmic Dancer, Electric Warrior Free Press, Rumblings and T. Rex Unchained. I also re-read the original T. Rex Fan Club Newsletters.

Of course not everything in this book is down solely to my research. I had considerable help from many individuals. Major assistance above and beyond the call of duty has come from Uwe Klee for detailed proofing, correction, research in German libraries and other services. Irving Campbell also contributed with useful information and acute analysis. Mick Grey a.k.a. Mickey Marmalade provided detailed tour information. Clive Zone was inspirational with his insights into Bolan's early career, as well as providing some interesting information from important sources. Rick Dalvano provided Internet assistance and expended a lot of energy publicising the project among the T. Rex Internet community. Peter Todd provided considerable amount of information regarding Marc's recording sessions. This helped me to correct a lot of suppositions regarding dates. Jorg Gunther and Claus Rasmussen helped with information about a variety of European and non-British television appearances. Nikki Sudden provided flashes of inspiration. Russ Thomas also helped provide Internet publicity. Finally I'd like to thank Jorgen Angel for the beautiful photos.

Numerous individuals also helped (wittingly and unwittingly) with snippets of information. Oh the joys of E-mail (and the pain of huge phone bills)! In alphabetical order: Ruth Anderson, Göran Assner, Keith Badman, Martin Barden, Alastair Barrow, Boz Boorer, Billy Chainsaw, Pierre Champion for French reviews and translations, Jorgen Claesson for the same, but in Swedish, Ros Davies, Jeff Dexter, Peter Doggett, Thomas Freitag, Caesar Glebbeek, Christian Douglas Goodwillie, Bolle Gregmar at the Blue Oyster Fan Club in Los Angeles, Steve Gridley, Clinton Heylin, Douglas Hinman, Colm Jackson, Syd Jerram, Paul Johnson, Klemens Jäger, Brian Joseph Kotz, Wolfgang Kowalski, Alan Lauchlan, Bill Legend, Natalie McDonald, Bill Manny at Medford Mail Tribune, Mark McLellan, Serge Mironneau, Randy Mitchell, Bob Moesse, Patrick Motteau, Anne Nightingale, Alys Palmer, Mark Paytress, John Peel, Nigel Pickup, Mike Plumbley at Isle Of Wight Rock, George Rab, Ian Russell, Steven Severin, The Till Dawn subscribers list, Johan Tommervik, Peter Van Houten, Tony Visconti for additions to recording session information, Barrie Wilkinson, Wesley Willis and Wolfgang Wüst. If there's anybody I've missed out, profuse apologies and blame it on the tequila.

No thanks are due to one or two members of the T. Rex "elite" who withheld information, hiding behind a "We know something you don't and we're not gonna tell you" attitude.

Finally, the big proviso. I cannot guarantee that everything in this book is 100% accurate. In the previous edition I did put two and two together and came up with five. I've been appraised of most of many of these errors and made necessary corrections. But, maths is still not my strongest subject, so I've now probably come up with six in one or two instances.

Concert dates get cancelled; new dates are added to a tour at the last minute; others are rescheduled, or the venue is changed. The situation regarding recording sessions is even worse where the dates and contents written on track sheets of tape boxes, which one would imagine to be accurate and consistent, often contradict each other. I've not had the luxury of hearing a tape of every single recording session Bolan undertook, but I have heard a substantial number and done my best. Frequently, the track sheets of a tape and the actual contents of the tape don't match. If I've got it wrong somewhere, I'd love to know, but please, in the nicest way possible. Any further information would be gratefully received. I can be contacted via e-mail at klif@hotmail.com. Please use "Bolan info" as the subject header. At some point in the future, probably via my website, I'll provide details of new information and corrections.

Finally, this book is dedicated to all the people who have had to put up with me during the course of its writing. As before, it's especially dedicated to my parents and my wife Martina.

Cliff McLenehan
Brno, Czech Republic May 2002

Chronology note:

Not every date listed here can be confirmed. Where I've had to make an educated guess, either about the date or place, a question mark appears immediately after the entry in question. Where I haven't been able to confirm if a concert actually took place, despite being scheduled, a note to the effect appears in the text.

All given British counties are subject to the Local Government Reorganisation Act of 1974.

The Early Years

Bolan's formative years are clouded in mystery. Much of this can be attributed to Marc spinning a yarn for the benefit of good press copy and deliberately obscuring the reality, in order both to embellish the truth and to bolster the image he had created for himself. This was pretty standard practice for the early Sixties pop industry, and was nothing more than an adoption of the old Hollywood film studio trick of inventing an exotic past for the star, in order to hide a more mundane reality. It's a trick Bolan learnt extremely well and which he used constantly throughout the remainder of his career.

This deliberate masking of reality also had the added advantage of, should Bolan ever become successful, making it extremely difficult for any future journalist to go scrabbling around in the dirt, looking for skeletons in the closet. It also makes the job of a more serious biographer much harder. After all, it's much better to be thought of as a strange elvan child rather than an archetypal street hustler from Hackney; the truth lying somewhere between the two.

What follows in this section are a variety of early events that can, to an extent, be verified by outside sources, the Press or other contemporary documentation. Other entries are included as the balance of probabilities is such that they are likely to be grounded more in reality than fantasy.

For the entries chronicling the early years, I have referred to 'Bolan' by his true name, Mark Feld, rather than the 'professional' name Marc Bolan. I have maintained this up until the time of the release of 'The Wizard', when the professional name made its debut.

1947
30th September
Hackney Hospital, Hackney, London, England
Mark Feld is born at the above hospital in East London. The family home is located at 25 Stoke Newington Common, London.

1952
September
Northwold Road Primary School, Stoke Newington, London, England
Mark begins to attend the above school.

1959
September
William Wordsworth Secondary Modern School, Wordsworth Road, London, England
Mark begins to attend the above secondary school.

1960
Summer (?)

Mark forms his first group, Suzie And The Hula-Hoops. The band consists of Stephen Gould, Melvyn Fields, Helen Shapiro, Susan Sugar and Mark Feld. Rehearsals are held in Mark's front room and two performances are given, one at a local cafe and another at a local school.

1962
May / June (?)

Mark gains his first press exposure when he and a group of his friends are photographed and interviewed for an article about mods in the magazine 'Town'. The article was titled 'Faces Without Shadows' and was published in the September edition of the magazine. The portrait is not entirely flattering and it's prediction of young men running nowhere fast proved, in Mark's case, to be wide of the mark.

Summer (?)

The Feld family moves from Hackney to Summerstown near Wimbledon in south-west London.

1963
Spring (?)

Joe Meek's Studio, 304 Holloway Road, London, England

Mark visits record producer Joe Meek in an attempt to get Meek to produce him and to launch his career as a singer. It's probable that one song was recorded, 'Mrs. Jones'. However, there is no documentation on the surviving acetate to confirm that it is Bolan. The consensus of opinion among Meek fans and certain Marc Bolan fans is that it is Mark Feld; others disagree. In the event, nothing substantial resulted from the connection.

1964
Summer (?)

Mark does modelling work for the Littlewood's Autumn/Winter mail-order catalogue. He also models for John Temple's 'Styles To Suit You, Suits To Style You' brochure.

October (?)

Mark moves to 81 Lexham Gardens, Kensington, London. He shares a flat with Allan Warren who acts as his manager.

December (?)

Regent Sound Studios, London, England

A possible date for Mark's first proper demo session. Another unidentified guitar player accompanied him. Speculation remains as to which songs were recorded at the two-hour session. Allan Warren recalls the Bob Dylan song 'Blowin' In The Wind' and one other song being committed to tape and has suggested 'The Perfumed Garden Of Gulliver Smith' as a contender for the second title. However, it is possible that Warren has confused this session with the following one.

1965

January (?)
Maximum Sound Studios, 47 Dean St., London, England
Mark's second (?) demo session took place at the above studio. He sang and played harmonica and was accompanied by an unknown guitar player, probably the same one who worked at the earlier session at Regent Sound Studios, (assuming there was a session there). Multiple takes of two songs were recorded; a (second) version of 'Blowin' In The Wind' and a version of the Dion song 'The Road I'm On (Gloria)'. The tape originally featured the song credited to Mark Feld. However, this has been scribbled out and in its place, in Mark's handwriting, the name Toby Tyler has been written.

January (?)
Mike McGrath's Flat, Earls Court Square, London, England
Probably the first photo session of Mark as a musician was taken by Mike McGrath at his Earls Court Square flat and outside in the street.

Tuesday 16th February
EMI Studio 3, Abbey Road, London, England
Mark attended a short demo session for EMI subsidiary Columbia Records. The session lasted all of fifteen minutes, from 3.45 p.m. until 4.00 p.m. He performed Betty Everett's 'You're No Good' and was rejected by A&R man John Pearson. It's not known whether Marc accompanied himself on guitar or if he sang solo. Piano player Syd Hadden was on hand at the session to provide any required musical assistance.

Wednesday 12th May
Levy's Recording Studio, New Bond Street, London, England
Mark allegedly attended a Bob Dylan recording session held on this date at the above studio. The session involved John Mayall's Bluesbreakers as Dylan's backing band.

Saturday 29th May
Mark attends a Campaign for Nuclear Disarmament rally in London and is photographed at the head of the crowd alongside Joan Baez, Donovan and Tom Paxton.

Summer (?)
The Pontiac Club, Putney, London, England
Mark's only known concert performance from this period took place at the above club. He was

probably still using the name Toby Tyler at the time. However, this name does not appear in any of the club's concert schedules from the period; neither do the names Mark Feld or Marc Bolan. The appearance was probably a support slot. The concert was given a brief mention in a folk magazine.

Summer (?)
Around this time Mark allegedly obtains parts as an extra in the children's TV series 'Orlando'. This remains unconfirmed.

Monday 9th August
Marc officially signs to Decca Records on this date. The deal was obtained after Mike Pruskin, acting as his manager, took a tape of him performing an acoustic version of 'The Wizard' to Decca.

According to an issue of 'London Life' magazine, dated September 1965, Marc had originally planned to use the professional name of Bolam, but a misspelling on the contracts resulted in the name Bolan.

September (?)
Marc moves to 22 Manchester Street, London, where he shares a basement flat with Mike Pruskin.

Tuesday 14th September
Decca Studios, Broadhurst Gardens, West Hampstead, London, England
The date for Bolan's first full recording session. Jim Economides acted as producer, with Mike Leander employed as musical arranger. A total of three songs were recorded at the two-hour session. These were 'The Wizard', 'Beyond The Rising Sun' and 'That's The Bag I'm In'. The Ladybirds provided backing vocals, with other instrumentation supplied by unidentified session musicians. 'That's The Bag I'm In' was left unreleased at the time and this remains the case to this day.

Friday 1st October
Photographer David Wedgebury did a photo session of Marc for Decca.

Sunday 17th October
22 Manchester Street, London, England
An interview, along with a photo session, was conducted at Mike Pruskin's flat for 'Queen' magazine.

Tuesday 9th November
Studio One, Wembley, Middlesex, England
With Decca's weight behind him, Marc was able to secure a slot performing 'The Wizard' on Redifussion's 'Ready, Steady, Go'. The show was broadcast on the 12th November. Bolan later described his television debut as a disaster with the studio band playing the song in the wrong key and at the wrong tempo.

Thursday 11th November
Decca Studios, Broadhurst Gardens, West Hampstead, London, England
A production tape was made of 'The Wizard' and 'Beyond The Rising Sun'.

Friday 12th November
Broadcast date for Marc's appearance on 'Ready, Steady, Go'.

Thursday 18th November (?)
ATV Studios, London, England
Marc's second TV performance to promote 'The Wizard' took place on the programme 'Five O' Clock Fun Fair'. The programme was broadcast on 23rd November.

Friday 19th November
The Wizard / Beyond The Rising Sun (Decca F12288)
Despite failing commercially, the single did receive some reasonable reviews:
"... it has a most intriguing lyric, and his Sonny Bono-like voice is offset by a solid thumping beat and ethereal voices ..."

Derek Johnson, NME

"It's a very raw sound, like Barry McGuire, which is a bit too raucous for the hit parade. It doesn't do anything for me."

Judith Durham (The Seekers), Blind Date, Melody Maker

"On the strength of this strange young man's looks and weird background I suspect we'll hear more of this odd record... I prefer the other side, 'Beyond The Rising Sun' which has more tune. Jim Economides, ace producer, does lovely things on this. I'm a bit put off by the way this boy sings with Dylan phrasing, but that's all."

Disc

Glad Rag Ball, Empire Pool, Wembley, Middlesex, England
Bolan played a short three-song set, sandwiched between more heavyweight artists such as The Who, Donovan and The Hollies among others. He was a last-minute addition to the bill, replacing blues artist John Lee Hooker. The television company ATV filmed the concert and edited highlights were broadcast on 8th December. It's not known if any of Bolan's performance was included in the final programme.

Tuesday 23rd November
Broadcast date on ITV networks of the edition of 'Five O' Clock Fun Fair' featuring Marc's performance of 'The Wizard'. See entry for 18th November.

Monday 6th December
Highgate Cemetary, Highgate, London, England
A photo shoot of Marc is held at the cemetery by photographer Tony Prime from the British newspaper 'The Observer'.

Tuesday 7th December
Alpha Studios, Aston, Birmingham, Warwickshire, England
Marc recorded an appearance on ABC Television's 'Thank Your Lucky Stars', again performing 'The Wizard'. He was paid thirty-seven pounds and sixteen shillings for the performance and also received a Second Class return train ticket. He appeared alongside Freddie And The

Dreamers, Vince Hill and The Merseybeats amongst others. The show was broadcast on the 18th December.

Wednesday 8th December

Broadcast date on ITV networks for 'Glad Rag Ball'. Though it's not certain if Bolan's perform-ance was included in the final edit of the programme, his name appears in an article that accompanied the programme in that week's edition of 'TV Times'. See entry for 19th November.

December

Fleetway House, London, England

In the middle of the month Marc attends the 'Fab 208' magazine Christmas party, being pho-tographed with Helen Shapiro.

Saturday 18th December

Broadcast date on ITV networks for the edition of 'Thank Your Lucky Stars' of Marc's perform-ance of 'The Wizard'. See entry for 7th December.

Thursday 30th December

Decca Studios, Broadhurst Gardens, West Hampstead, London, England

Despite the lack of success with 'The Wizard', Decca called for further recordings from Bolan. This second studio session, with Jim Economides and Mike Leander in control again, saw four songs recorded: 'Rings Of Fortune', 'A Song For A Soldier', 'Highways' and 'Reality'. All four songs were left in the can and to date have not been released. 'A Song For A Soldier' is some-times erroneously entitled 'A Soldier's Song'. Bolan provided vocals at the session; session musicians probably provided other instrumentation. However the master tape for the session has gone missing from the Decca tape library.

As this book was being completed, four acetates, each containing one of the above songs, were due to be auctioned at Christie's in London. The versions of the songs on the acetates are all solo acoustic demos. It is a possibility that the reason that a tape of the session cannot be found in Decca's vaults is that there never was one in the first instance; the songs never having proceeded beyond the acoustic demo stage.

1966

Spring

Unconfirmed studio, London, England

Following Bolan's December session for Decca, the company called for no more studio sessions from their recent signing. As a result of this decision, Jim Economides arranged for 'The Third Degree' and 'San Francisco Poet' to be independently produced and offered to interested companies. Marc played guitar with other instrumentation provided by session musicians, possibly Jimmy Page and John Paul Jones among them.

Friday 3rd June

The Third Degree / San Francisco Poet (Decca F12413)

Despite being unwilling to bankroll studio sessions at their own studios, Decca decided to lease the independently produced recordings from Economides. Like 'The Wizard' before it, 'The Third Degree' was a commercial flop and Decca stopped pursuing their interest.

"... (a) contagious driving shake beat (which) keeps you moving to the rhythm, as Marc dual tracks this swinger."

Anonymous review

October (?)

De Lane Lea Studios, 129 Kingsway, London, England

Studio session(s) Marc Bolan – vocals, acoustic guitar.

Having gained the attention of noted record producer Simon Napier-Bell by using the pretext of wishing to deliver a demo tape and then turning up on the producer's doorstep to actually perform his songs, Marc was back in a recording studio putting down acoustic demos of his material. The sessions were probably held during time left over at the end of studio sessions by Napier-Bell's other acts.

In all likelihood, all the songs that were recorded were cut over two evening sessions. A total of fourteen known titles were committed to tape: 'Hippy Gumbo', 'I'm Weird', 'Charlie', 'Jasmine 49', 'Eastern Spell', 'Horrible Breath', 'Mustang Ford', 'Cat Black', 'Hot Rod Mama', 'Black And White Incident', 'Observations', 'You Got The Power', 'Pictures Of Purple People' and 'The Perfumed Garden Of Gulliver Smith'.

Some additional production work was done to 'Observations', possibly at a later date. One version contains a single piano overdub. Another mix features two piano tracks.

November (?)
De Lane Lea Studios, 129 Kingsway, London, England
After having chosen 'Hippy Gumbo' as a candidate for possible single release, Napier-Bell booked a further session to re-record the song with the addition of strings, which he felt were needed to give the recording a stronger presence. Dave Siddle was the engineer at the session. Two takes were recorded. It's unclear whether the basic track for 'Misfit' was recorded at this session. It may well have been recorded at a different time.

Friday 25th November
Hippy Gumbo / Misfit (Parlophone R5539)
Owing to his success as manager of The Yardbirds, Napier-Bell was able to secure a one-off single deal with EMI subsidiary Parlophone. Like the preceding singles, 'Hippy Gumbo' was a commercial flop. It did, however, bring Bolan to the attention of DJ John Peel.

Tuesday 13th December
Studio One, Wembley, Middlesex, England
Marc's second appearance on 'Ready, Steady Go' coincided with Jimi Hendrix's debut on British television. Marc sang 'Hippy Gumbo'. The programme was broadcast on 16th December. Marc had originally been scheduled to appear on the previous week's edition, but that appearance appears to have been cancelled.

Friday 16th December
Broadcast date for Marc's performance of 'Hippy Gumbo' on 'Ready Steady Go'.

1967

Despite the failure of 'Hippy Gumbo', it seems that Napier-Bell was willing to record a potential follow-up single, 'Jasper C. Debussy'. Unfortunately, it seems he was unable to secure a release for the prospective disc. Napier-Bell then suggested that Bolan join another of the artists under his management, the psychedelic mod group John's Children. It's highly possible that both Bolan and Napier-Bell envisaged a separate solo career running in tandem with the participation in John's Children.

January (?)

Advision Studios, 23 Gosfield Street, London, England (?)
The planned follow-up single, 'Jasper C. Debussy' was recorded with heavyweight session musicians Big Jim Sullivan on guitar, John Paul Jones on bass, Nicky Hopkins on piano and Clem Cattini on drums. Two mixes were prepared. One featuring additional handclaps. The song was not properly issued until 1974.

JOHN'S CHILDREN

ANDY ELLISON – vocals. MARC BOLAN – guitar, backing vocals. JOHN HEWLETT – bass guitar. CHRIS TOWNSON – drums

Bolan was later to suggest that he was only in John's Children for a few weeks. In fact his tenure in the band, though brief, was much longer than he was ever willing to admit to. He probably began rehearsing with the band in late February and didn't leave their ranks until early July.

March

Unconfirmed venue, Watford, Middlesex, England
Marc's debut with the band allegedly took place in Watford, probably at a youth club hall.

Friday 10th March

Bluesette Club, Leatherhead, Surrey, England
Prior to the concert, during rehearsal, John's Children were interviewed by New Musical Express journalist Keith Altham. By this stage Marc was definitely a member of the group.

---

bluesette club
BRIDGE STREET, LEATHERHEAD

FRIDAY, 10th MARCH

grand opening night

JOHN'S CHILDREN

and

THE A-JAES

Admission, 7/-.

The club has been completely re-decorated!

SUNDAY, 12th MARCH

THE GRAHAM BOND ORGANISATION

Admission, 7/-.

Friday 24th March
Tiles Club, Oxford Street, London, England
John's Children play support to The Easybeats.

Tuesday 28th March
Advision Studios, 23 Gosfield Street, London, England
Photographs were taken at Advision Studios for North London Newspaper.

Sunday 2nd April
Bluesette Club, Leatherhead, Surrey, England

GERMAN TOUR

Stories regarding John's Children's tour of Germany supporting The Who have now passed into rock legend. Previously, it was thought that the band played only three or four shows before being thrown off the tour by The Who's management, after provoking a riot in Ludwigshafen, which prevented The Who from taking the stage. Recent research has shown that they managed five and The Who did play in Ludwigshafen.

John's Children arrived in Germany, at Essen Airport, on 7th April. The tour started the following day, 8th April. By the 14th April, when The Who played in Münster at Münsterlandhalle, they were no longer part of the tour.

The band had stirred up some strong reactions, with at least one audience member, a British soldier stationed in Germany, who had caught the Düsseldorf show, feeling compelled to write to the press voicing his disgust at the band's antics.

A hand-written note in one of Marc's notebooks from the time indicates that the band's probable set list for the concerts was: 'The Third Degree', 'Jagged Time Lapse', 'Smashed Blocked', 'Desdemona', 'Mustang Ford', 'Hot Rod Mama', 'Remember Thomas A Beckett (Freak Out)'.

Saturday 8th April
Messehalle, Nuremburg, West Germany
Support to The Who.
The concert was originally scheduled to take place at the Meistersingerhalle. It's possible that the Meistersingerhalle and Messehalle are one and the same.

"Before (The Who went on stage), the four snow-white dressed John's Children ... demonstrated what the listeners were to expect: the guests from England rolled over the floor, writhing convulsively, beat themselves up, smashing lamps and chairs. "

ab, Nürnberger Zeitung

Sunday 9th April
Thalia-Theater, Wuppertal, West Germany
Support to The Who.

Monday 10th April
Jaguar Club, Herford, West Germany
Support to The Who.
Apparently parts of the concert were filmed by the club owner.

Tuesday 11th April

Rheinhalle, Düsseldorf, West Germany

Support to The Who.

   "The climax of the spectacle came with John's Children ... they wildly stamped around the stage, jumped into the audience, lashed out with metal chains and guitars, kicked around the amps, slit open a pillow and finally rolled among the feathers. One guitarist was so exhausted, he had to be carried off stage."

Uwe Witsch, Rheinische Post

Wednesday 12th April

Frederich Eberthalle, Ludwigshafen, West Germany

Support to The Who.

   "... John's Children turned out to be very "lively" children. They were dressed in bright white, the same colour that the hall owner's face was changing into, as they jumped around the stage. As if chased by a thousand devils, the singer jumped into the audience, running through the aisles, throwing confetti over people. Immediately he was back on stage to sing 10 bars before leaping back into the lion's den. Now the hall went crazy. Each new attempt of the wandering singer to run through the hall was forcibly stopped by the bouncers... The stage wasn't capable of containing the fit of raving madness of these ecstatic musicians. Amps fell down, making nerve-killing sounds and the stage lighting also collapsed. In addition to this, the drummer stoically kept on drumming. So these are John's Children. "Poor John!""

Volker Einberger, Mannheimer Morgen

April

Advision Studios, 23 Gosfield Street, London, England

Probable date and studio (though it's possible that Spot Studios were used) for the sessions that produced the 'Desdemona' single.

Wednesday 26th April

Bluesette Club, Leatherhead, Surrey, England

Saturday 29th April

'14 Hour Technicolour Dream', Alexandra Palace, Muswell Hill, London, England

Though not mentioned on any of the posters produced for the event, film of the concert included in the video 'Pink Floyd In 1966–67' does provide fleeting glances of John's Children on stage. These can be seen during 'Interstellar Overdrive'. The band are also rumoured to have been filmed by Pete Townshend.

Wednesday 3rd May

Bluesette Club, Leatherhead, Surrey, England

Friday 5th May

Desdemona / Remember Thomas A Beckett (Track 604003)

Though not a huge hit, the single garnered good reviews.

"This is an instinctive tip for the Fifty… Verse is well sung and the chorus, with 'answering' voice in the background, is both catchy and impacty. Strong guitar in parts and the beat is just right."

Peter Jones, Record Mirror

"I like the idea of the song. It's very repetitious with just enough lyrical content to make you think "Aye, aye"… I like it. The member of the group who answers the lead singer (Marc Bolan) has a great voice. I'd like to hear more of him."

Alan Freeman, Blind Date, Melody Maker

Spot Studios, South Molton Street, London, England

A rehearsal session which saw rough versions of 'Midsummer Night's Scene' and 'Jasper C. Debussy' committed to tape.

Monday 8th May

Spot Studios, South Molton Street,
London, England
Further recording sessions, producing two takes of 'Midsummer Night's Scene'.

Tuesday 16th May

Spot Studios, South Molton Street,
London, England
Recording session producing versions of 'Sally Was An Angel' and 'The Perfumed Garden Of Gulliver Smith'.

Friday 19th May

Youth Club, Beaconsfield,
Buckinghamshire, England

Sunday 21st May

Tally Ho Electric Store, Finchley, London,
England
John's Children visit the above record shop to sign copies of the 'Desdemona' single.

Beaconsfield
YOUTH CLUB
AMBOY DUKES
FRIDAY, 5th MAY

JOHN'S CHILDREN
FRIDAY, 19th MAY

SIMON DUPRÉE
FRIDAY, 2nd JUNE

concert poster

May / June

Spot Studios, South Molton Street, London, England
Studio sessions for a planned John's Children album. The album was provisionally titled 'Playing With Themselves'. In the final event, Track Records passed on the option of releasing the album, despite a final production master being completed.

Among the tracks recorded were 'Midsummer Night's Scene', 'Mustang Ford', 'Hippy Gumbo', 'The Perfumed Garden Of Gulliver Smith', 'Leave Me Alone', 'Sara Crazy Child', 'Sally Was An Angel', 'Daddy Rolling Stone', 'Jasper C. Debussy', 'The Third Degree' and 'Hot Rod Mama'.

Thursday 1st June

Spot Studios, South Molton Street, London, England
Recording session which produced another version of 'Midsummer Night's Scene'.

Friday 2nd June

Spot Studios, South Molton Street, London, England
A further session which was concerned with providing overdubs to 'Midsummer Night's Scene'.

June

Playhouse Theatre, Northumberland Avenue, London, England
Some point after the 6th June John's Children recorded four songs for the BBC's 'Saturday

Club' programme (Chris Townson deputised for Keith Moon at The Who concerts on 5th and 6th June). The band were recorded without an audience being present in the theatre. The songs were broadcast on the 17th June. The recorded titles were 'Jagged Time Lapse', 'The Perfumed Garden Of Gulliver Smith', 'Hot Rod Mama' and 'Daddy Rolling Stone'. An interview between John Hewlett and Brian Mathew, which mentioned Townson performing with The Who, was also recorded.

Monday 12th June
Spot Studios, South Molton Street, London, England
Yet more overdubs on 'Midsummer Night's Scene' were recorded at this session. This may well have been Bolan's last session with the band.

Saturday 17th June
Transmission date for the John's Children session for BBC's 'Saturday Club' programme.

Saturday 24th June
Football Ground, Warminster, Wiltshire, England
This concert was a last minute booking as a replacement for Wayne Fontana.

Friday 7th July
Midsummer Night's Scene / Sara Crazy Child (Track 604005)
The scheduled release date for 'Midsummer Night's Scene'. Though a small number of copies were manufactured, the single was withdrawn before it could reach the shops The catalogue number was reassigned to the 'Come And Play With Me In The Garden' single.

Early July
Bolan officially leaves John's Children. A press statement to the effect appears in Record Mirror dated week ending 15th July. A week later Tyrannosaurus Rex made their concert debut.

July (?)
Advision Studios, 23 Gosfield Street, London, England (?)
Some time around leaving John's Children and the launch of Tyrannosaurus Rex, Bolan, with members of John's Children as his backing band, recorded 'The Lilac Hand Of Menthol Dan', maybe for use as a single. The track is almost certainly a John's Children demo which then had further production work added to it.

TYRANNOSAURUS REX

Marc Bolan – vocals, guitar. Steve Peregrine Took – percussion.

Little is known about the early Tyrannosaurus Rex concerts. Definite facts are that the band's debut gig was as a four or five-piece electric band. The gig was supposedly a complete disaster. However, all this is hearsay; the source being Simon Napier-Bell. Allegedly, the band had not rehearsed together properly, seemingly having been quickly put together by Bolan, who seemed to expect everything to come together as if by magic.

Following the gig it's probable that, though still signed to Track Records (the contract probably expiring at the end of 1967), the record label repossessed the electric equipment that Bolan had been using, which could explain why right from the very outset all the early Tyrannosaurus Rex material was basically acoustic.

How long a period there was between the debut gig and the first shows as a duo is unknown. Certainly by late August/early September the band was back on the club and college circuits in and around London. Many gigs were probably unannounced performances at colleges or, with the support of Track Records, at music business watering holes such as Tiles and The Speakeasy, where Frank Zappa caught an early show. Later the band graduated to gigs at London's Middle Earth, which following the closure of the UFO, had become London's premier underground club.

Friday 21st July (?)

Come And Play With Me In The Garden / Sara Crazy Child (Track 604005)
Release date for the second John's Children single to feature Marc. It's likely that he only appears on the B-side of the disc.

UFO Club, The Blarney, Tottenham Court Road, London, England (?)
Posters from the period indicate that Tyrannosaurus Rex were scheduled to make their debut at the above venue on this date. However this remains unconfirmed and it's far more likely that the group's debut took place the following night at the Electric Garden. DJ Jeff Dexter has stated that Marc never played at the UFO and the venue had closed its doors by October 1967.

Saturday 22nd July

Electric Garden, King Street, Covent Garden, London, England
Tyrannosaurus Rex played fourth on the bill to Pandemonium. Though the date at the UFO Club the previous night remains unconfirmed, this particular concert certainly went ahead.

At this stage Tyrannosaurus Rex were probably a four-piece band featuring Bolan on vocals and guitar, Steve Took on drums plus Ben Cartland on bass and a second unknown guitar player. Following the concert Cartland and the guitar player services were dispensed with, leaving Bolan and Took on their own. Track apparently repossesed the sound equipment. Took got rid of his drum kit and took to playing a pair of bongos.

July (?)

Spot Studios, South Molton Street, London, England (?)
The first Tyrannosaurus Rex demo session was done for Track Records. An unknown bass player augmented the band for certain songs, the aforementioned Ben Cartland being the most likely candidate. In addition a couple of female "backing singers" were also present, one of these being Marc's girlfriend Teresa Whipman.

fri., 21 july
9.30 p.m.-2.30 a.m.

* **RIOT SQUAD**
  * Apostolic Intervention

sat., 22 july
10.30 p.m. 'til dawn

* **PANDEMONIUM**
* **117**
  * Apostolic Intervention
    Marc Bollam
    & Tyrannosauras Rex

sun., 23 july
6.0 p.m.-11.0 p.m.

* **EXPLODING GALAXY**
  Admission 5/- & 8/-
  Licensed restaurant until 1 a.m.
  LIGHT SHOW and FLICS

ELECTRIC garden
43 KING ST. COVENT GDN.
TEL: 240 1327.

A total of eleven known tracks were recorded: 'Rings Of Fortune', 'Sara Crazy Child', 'Lunacy's Back', 'Highways' (a.k.a. 'Misty Mist'), 'Beyond The Rising Sun', 'One Inch Rock', 'Sleepy Maurice', 'Jasper C. Debussy', 'Hot Rod Mama', 'The Beginning Of Doves' and 'Sally Was An Angel'.

In a letter to John Peel Marc mentioned that a session had been held on a Monday night and that twelve songs had been recorded (which would indicate that one of the recorded songs is missing from the above listing), allegedly for White Whale in the USA. It's not known if the letter is referring to this particular session, however if so, this would suggest that likely dates for the session would be the 24th or 31st July or 7th August.

August (?)
Spot Studios, South Molton Street, London, England (?)
A second demo session for Track Records probably produced only two known tracks: 'Lunacy's Back' and 'Beyond The Rising Sun'. By now the band had slimmed down to a duo. By 14th August, Tyrannosaurus Rex had cut several acetates, with John Peel playing two of them, 'Rings Of Fortune' and 'Highways' on his final Radio London 'Perfumed Garden' programme, broadcast during the early hours of the 14th.

Sunday 27th August
'Festival Of The Flower Children', Woburn Abbey Festival, Woburn, Bedfordshire, England
Unconfirmed date.

August (?)
Tiles Club, Oxford Street, London, England
Tyrannosaurus Rex perform at one of John Peel's 'Perfumed Garden' evenings, though the date is speculative. The appearance may have happened in September and there may have been more than one.

Monday 18th September
Speakeasy, 48 Margaret Street, London, England
Though difficult to confirm, this is the likely date for a gig attended by Frank Zappa who went on to the Speakeasy following a Crazy World Of Arthur Brown concert at The Marquee.

Saturday 23rd September
Middle Earth, 43 King Street, Covent Garden, London, England
Set list: 'Hot Rod Mama', 'Sara Crazy Child', 'Scenescof', 'Hippy Gumbo', 'Graceful Fat Sheba',

'Highways', 'The Wizard', 'Mustang Ford', 'The Lilac Hand Of Menthol Dan', 'The Beginning Of Doves', 'Child Star', 'Dwarfish Trumpet Blues', 'Knight', 'Chateau In Virginia Waters', 'Pictures Of Purple People', 'Lunacy's Back'.

Tyrannosaurus Rex played third on the bill to Denny Laine's Electric String Band and The Piccadilly Line.

Saturday 7th October

Middle Earth, 43 King Street, Covent Garden, London, England

Tyrannosaurus Rex appeared third on the bill to The Action and Sam Gopal Dream.

Friday 20th October

Go Go Girl / Jagged Time Lapse (Track 604010)

Release date for the final John's Children single to feature Marc. He only appears on the A side track. The backing track was the instrumental that had been cut for John's Children's version of 'Mustang Ford'. The lyrics were probably rewritten by Simon Napier-Bell.

Monday 30th October

BBC Studio 1, 201 Piccadilly, London, England

Recording date for the first radio session for BBC Radio One's 'Top Gear' programme. This session began a long association between Tyrannosaurus Rex and the show's DJ John Peel. This session was treated as an audition by a BBC panel, on which future appearances were dependent. The reaction from the panel was mixed, with at least one member describing the duo's music as "pretentious crap". However despite the response, the band were passed for future programmes.

A total of six songs were recorded. Five of those songs, 'Scenescof', 'Child Star', 'Highways', 'Hot Rod Mama' and 'Dwarfish Trumpet Blues', were broadcast on 5th November. The final song, 'Pictures Of Purple People', was held over until 4th February the following year.

Autumn

Holland Park, Holland Park, London, England

A photo session with lensman Ray Stevenson was conducted in this London park.

Sunday 5th November

Transmission date for the 'Top Gear' session on BBC Radio One. See entry for 30th October. Five of the songs which had been taped were broadcast: 'Scenescof', 'Child Star', 'Highways', 'Hot Rod Mama' and 'Dwarfish Trumpet Blues'.

Friday 24th November

Middle Earth, 43 King Street, Covent Garden, London, England

Tyrannosaurus Rex appeared third on a bill headlined by The Pretty Things and Eyes Of Blue.

December (?)

Sound Techniques Studio, Old Church Street, Chelsea, London, England

A third demo session was recorded with Joe Boyd taking the producer's role. Danny Thompson of Pentangle was drafted in on acoustic bass, probably in order to flesh out the duo's sound. At least one song, 'Chateau In Virginia Waters', was recorded and fully mixed. It's probable that 'Child Star', 'Highways' and 'Dwarfish Trumpet Blues' were also put down on tape, though it appears that these did not reach the mixing stage. The session received a glowing mention in John Peel's column in 'International Times'. Track Records, however, passed on their option to release the band's recordings, though this probably made little difference as Bolan's publishers, Essex Music, appear to have had other plans.

Friday 22nd December

'Christmas On Earth Continued', Olympia, Kensington, London, England

Though uncredited on the posters, Tyrannosaurus Rex appeared low on the bill alongside other artists such as the Jimi Hendrix Experience.

1968

The early months of 1968 saw Tyrannosaurus Rex slowly move further up concert bills, gaining further prestigious support slots at the Middle Earth club as well as doing several college concerts. A setback had occurred at the end of 1967 when Track Records decided not to pursue their interest in releasing the band's recordings. Instead, Tyrannosaurus Rex signed to Essex Music's production company (Straight Ahead Productions) whose releases appeared on the EMI distributed label, Regal Zonophone.

Simon Napier-Bell also withdrew as the band's manager. Tyrannosaurus Rex then signed with Blackhill Enterprises, run by Andrew King and Peter Jenner, the same people who worked with Pink Floyd. It was at their offices that Marc met June Child, who was working there as a secretary. A major break for the band was gaining the support slot at Donovan's Royal Albert Hall concert. Surprisingly they didn't headline the Middle Earth until one month after 'Debora' had been released, by which time they had headlined the Purcell Room at London's Southbank prestigious arts complex. There were numerous other out of London gigs in the company of John Peel.

The first documented European gigs took place in the summer months of 1968. These coincided with Tyrannosaurus Rex's first television appearances. These were on European television channels. Despite the support of BBC Radio One, and John Peel in particular, the band were unable to secure spots on any of the major rock and pop music programmes emanating from the UK at the time. This was despite the fact that both 'Debora' and 'One Inch Rock' had been minor chart successes.

For the first album, 'My People Were Fair And Had Sky In Their Hair, But Now They're Content To Wear Stars On Their Brows', Bolan had a huge backlog of songs on which to draw. The album was completed by mid-April 1968 and was originally scheduled for release in the first half of May. In the final event, it didn't appear until some two months later.

The follow-up album, 'Prophets, Seers, And Sages, The Angels Of The Ages' appeared only four months later and failed to emulate the success of the debut album, probably due to the fact that it followed so soon on the heels of the debut release. Tyrannosaurus Rex finished the year headlining a variety of venues in the UK to promote the disc. They had originally been mooted to tour North America for the first time, as support act to Pink Floyd. The tour never happened.

Friday 12th January
Middle Earth, 43 King Street, Covent Garden, London, England
Tyrannosaurus Rex appear third on the bill to The Nice and Limousine.

Friday 26th January

University Of Southampton, Highfield, Southampton, Hampshire, England

Tyrannosaurus Rex appear on a bill headlined by Pink Floyd and The Incredible String Band.

Sunday 4th February

BBC Radio Studios, Broadcasting House, London, England

In addition to repeating the songs previously transmitted on 'Top Gear' (see entry for 5th November), the previously unbroadcast 'Pictures Of Purple People' was also included in this edition of 'Top Gear'. Marc also joined John Peel in the studio and gave a short interview as well as providing commentary on the songs.

Friday 23rd February

Middle Earth, 43 King Street, Covent Garden, London, England

Tyrannosaurus Rex appear third on the bill to Blossom Toes and Fairport Convention.

Wednesday 28th February

BBC Studio 2, Broadcasting House, London, England

The second Tyrannosaurus Rex BBC radio session was recorded for the 'John Peel's Night Ride' programme and was broadcast on 13th March. The duo recorded a total of six songs: 'The Beginning Of Doves' (1.36), 'Wielder Of Words' (3.32), 'The Wizard' (2.47), 'Afghan Woman' (2.00), 'Hippy Gumbo' (2.00) and 'Frowning Atahuallpa (My Inca Love)' (5.34). No other Tyrannosaurus Rex studio versions of either 'The Wizard' or 'Hippy Gumbo' are known to exist. Also included was a short interview with Marc. BBC records suggest that this lasted all of 17 seconds.

Saturday 9th March

Middle Earth, 43 King Street, Covent Garden, London, England

Slowly Tyrannosaurus Rex were beginning to creep up the bill at the Middle Earth. For this appearance they were on second to the Jeff Beck Group.

Monday 11th March

BBC Studio 1, 201 Piccadilly, London, England

Recording date for the second session for BBC Radio One's 'Top Gear' programme. As at the previous session for 'John Peel's Night Ride', a total of six songs were recorded. Four of these, 'Knight' (2.20), 'Debora' (3.10), 'Afghan Woman' (1.55) and 'Frowning Atahuallpa' (My Inca Love) (4.25) were broadcast on the 24th March. The final two songs, 'Mustang Ford' (2.50) and 'Strange Orchestras' (1.40), were held over until a later programme, not being broadcast until 3rd May. 'Debora' was later rebroadcast on 'Saturday Afternoon Pop – The Barron Show' on 15th April 1972.

IMPERIAL COLLEGE CHARITY CARNIVAL

Present a

Folk Concert

in aid of the LEUKEMIA RESEARCH FUND

STARRING

DONOVAN

with

TYRANNOSAURUS REX
THE FLAME

COMPERE **JOHN PEEL**

THURSDAY 21st MARCH

ROYAL ALBERT HALL
Manager F. J. MUNDY

1/-

Wednesday 13th March

Transmission date for the session recorded for the 'John Peel's Night Ride' programme on BBC Radio One. See the entry for 28th February. Unusually for a BBC programme, all six songs were broadcast on the one show.

Thursday 21st March

'Imperial College Charity Carnival', Royal Albert Hall, Kensington, London, England

As an indication of Tyrannosaurus Rex's rapidly growing popularity the band were booked as support act to Donovan at the 6,000 capacity Royal Albert Hall. The concert was held in support of the 'Leukaemia Research Fund'.

Sunday 24th March

Broadcast date for 'Top Gear' session recorded on 11th March. Four songs were broadcast: 'Knight', 'Debora', 'Afghan Woman' and 'Frowning Atahuallpa (My Inca Love)'.

March (?)

Tony Visconti's Flat, 108 Lexham Gardens, Earls Court, London, England

Prior to the recording of the first album, a session took place at Tony Visconti's flat where the band demoed the complete 'My People Were Fair And Had Sky In Their Hair... But Now They're Content To Wear Stars On Their Brows' album, plus a handful of songs which didn't make the final track listing. These were 'Hippy Gumbo', 'Puckish Pan' (a.k.a. 'Rock Me') and 'Lunacy's Back'.

March (?)

Advision Studios, 23 Gosfield Street, London, England

The studio sessions which produced the 'My People Were Fair And Had Sky In Their Hair, But

Now They're Content To Wear Stars On Their Brows' album and 'Debora' single were held over four days at the above studio. These sessions probably took place in late March. An acetate of the album was produced on 16th April.

Friday 5th April
'Oak, Ash And Thorn', Purcell Room, Southbank, London, England
Tyrannosaurus Rex's first headline appearance in the London area took place at the prestigious Purcell Room, part of London's Southbank complex. Narration was by John Peel.

Saturday 13th April
'Oak, Ash And Thorn', Purcell Room, Southbank, London, England
Narration at the concert was provided by John Peel.

Friday 19th April
Debora / Child Star (Regal Zonophone RZ 3008)
Release date for the first Tyrannosaurus Rex single. The disc peaked at 34 in the singles chart.

"Once you've staggered over that name this is a very interesting record ... a new weird sound from Marc Bolan's highly distinctive vocal. Few words, lots of sounds and it's pretty in a strange way too. Unexpectedly nice ...".

Penny Valentine, Disc And Music Echo

"A versatile and very underrated group which discerning listeners will have heard many times on Top Gear. This is a fascinating disc debut that's probably much too offbeat to succeed.

Rattles along at a hectic pace, with acoustic guitar and bongos. All very clever and intricate – probably too complex to register."

Derek Johnson, NME

"This is ever so clever, ever so different – and I hope ever so that it makes the charts. When something really offbeat and unusual comes along, one raises a cheer. This complex, catchy, ad-lib type single gets three cheers from me."

Peter Jones, Record Mirror

Sunday 5th May
Repeat broadcast date for the 'Top Gear' session recorded on 11th March. In addition to 'Debora' and 'Afghan Woman', the two songs that were not used on the original date, 'Mustang Ford' and 'Strange Orchestras', were included in this edition of the show.

Monday 13th May
Middle Earth, 43 King Street, Covent Garden, London, England
The first Tyrannosaurus Rex headline appearance at the famous underground music venue. Junior's Eyes were the support band.

Saturday 18th May
University Of Southampton, Highfield, Southampton, Hampshire, England
Tyrannosaurus Rex played alongside Captain Beefheart And His Magic Band.

Sunday 19th May

'Gandalf's Garden Benefit', Middle Earth, 43 King
Street, Covent Garden, London, England

This concert was a special benefit for the underground magazine 'Gandalf's Garden'. The concert began in the afternoon and continued into the evening. Other bands on the bill included Junior's Eyes, Hapshash And The Coloured Coat, Edgar Broughton Band, Third Ear Band, David Bowie, Flame and others. John Peel hosted the event.

Wednesday 22nd May

'Celebration For Albion', Middle Earth, 43 King
Street, Covent Garden, London, England

Tyrannosaurus Rex headlined over Hapshash And The Coloured Coat and Third Ear Band. John Peel also appeared.

Saturday 25th May

London School Of Economics, Houghton Street,
London, England

Tyrannosaurus Rex appeared alongside Chicken Shack.

BLACKHILL ENTERPRISES
presents for one night only

TYRANNOSAURUS   ROY
REX   HARPER

with

STEFAN GROSSMAN & DAVID BOWIE

Vibrations by

JOHN PEEL

at THE ROYAL FESTIVAL HALL
(General Manager John Denison C.B.E.)

on WHIT MONDAY, JUNE 3rd, 1968

Tickets from :—
THE ROYAL FESTIVAL HALL Box Office (WAT 3191)
and
MUSICLAND, 230 Portobello Rd. (01-229 3077)

May (?)

Marc, who had, up until then, probably continued to live with his parents in Wimbledon, moved in with new girlfriend June Child to 57 Blenheim Crescent, Ladbroke Grove, London.

Monday 3rd June

'The Babylonian Mouthpiece Show', Royal Festival Hall, Southbank, London, England

Further evidence of Tyrannosaurus Rex's increasing popularity was shown by a return to London's Southbank complex, this time appearing at a much larger hall. Support came from Roy Harper, Stefan Grossmann and David Bowie.

"What a bring down from the Tyrannosaurus Rex. It was an unwise move for them to do such a long set, and the reason is, their arrangements do not vary enough. If they had done two sets of say half an hour, I think it would have been much more enjoyable.

…Then came Tyrannosaurus Rex. They have a beautiful sound, but too much of it all at once is like using a typewriter all day – it gets boring. If they had stopped after 'Debora', the interest in their sound would still have been at its peak, but they went on and spoiled it by Marc Bolan singing without music. He asked the audience to clap, which was a wise move on his part, because it covered up some of his off-key notes, but not all of them. Their performance was not up to standard. The reason might have been that they were nervous at playing to such a large audience. Every time I have seen them at the Middle Earth they have always been of a fairly high standard."

Uncredited, International Times

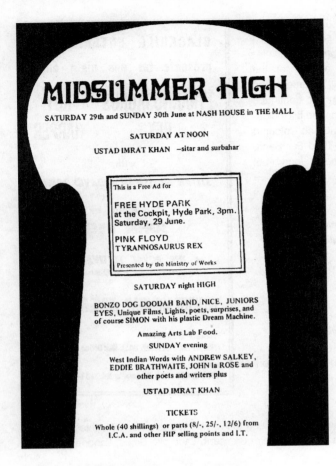

MIDSUMMER HIGH

SATURDAY 29th and SUNDAY 30th June at NASH HOUSE in THE MALL

SATURDAY AT NOON

USTAD IMRAT KHAN —sitar and surbahar

This is a Free Ad for

FREE HYDE PARK
at the Cockpit, Hyde Park, 3pm.
Saturday, 29 June.

PINK FLOYD
TYRANNOSAURUS REX

Presented by the Ministry of Works

SATURDAY night HIGH

BONZO DOG DOODAH BAND, NICE, JUNIORS
EYES, Unique Films, Lights, poets, surprises, and
of course SIMON with his plastic Dream Machine.

Amazing Arts Lab Food.

SUNDAY evening

West Indian Words with ANDREW SALKEY,
EDDIE BRATHWAITE, JOHN la ROSE and
other poets and writers plus

USTAD IMRAT KHAN

TICKETS

Whole (40 shillings) or parts (8/-, 25/-, 12/6) from
I.C.A. and other HIP selling points and I.T.

Tuesday 11th June

BBC Studio 1, 201 Piccadilly,
London, England

Recording date for another session for BBC Radio One's John Peel hosted 'Top Gear' programme. Five titles were committed to tape: 'Stacey Grove' (1.55), 'One Inch Rock' (1.40), 'Salamanda Palaganda' (2.10), 'Eastern Spell' (1.35) and 'Wind Quartets (2.55)'. The first four were broadcast on the 14th July while the last was held over until a repeat transmission on the 25th August.

Saturday 15th June

Students Union, Birmingham
University, Warwickshire,
England

This gig took place with John Peel, who was billed above Marc and Steve. The event began at 8 p.m. and finished at 1.a.m.

Monday 17th June

City Memorial Hall, Sheffield, Yorkshire, England

Sunday 23rd June

Mothers, Erdington, Birmingham, Warwickshire, England

Surprisingly, only twelve days after they had last appeared in Birmingham, Tyrannosaurus Rex returned to perform in the city. John Peel, once again, also appeared.

Saturday 29th June

'Midsummer High', The Cockpit, Hyde Park, London, England

The first of the free Hyde Park concerts organised by Blackhill Enterprises, Marc's then management company. The idea of a free concert was allegedly Marc's. Tyrannosaurus Rex supported Pink Floyd. The bill attracted a crowd of some 2,000 people. The concert began at 3 p.m.

Following Floyd's appearance there was a break. The music recommenced at 8 p.m. under the title 'Flesh Party' with appearances from The Nice and Bonzo Dog Doo Dah Band among others.

Friday 5th July

My People Were Fair And Had Sky In Their
Hair ... But Now They're Content To Wear
Stars On Their Brows (Regal Zonophone LRZ
& SLRZ 1003)

'Hot Rod Mama', 'Scenescof', 'Child Star', 'Strange Orchestras', 'Chateau In Virginia Waters', 'Dwarfish Trumpet Blues', 'Mustang Ford', 'Afghan Woman', 'Knight', 'Graceful Fat Sheba', 'Wielder Of Words', 'Frowning Atahuallpa (My Inca Love)'

In addition to the above track listing, John Peel read a short story.

Marc Bolan – vocals, acoustic guitar;
Steve Peregrine Took – backing vocals, drums, pixiephone, percussion.
Recorded at Advision Studios, London
Produced by Tony Visconti; Engineered by Gerald Chevin
The album peaked at 15 in the album charts.

"Do not adjust your record players, this is how Marc Bolan and Steve Peregrine sing – as if they're about to break out crying. Using some weird backing instruments, ... they do get a "different" sound, as they sing a dozen new songs by Marc Bolan."

Allen Evans, NME

"Traditionally John Peel's favourite group. Tyrannosaurus Rex's firs LP shows off beautifully the many talents of the gifted Marc Bolan...

Marc is one of the most prolific composers we know and the strength of the album lies in his excellent, totally individual songs of love, beauty, fantasy and nature. And then Marc says that, for him, the album is months out of date! Which bodes extremely well for the future."

Uncredited, Disc And Music Echo

"This duo's sound is the brainchild of Marc Bolan whose career has spawned many phases. Most of the tracks are a kind of jug-band psychedelia with a set of vocals that sound like the earliest possible blues recordings. The overall sound is same-y... Original, deserves to be a big seller, maybe it will be."

Uncredited, Record Mirror

Saturday 6th July

'Woburn Music Festival', Woburn Abbey, Woburn, Bedfordshire, England
Tyrannosaurus Rex played third on the bill to the Jimi Hendrix Experience and Geno Washington

KEMPTON PARK RACECOURSE
Staines Road (A308)

SUNBURY

Previously held at
Richmond & Windsor

8TH NATIONAL
JAZZ · POP · BALLADS &
BLUES FESTIVAL

An NJF/MARQUEE presentation

FRIDAY, 9th AUGUST, 8-11.30 p.m.   Tickets 15/-
THE HERD   MARMALADE   THE TASTE
Time Box and, from the U.S.A., JERRY LEE LEWIS

SATURDAY, 10th AUGUST, 2.30-5.30 p.m.   Tickets 10/-
JON HENDRICKS   RONNIE SCOTT QUINTET
THE DON RENDELL/IAN CARR QUINTET
ALAN HAVEN TRIO plus THE MIKE WESTBROOK BIG BAND

SATURDAY, 10th AUGUST, 7-11.30 p.m.   Tickets 15/-
ARTHUR BROWN   THE NICE   JEFF BECK
TEN YEARS AFTER   TYRANNOSAURUS REX
JOE COCKER   DEEP PURPLE   plus GINGER BAKER

SUNDAY, 11th AUGUST, 2.30-5.30 p.m.   Tickets 10/-
THE INCREDIBLE STRING BAND
AL STEWART   FAIRPORT CONVENTION   ECLECTION, etc.

SUNDAY, 11th AUGUST, 7-11.30 p.m.   Tickets 15/-
TRAFFIC   SPENCER DAVIS   JOHN MAYALL
JETHRO TULL   CHICKEN SHACK   JOHN PEEL, etc., etc.

Why not make a weekend **CAMP**   Bring your own tent, etc.
of it and stay at our **SITE**   We provide water and toilets
Details and Tickets from NJF Secretary
Marquee, 90 Wardour St., London, W.1.   Tel. 01-437 6601

N.B.: SPECIAL TICKETS available IN ADVANCE ONLY
Season £2.5.0   Weekend (Sat. and Sun.) £1 15.0

And The Ram Jam Band. Fourth on the bill were Family. All these bands were recorded direct from the soundboard. Tyrannosaurus Rex, unfortunately, were not.

Tuesday 9th July

Middle Earth, 43 King Street,
Covent Garden, London, England

Sunday 14th July

Broadcast of the 'Top Gear' session recorded on 11th June on BBC Radio One. Four titles were broadcast on this date: 'Stacey Grove', 'One Inch Rock', 'Salamanda Palaganda' and 'Eastern Spell'.

Wednesday 24th July

Country Club, Havestock Hill,
London, England
Support came from John Bull's Blues Band.

July (?)

Trident Studios, St. Anne's Court, Soho, London, England
Probable date for studio sessions for a new album and single. Certainly by the end of the month 'Prophets Seers And Sages, The Angels Of The Ages' had been completed.

July (?)

Trident Studios, St. Anne's Court, Soho, London, England
Probable month for a session which saw 'O Harley (The Saltimbaques)', 'Nickelodeon' and 'Juniper Suction' committed to tape.

Saturday 10th August

'18th National Jazz, Blues And Pop Festival', Kempton Park, Sunbury On Thames, Surrey, England
Also on the bill for that day Joe Cocker, Jeff Beck, The Nice, Ginger Baker and The Crazy World Of Arthur Brown. Tyrannosaurus Rex appeared on the bill between Joe Cocker and Jeff Beck. Three songs from the concert were filmed, probably by Tony Visconti. These were 'One Inch Rock', 'Conesuala' and 'Mustang Ford'. The songs are complete with sound.

Roundhouse, Chalk Farm, London, England
Following the afternoon appearance at Kempton Park, Tyrannosaurus Rex appeared at an all-nighter at the Roundhouse. The concert began at 10.30 p.m. and lasted until dawn. Support came from Ansley Dunbar Retaliation and Fusion.

Friday 23rd August

One Inch Rock / Salamanda Palaganda (Regal Zonophone RZ 3011)

Tyrannosaurus Rex's only Top Thirty single was released on this date. The song peaked at number 28. Unfortunately BBC producers decided not to reward the band with an appearance on 'Top Of The Pops'.

"A group that's becoming increasingly popular around the club circuit... Can't make up my mind about this disc – it's happy, light-hearted and thoroughly infectious, yet I wonder if it has enough substance and punch to meet today's demands.

It has a deliberately dated sound, a toe-tapping bouncy shuffle beat, and vocal that's sung largely in scat. All credit to Tyrannosaurus Rex for coming up with something that's undemanding, good fun and blues chasing...".

Derek Johnson, NME

"We're all pretty unanimous that this will be a big hit for the two lads. It's a gently produced piece, with interesting sounds behind a very basic, catchy guitar phrase running through the whole thing. Really it's very commercial material, and a genuine effort to find something different. Should be a goodie for them."

Peter Jones, Record Mirror

"It has taken me much longer than all those hip people who have been digging them for ages to appreciate this group.

I now admit I find their sound rather endearing, certainly very individual, and totally fascinating.

I'm glad they put a title on this ... I couldn't understand a thing Marc Bolan was singing about. But there's power in those vocal chords, by Jove! And they do get a very good sound."

Penny Valentine, Disc And Music Echo

Marc and Steve Took fly to Maastricht Airport in The Netherlands.

Unconfirmed television studio, Belgium

TV recordings for an unconfirmed Belgian TV station. Neither details of which song(s) were performed, or on which programme the band appeared are available.

Saturday 24th August

'Jazz Bilzen 68', Limburg, Belgium

Tyrannosaurus Rex were featured on a bill which also included The Action, The Pretty Things, Simon Dupree And The Big Sound, Idle Race and The Move. They appeared between The Pretty Things and Simon Dupree And The Big Sound.

"Determined, mainly through the promptings of their manager Bryan Morrison... to watch them and listen, I saw Tyrannosaurus Rex again. Marc Bolan sat cross-legged on the floor and Steve Peregrine Took, who later had to sleep on the floor so that Bryan could have a bed, crouched over his various sets of drums.

"One Inch Rock", the duo's new single, was well received and arch-cynic Green has to admit that he quite liked it. But I'll deny it if approached in public. Many of Marc's words are sung in a strange fashion and the vocals become what could be called scat if it was jazz."

Richard Green, NME

Sunday 25th August

Repeat broadcast of the 'Top Gear' session recorded on 11th June. 'Salamanda Palaganda', 'One Inch Rock' and 'Stacey Grove' were played a second time. One song that had not been previously broadcast, 'Wind Quartets', was included on this day's show.

Paradiso Theatre, Amsterdam, Holland

Unconfirmed appearance.

Saturday 31st August

'The Great South Coast Bank Holiday Pop Festival', Hayles Field, Ford Farm, Godshill, Isle Of Wight, England

This was the first of the Isle Of Wight festivals and was held over two days, the 31st August to 1st September. Among the other acts performing were The Crazy World Of Arthur Brown, The Pretty Things, The Move and Fairport Convention.

Tuesday 3rd September

Studio Wandsbeck, Hamburg, West Germany

TV recordings for the German ZDF programme '4–3–2–1 Hot And Sweet'. The show was broadcast on the 14th September. The appearance on the programme was organised by David Bowie's manager Ken Pitt. Details of which songs were performed are unfortunately lost though 'One Inch Rock' would be a prime candidate.

September (?)

Mönckeberg Brunnen, Mönckebergstrasse, Hamburg, West Germany

Around the time of the first performance on '4–3–2–1 Hot And Sweet', Bolan and Took gave an open-air concert in the street at the above site, a pedestrianised area of Hamburg.

Saturday 14th September

Transmission date for the Tyrannosaurus Rex slot on '4–3–2–1 Hot And Sweet' on ZDF. See entry for 3rd September.

Sunday 15th September

Mothers, Erdington, Birmingham, Warwickshire, England

Support came from Bakerloo Blues Line.

Monday 16th September (?)

Unconfirmed BBC Radio Studio, London, England

Marc recorded an interview for 'The Voice Of Pop' which was broadcast on 21st September.

Friday 20th September

Albert Hall, Nottingham, Nottinghamshire, England

Saturday 21st September

Broadcast date on BBC Radio One for the interview recorded for 'The Voice Of Pop' on 16th September. The programme focused on pop lyrics and censorship. Also appearing were Mick Jagger, Pete Murray and Barry Mason. John Peel hosted the programme.

Thursday 26th September
BBC Television Centre, Wood Lane, Shepherd's Bush, London, England

Tyrannosaurus Rex recorded a performance of 'One Inch Rock' for the BBC television arts and music programme 'How It Is'. This was broadcast the following day on BBC 1.

Friday 27th September
The edition of 'How It Goes' featuring the Tyrannosaurus Rex performance, recorded the previous day, was broadcast at 6 p.m.
Technical College, Billingham, County Durham, England

Saturday 28th September
'Malvern Big Beat Sessions', Winter Garden, Malvern, Worcestershire, England

Sunday 29th September
Country Club, Havestock Hill, London, England

Wednesday 2nd October
Red Lion, Leytonstone, London, England

Thursday 3rd October
NME reported that Pink Floyd, The Nice, The Moody Blues, Cream and Tyrannosaurus Rex music would appear in the Thames Television children's programme 'The Tyrant King', due to begin broadcasting on this date. No other details exist as to whether this actually happened, however the programme was certainly made.

Saturday 5th October
Town Hall, Glastonbury, Somerset, England

Saturday 12th October
University Of East Anglia, Norwich, Norfolk, England

Monday 14th October
BBC Studio 1, 201 Piccadilly, London, England

Recording date for another 'Top Gear' radio session. Again, a total of six songs were recorded. Four of these, 'The Friends', 'Conesuala', 'The Seal Of Seasons' and 'Evenings Of Damask' were all broadcast on 10th November. Two songs, 'The Travelling Tragition' and 'Trelawny Lawn' were broadcast at a later date, the 22nd December.

Friday 18th October
Mistrale Club, Beckenham, Kent, England

October (?)
L'Antenne Culturelle, Kremlin Bicetre, Paris, France

TV recordings for 'Tous En Scene', a programme broadcast on French TV Channel 2. Two songs were filmed. One song, a mimed edited version of 'Stacey Grove', was recorded in the open air. The second, a live take of 'Salamanda Palaganda', was filmed from within a circus tent.

The recording most likely took place in late October, with broadcast taking place on 26th November.

Friday 1st November
Prophets, Seers And Sages, The Angels Of The Ages (Regal Zonophone LRZ & SLRZ 1005)
'Deboraarobed', 'Stacey Grove', 'Wind Quartets', 'Conesuala', 'Trelawny Lawn', 'Aznageel The Mage', 'The Friends', 'Salamanda Palaganda', 'Our Wonderful Brownskin Man', 'O Harley (The Saltimbaques)', 'Eastern Spell', 'The Travelling Tragition', 'Juniper Suction', 'Scenescof Dynasty'
Marc Bolan – vocals, guitar; Steve Peregrine Took – bongos, African drums, kazoo, pixiephone, Chinese gong.
Recorded at Trident Studios, London
Produced by Tony Visconti; Engineered by Malcolm Toft
The album surprisingly failed to chart.

"Innocence is what Rex is all about, innocence mixed with a search for ancient wisdom ... It could be so pretentious except when it's in the hands of a genuine bopping imp, Marc Bolan, aided by sprite Steve Peregrine Took ... A mere acoustic guitar jumbles merrily, while bongos plink and plonk like gnomes tap dancing on flower pots ... Marc's guitar seems to be improving and Steve is adding more percussive effects ...".

Melody Maker

"They have a quivering and tremulous style of singing which is different. Marc Bolan's beautiful lyrics almost compensate for the rather unmelodic arrangements, which after fourteen tracks of acoustic guitar and monotonous percussion, become virtually indistinguishable."

Allen Evans, NME

Saturday 9th November
Mothers, Erdington, Birmingham, Warwickshire, England

Sunday 10th November
Broadcast date on BBC Radio One for the 'Top Gear' session recorded on 14th October. Four songs were broadcast on this date: 'The Friends', 'Conesuala', 'The Seal Of Seasons' and 'Evenings Of Damask'.

Thursday 21st November
Free Trade Hall, Manchester, Lancashire, England
In addition to the above concert, Tyrannosaurus Rex were also scheduled to record a session for 'Radio One Club' on this date. BBC records indicate no transmission date, so it's extremely unlikely that one was recorded.

Saturday 23rd November
Neeld Hall, Chippenham, Wiltshire, England

Tuesday 26th November
Transmission date for the Tyrannosaurus Rex performance on French Television's Tous En Scene'.

Sunday 1st December
Cambridge Arts Theatre, Cambridge, Cambridgeshire, England
Two shows. One at 7.30 p.m. and the second at 10.00 p.m.
Support came from Blonde On Blonde and Paul Wheeler.

Tuesday 3rd December
Studio Wandsbeck, Hamburg, West Germany
A second performance slot for ZDF's '4–3–2–1 Hot And Sweet' was recorded on this date. This performance was broadcast on 14th December. As with the previous appearance, details of which material was performed are lost.

Saturday 7th December
Winter Gardens, Ventnor, Isle Of Wight, England
Support acts were The Knights and Halcyon Order.

Saturday 14th December
Transmission date for the second Tyrannosaurus Rex performance on '4–3–2–1 Hot And Sweet' on ZDF. See entry for 3rd December.

Wednesday 18th December
Highbury Technical College, London, England
Tyrannosaurus Rex played the Highbury Technical College Dance accompanied by Elmer Gantry's Velvet Opera, Heaven, and Coconut Mushroom.

Sunday 22nd December
Date for a repeat broadcast of the 'Top Gear' session recorded on 14th October. 'The Travelling Tragition' and 'Trelawny Lawn', which had not been included in the original broadcast, were played on this date.

Saturday 28th December
Paradise II, Margriethal – Jaarbeurs, Utrecht, Netherlands
Marc and Steve Took fly into Schiphol Airport, Amsterdam and appeared at the above venue supporting Pink Floyd and The Bonzo Dog Doo Dah Band. Also on the bill were Eire Apparent and The Pretty Things. Eire Apparent featured among their line-up drummer Davey Lutton who was to re-enter the T. Rex story some five years later.

Originally Tyrannosaurus Rex were scheduled to play at the Glyderdome in Boston, Lincolnshire in England. However this performance was cancelled in favour of an appearance at a larger event in The Netherlands. Jeff Beck and The Jimi Hendrix Experience were due to appear at this event, but cancelled.

December
Trident Studios, St. Anne's Court, Soho, London, England
Probable month for sessions which produced the 'Pewter Suitor' single and some of the early 'Unicorn' tracks.

1969

Despite Tyrannosaurus Rex's continuing popularity in underground music circles, singles success continued to elude the band – neither of the band's 1969 releases, 'Pewter Suitor' and 'King Of The Rumbling Spires', set the charts on fire. The story regarding albums was significantly different though. Despite the chart failure of 'Prophets, Seers And Sages, The Angels Of The Ages', 'Unicorn' met with both critical acclaim and commercial success. However, the album masked increasing tensions between Bolan and Took.

The early part of the years continued with a series of acoustic concerts. In March Bolan bought a Fender Stratocaster (the famous guitar with the teardrop symbol), and slowly began to introduce electric guitar into the live set. The first "electric gig" was at London's Lyceum in April and was, in Marc's words, "a disaster". However, aural evidence, via a tape of the concert, indicates that this judgement was rather harsh.

Though it was clear that Bolan wanted to go electric, it seems that he wasn't quite sure how to achieve his aims. The first John Peel session with Mickey Finn in November 1969 was the first to indicate the more electric direction.

Tyrannosaurus Rex also made their debut tour of the USA, a country which was to become something of a bete-noire for Bolan. If nothing else, the tour clearly defined the differences between Bolan and Steve Took. It's unclear if Took went on the trip purely as a contractual obligation, knowing that he would no longer be a member of Tyrannosaurus Rex after the dates were completed, or whether the decision to kick him out was made when Bolan and June Child returned to England.

Monday 13th January
'For The Lion And The Unicorn In The Oak Forests Of Faun', Queen Elizabeth Hall, Southbank, London, England
Set list: 'Conesuala', 'The Seal Of Seasons', 'One Inch Rock', 'Eastern Spell', 'Wind Quartets', 'Mustang Ford', 'Salamanda Palaganda', 'Strange Orchestras', 'Evenings Of Damask', 'Chariots Of Silk', 'Pewter Suitor', 'The Travelling Tragition' (Later show)
Two shows, one at 6.15 p.m., the other at 9.00 p.m.
Support came from Vytas Serelis and David Bowie performing mime.

"A handful of musical fairydust was thrown in the air... which baffled some and choked others.

Marc Bolan squatted on the floor in a black vest and sang with fervour strumming a competent, if not exactly advanced guitar. Steve Peregrine Took juggled with a rare selection of African talking drums, pixie phones and bongos.

There was a touch of Noddy meets Pete Townshend when Steve stopped rattling pots and began roughly using a Chinese Gong. This was during the climax of the evening on 'The Wizard' – a freakout designed to make the most miserable Hobgoblin jive in the aisles.

... A pretty evening of wafer thin material presented in such a civilised way it became charming and satisfying."

Chris Welch, Melody Maker

Friday 17th January

Pewter Suitor / Warlord Of The Royal Crocodiles (Regal Zonophone RZ 3016)

The single failed to emulate the success of the previous two and failed to reach the singles' charts.

"... I admire his courage ... Seriously, I can't find anything constructive about the words, although he gets a fantastic rhythm going. I should imagine if you were in a stoned state at a party, you'd think this record was fantastic."

Tony Hatch, Blind Date, Melody Maker

"Here comes Marc Bolan and Steve Peregrine Took with another bopping opus, this time distinguished by a rather natty guitar figure from Marc ... Their rattling pots and tiny voices get quite heated at the end, rather like a couple of rough gnomes, bashing each other with toadstools."

Chris Welch, Melody Maker

"One of these days, Tyrannosaurus Rex are going to get themselves a hit. I don't rate this as their best single to date – but it's uncomplicated, easily absorbed material, so you never know.

Written by Marc Bolan, it's virtually a scat vocal, with complex counter-harmonies underlying the solo. Set to an urgent fast driving beat which intensifies throughout, it also spotlights some really exciting guitar playing.

The material has little substance, however."

Derek Johnson, NME

concert flyer

"After having owned up to liking the overall sound ... (I am now) rather confused as to why all their singles have this hard tight chanting vocal, but very little lyric. It's okay if you want to leap about in a white hat ... but to sit and listen to ... it's a bit mind boggling."

Unsourced

Friday 24th January
Bolan and Steve Took enter Denmark for television and radio slots and one concert.

Saturday 25th January
In the morning Tyrannosaurus Rex recorded a slot for the Danish radio programme 'After Beat'. Whether this was a music session or an interview is not known. They then recorded a slot for the 'Toppop' programme which was broadcast on Danish TV between 5.25 p.m. and 5.50 p.m. Details of what material the band performed are now lost. (Part of) the Tyrannosaurus Rex segment was included in the end of year special broadcast on 26th December.

Brøndby Popclub, Nørregaard Hallen, Brøndby, Denmark

Set list: 'Unicorn Hot Rod Mama (medley)', 'Debora', 'Stacey Grove', 'Mustang Ford', 'One Inch Rock', 'Eastern Spell', 'Wind Quartets', 'Conesuala', 'Strange Orchestras', 'Salamanda Palaganda', 'The Wizard'

"...As is known, it has not been possible to develop amplification for vocals, that reproduce the song as clearly and powerfully as guitar amplifiers. The group did not demand the silence of the crowd for their act as was feared. Still, the performance was much different to that usually seen from an electric group."

Carsten Grolin, Ekstra Bladet

"...The two talented Englishmen have been on television twice in England, and both occasions were local broadcasts. A shame, as they are quite photogenic and exciting on the television, as was seen on this Saturday afternoon's 'Toppop'. However, the finer aspects of their music are somewhat lost in the live situation, as was seen in Brøndby on Saturday night... The reception in Brøndby was overwhelmingly positive."

Sven Wezelenburg, Berlingske Tdende

Wednesday 29th January
Tyrannosaurus Rex leave Denmark.

Friday 7th February
Kee Club, Bridgend, Glamorgan, Wales
The concert may have taken place on Saturday 8th February.

'FOR THE LION AND THE UNICORN IN THE OAK FORESTS OF FAUN' TOUR

A short series of dates, ending with the concert in Brighton on 8th March. Sitar player Vytas Serelis and David Bowie, who performed a mime piece, provided support.

Saturday 15th February
Town Hall, Birmingham, Warwickshire, England

Sunday 16th February
Fairfield Halls, Croydon, Surrey, England

Wednesday 19th February
Playhouse Theatre, Northumberland Avenue, London, England
Marc was interviewed for BBC Radio 'Radio One Club'. The interview was broadcast live. 'Pewter Suitor' was also played.

FREE TRADE HALL · · MANCHESTER
NEMS ENTERPRISES Present
TYRANNOSAURUS REX & FRIENDS
SATURDAY, 22nd FEBRUARY, 1969
at 7-45 p.m.

SIDE CIRCLE - - 12/6
A 15

Saturday 22nd February
Free Trade Hall, Manchester, Lancashire, England

Sunday 23rd February
Colston Hall, Bristol, Gloucestershire, England

Saturday 1st March
Philharmonic Hall, Liverpool, Lancashire, England

Saturday 8th March
The Dome, Brighton, East Sussex, England

Saturday 15th March
Official publication date of Marc's poetry book 'The Warlock Of Love'.

FOR THE LION AND THE UNICORN

IN THE OAK FORESTS OF FAUN

ROY GUEST

presents

TYRANNOSAURUS REX

in concert

with

JOHN PEEL

and

VYTAS SERELIS—SITAR

and

DAVID BOWIE—MIME

No smoking in the Auditorium. The taking of photographs in the Auditorium is not permitted.

A NEMS ENTERPRISE

2/6

Thursday 20th March

West Ham College, West Ham, London, England

Though scheduled, this concert may have been cancelled at the last minute.

Friday 21st March

Unconfirmed venue, Cambridge, Cambridgeshire, England

A concert which was mentioned in the Tyrannosaurus Rex Fan club newsletter and which may have been cancelled.

March / April (?)

Trident Studios, St. Anne's Court, Soho, London, England

Probable months for the sessions that produced the bulk of the 'Unicorn' material.

Saturday 5th April

New Middle Earth Royalty Theatre, Ladbroke Grove, London, England

Though scheduled, this concert may also have been cancelled.

Monday 7th April

The Great Hall, Alexandra Palace, Muswell Hill, London, England

Another concert that was mentioned in the Tyrannosaurus Rex Fan Club newsletter, but in the final analysis never took place. It was replaced by the following show.

NEW MIDDLE EARTH
ROYALTY THEATRE
LANCASTER ROAD,
LADBROKE GROVE
229 1438

March: Sat 22nd
CARAVAN
PETE BROWN & HIS
BATTERED
ORNAMENTS
THE WRITING ON
THE WALL.

Fri 28th
COUNTRY JOE & THE
FISH + full supporting
programme.

Sat 29th
COUNTRY JOE & THE
FISH + full supporting
programme

April: Sat 5th
TYRANNOSAURUS
REX

Coming Soon
STEPPENWOLF

Friday 11th April

'Midnight Court', Lyceum, Strand, London, England

Set list: 'Unicorn-Hot Rod Mama (medley)', 'Afghan Woman', 'Debora', 'Mustang Ford', 'Stacey Grove', 'Salamanda Palaganda', 'Wind Quartets', 'One Inch Rock', 'Chariots Of Silk', 'Seal Of Seasons', 'Conesuala', 'Nijinsky Hind', 'Once Upon The Seas Of Abyssinia', 'Do You Remember', 'The Wizard'

Support came from Jerome Arnold Band and Eire Apparent.

This gig was one of the earliest to feature expanded instrumentation. Towards the end of the set Marc strapped on an electric guitar for 'Do You Remember'. Took was also starting to use a fuller drum kit than at previous shows and, on a couple of songs, moved from percussion to bass guitar.

April (?)

Unconfirmed Granada TV venue, Manchester, Lancashire, England

Television recording for 'John Peel's In Concert'. This was a pilot show for Granada Television and was never broadcast. Details of which songs were included are not known. No copies of the show appear to survive, though a photograph taken at the event appeared on the inside gatefold sleeve of 'The Words And Music Of Marc Bolan' album. John Peel remembers little about the evening's proceedings other than that it was possibly filmed in a barn and that during the Tyrannosaurus Rex set a dog wandered on stage and decided to join in with the duo.

Monday 5th May

Playhouse Theatre, Northumberland Avenue, London, England

The final 'Top Gear' session to feature Steve Took as a member of the band saw five songs being recorded. Four of these were broadcast on the 11th May: 'Once Upon The Seas Of Abyssinia' (2.05), 'Nijinsky Hind' (2.15), 'Misty Coast Of Albany' (2.15) and 'Chariots Of Silk' (2.30). 'Iscariot' was held over until 15th June.

Sunday 11th May

Broadcast date on BBC Radio One for the 'Top Gear' session recorded on 5th May. Four songs were transmitted on this date: 'Once Upon The Seas Of Abyssinia', 'Nijinsky Hind', 'The Misty Coast Of Albany' and 'Chariots Of Silk'.

Monday 12th May

The Pavilion, Bath, Avon, England

Friday 16th May

Unicorn (Regal Zonophone SLRZ 1007)

'Chariots Of Silk', ''Pon A Hill', 'The Seal Of Seasons', 'The Throat Of Winter', 'Catblack (The Wizard's Hat)', 'Stones For Avalon', 'She Was Born To Be My Unicorn', 'Like A White Star, Tangled And Far, Tulip That's What You Are', 'Warlord Of The Royal Crocodiles', 'Evenings Of Damask', 'The Sea Beasts', 'Iscariot', 'Nijinsky Hind', 'The Pilgrim's Tale', 'The Misty Coast Of Albany', 'Romany Soup'

Before 'Romany Soup' John Peel read another children's story.

Marc Bolan – vocals, guitars, harmonium; Steve Peregrine Took – backing vocals, bongos, drums, bass, pixiephone, Chinese gong. Tony Visconti – piano on 'Catblack (The Wizard's Hat)'.

Recorded at Trident Studios, London

Produced by Tony Visconti; Engineered by Malcolm Toft and Rob Cabel

The album peaked at 12 in the charts.

"In spite of the uneasy peace or the domestic rifts that ensue whenever I play their records, I must admit to deriving a certain enjoyment from the joyful music of the monstrous duo...

I can't imagine why the Rex should attract such loathing... To me it's just a happy warming sound, absorbing, refreshing and stimulating... I should say that this LP, the third, is better than the second though different from the earlier too.

'Unicorn' marks the start of the duo's excursion into electronic backing. Half is traditional Rex. The rest, recorded after a six month break, is new Rex plus electricity – a coupling full of intriguing possibilities which they promise to take further on the fourth album.

Of the sixteen tracks... the ones I liked best were those with the fascinating electric backings and pop like harmonies like 'Catblack' and 'Nijinsky Hind'.

On the whole, certainly a more acceptable LP for mass appeal than previous ones."

Nick Logan, NME

Saturday 17th May

Mothers, Erdington, Birmingham, Warwickshire, England

Wednesday 21st May

Trident Studios, St. Anne's Court, Soho, London, England

Recording session for 'King Of The Rumbling Spires' and 'Do You Remember'.

Saturday 31st May

Cherokee's, Ryde Pavilion, Isle Of Wight, England

This show was originally scheduled to take place at Music Box at Ryde Airport.

May (?)

The Ballroom, University Of Strathclyde, Glasgow, Lanarkshire, Scotland

Though the date is unconfirmed, Tyrannosaurus Rex played at the Student's Union Rag Ball at the above university in 1969. Reports indicate that at least one electric song was played.

Wednesday 11th June

Unconfirmed BBC Radio Studio, London, England

Live poetry reading on the John Peel hosted 'Night Ride' on BBC Radio One. Marc read three

American Tour Programme 1969

poems. Two of these were taken from the recently published 'The Warlock Of Love' book. These were the untitled poems on pages 17 and 46 of the book. The third poem, titled 'The Winged Man With Eyes Downcast To The Moon', was previously unpublished. In addition to the reading Peel and Bolan discussed Marc's poetry writing.

Saturday 14th June
Bromley Technical College, Bromley, Kent, England

Sunday 15th June
Repeat broadcast on BBC Radio One for the 'Top Gear' session that had been recorded on 5th May. 'Iscariot', which had not been played at the time of the original transmission, was included on this date.

Friday 27th June
Bay Hotel, Whitburn, Sunderland, County Durham, England

Friday 25th July

King Of The Rumbling Spires / Do You Remember (Regal Zonophone RZ 3022)

The disc stalled at number 44 in the singles chart. The reviews for the single were mixed.

"More than a song, this is tantamount to a poem set to music ... The lyric is deep, thought-provoking, enigmatic, almost obscure.

But in contrast, the tune is quite simple and has a catchy hook line. It pounds along with a throbbing beat...

A fascinating track... but whether it will have mass appeal is a moot point."

Derek Johnson, NME

"'Light all the fires...' is the substance of Marc Bolan's electrified teenybop and there are few other lines that are readily identifiable.

But it doesn't matter. The phrase is flowing and melodic...

This is Bolan Child's most commercial production to date, and with Steve Took rocking feverishly on regular drums ... they could easily crack their chart problem."

Chris Welch, Melody Maker

AMERICAN TOUR

Originally scheduled to begin on 15th June, the first and only Tyrannosaurus Rex tour of the USA didn't take place until August. Tyrannosaurus Rex went to America in exchange for Bob Dylan being given a work permit for the 1969 Isle Of Wight festival.

The American tour was something of a disaster. The band mainly played support slots and a couple of the more minor festivals taking place in the USA that summer – missing out on the big one, Woodstock. In fact they were playing a near deserted New York club during the Woodstock weekend. The band's record label Blue Thumb didn't seem to know how to promote the band. In addition Steve Took's increasing drug intake was resulting in disrupted performances and increasing alienation from Bolan. After the tour had finished, he was no longer a member of Tyranosaurus Rex.

Wednesday 6th August

Bolan and June Child, Steve Took and Mick O'Halloran fly to Los Angeles. Steve Took allegedly nearly missed the flight after failing to wake up in time.

Friday 8th August

Family Dog at The Great Highway, San Francisco, California, USA

Third on the bill to Country Joe And The Fish.

Saturday 9th August

Family Dog at The Great Highway, San Francisco, California, USA

Third on the bill to Country Joe And The Fish.

Sunday 10th August

Family Dog at The Great Highway, San Francisco, California, USA

Third on the bill to Country Joe And The Fish.

Monday 11th August

Thee Experience, Los Angeles, California, USA

Tuesday 12th August

Thee Experience, Los Angeles, California, USA

Wednesday 13th August

Thee Experience, Los Angeles, California, USA

Friday 15th August

Cafe Au Go Go, Greenwich Village, New York, New York, USA

Saturday 16th August

Cafe Au Go Go, Greenwich Village, New York, New York, USA

Set list: 'Unicorn-Hot Rod Mama (medley)', 'Debora', 'Afghan Woman', 'The Misty Coast Of Albany', 'Mustang Ford', 'The Seal Of Seasons', 'Chariots Of Silk', 'Strange Orchestras', 'The Wizard', 'Stacey Grove', 'One Inch Rock', 'Conesuala', 'Nijinsky Hind', 'Once Upon The Seas Of Abyssinia', 'Salamanda Palaganda'

Sunday 17th August

Cafe Au Go Go, Greenwich Village, New York, New York, USA

   "Tyrannosaurus Rex, one of today's most unusual acts, had an engrossing last set ... The British duo might not appeal to all tastes, with their distinctive vocalising, but their effect is telling on those who dig them ... The effect can be spellbinding...

   Bolan's high voice can often sound eastern, which it did on 'Afghan Woman'. Eastern influences were also apparent in 'The Misty Coast Of Albany' ...

   The final number was wild, from its opening jungle like screeching by Took, through Bolan's singing ... Took cut a finger in the wildness ... Tyrannosaurus Rex is quite an act ...".

Fred Kirby, Billboard

Monday 18th August

Cafe Au Go Go, Greenwich Village, New York, New York, USA

Tuesday 19th August

Cafe Au Go Go, Greenwich Village, New York, New York, USA

Wednesday 20th August
Cafe Au Go Go, Greenwich Village, New York, New York, USA

Thursday 21st August
Cafe Au Go Go, Greenwich Village, New York, New York, USA

Friday 22nd August
Kinetic Playground, Chicago, Illinois, USA
Third on the bill to Country Joe And The Fish and MC5.

Saturday 23rd August
Kinetic Playground, Chicago, Illinois, USA
Third on the bill to Country Joe And The Fish and MC5. An interview was also given to an unknown journalist on this day. The interview was later released on disc by Rhino Records.

August (?)
Organ Pavilion, Balboa Park, San Diego, California, USA
Tyrannosaurus Rex were part of the bill at an outdoor festival at the above venue. The exact date is unconfirmed. It may have taken place in September.

Friday 29th August / Saturday 30th August
'Houston Pop Festival', Sam Houston Coliseum, Houston, Texas, USA
Tyrannosaurus Rex played on one of the days at this two day festival. Among the other bands performing were Jefferson Airplane, The Grateful Dead, The Byrds and Poco.

Sunday 31st August
'New Orleans Pop Festival', Prairieville, Louisiana, USA
Among the other bands that played the festival were The Byrds, Canned Heat, Janis Joplin, Country Joe And The Fish, Chicago Transit Authority, The Grateful Dead, It's A Beautiful Day and Santana. Tyrannosaurus Rex played on the first day of a two day festival.

Thursday 4th September
Boston Tea Party, Boston, Massachusetts, USA
Support to Raven.

Friday 5th September
Boston Tea Party, Boston, Massachusetts, USA
Support to Raven.

Saturday 6th September
Boston Tea Party, Boston, Massachusetts, USA
Support to Raven.

Tuesday 9th September
Electric Factory, Philadelphia, Pennsylvania, USA

Wednesday 10th September
Electric Factory, Philadelphia, Pennsylvania, USA

Thursday 11th September
Electric Factory, Philadelphia, Pennsylvania, USA

Friday 12th September
Grande Ballroom, Detroit, Michigan, USA
Support to The Turtles.
It was at these dates that Marc began his friendship with Mark Volman and Howard Kaylan who were at the time singers with The Turtles.

Saturday 13th September
Grande Ballroom, Detroit, Michigan, USA
Support to The Turtles.

Friday 19th September
Eagles Auditorium, Seattle, Washington, USA
Support to It's A Beautiful Day.

Friday 20th September
Eagles Auditorium, Seattle, Washington, USA
Support to It's A Beautiful Day.

October
Mickey Finn, an acquaintance of photographer Pete Sanders, joins Tyrannosaurus Rex. Finn, unlike Took, was essentially a non-musician. Although he is rumoured to have been a member of a few bands, including Hapshash And The Coloured Coat, no evidence has emerged to suggest that he had ever appeared on one of their (or anybody else's) records. Finn was employed mainly for his looks and personality. This also gave a clear statement of who was the leader of the duo.

23rd October
Guild Of Students, Liverpool Polytechnic, Liverpool, Lancashire, England
Though scheduled, it's almost certain this concert didn't take place.

Saturday 15th November
Unconfirmed BBC Radio Studio, London, England
Marc, along with other studio guests, took part in a thirty-five minute discussion for the BBC Radio One programme 'Speakeasy' concerning money in the music business. The discussion was chaired by Jimmy Saville and the programme was broadcast live

Monday 17th November
Playhouse Theatre, Northumberland Avenue, London, England
The first radio session to be recorded for 'Top Gear' to feature new partner Mickey Finn saw five songs committed to tape: 'Fist Heart Mighty Dawn Dart' (2.40), 'Pavilions Of Sun' (2.50), 'A

Day Laye' (2.50), 'By The Light Of A Magical Moon' (2.45) and 'Wind Cheetah'. The first four were all broadcast on 22nd November. 'Wind Cheetah' appears to have been an outtake that was not broadcast at the time.

BRITISH TOUR

This was the first tour to feature Mickey Finn as Steve Peregrine Took's replacement. The tour also previewed a number of songs from the forthcoming 'A Beard Of Stars' album.

Friday 21st November
Free Trade Hall, Manchester, Lancashire, England

Saturday 22nd November
Broadcast date for the 'Top Gear' session recorded on 17th November. Four songs were transmitted: 'Fist Heart Mighty Dawn Dart', 'Pavilions Of Sun', 'A Day Laye', and 'By The Light Of A Magical Moon'.
Philharmonic Hall, Liverpool, Lancashire, England

Friday 28th November
Fillmore North, Locarno, Sunderland, County Durham, England

Saturday 29th November
City Hall, Newcastle, Northumberland, England

UK autumn tour programme 1969

PHILHARMONIC HALL, HOPE STREET, LIVERPOOL

JOHN PEEL and FRIENDS

TYRANNOSAURUS REX
(A Nems Presentation)

SATURDAY, 22nd NOVEMBER, 1969, at 8.00 p.m.

BOXES 20/-

12   1   HOPE ST. ENTRANCE
DOORS OPEN 7.15 p.m.

Booked Seats cannot be exchanged or taken back

Sunday 30th November
Mothers, Erdington, Birmingham, Warwickshire, England

December (?)
Trident Studios, St. Anne's Court, Soho, London, England
Recording sessions for the 'A Beard Of Stars' album and a single. Some songs had been started while Steve Took was still a member of the group. His parts were replaced, allegedly by Mickey Finn, though it's equally likely that the job was done by either Bolan or Tony Visconti.

December (?)
Trident Studios, St. Anne's Court, Soho, London, England
Possible date for a session which saw 'Demon Queen' and 'Ill-Starred Man' recorded. Both tracks were left unreleased at the time.

Friday 26th December
Transmission date for 'Lrets Toppop' in Denmark which included a repeat of (some of) the material from the Tyrannosaurus Rex 'Toppop' performance recorded in January.

Saturday 27th December
Fairfield Halls, Croydon, Surrey, England

LIVE! AT THE FAIRFIELD
FAIRFIELD HALL, CROYDON
Manager: Thomas J. Pyper, M.I.M.Ent.
SATURDAY, 27th DECEMBER, at 7.45 p.m.
JOHN & TONY SMITH PRESENT
TYRANNOSAURUS REX
IN CONCERT
WITH BOPPING FRIENDS

SEATS: 17/-, 15/-, 13/-, 10/-, 8/-. Bookable in advance from: BOX OFFICE, FAIRFIELD HALL, CROYDON. TEL: CRO 9291. Open 10 a.m. to 8 p.m.

1970

1970 was the year that Bolan achieved his big breakthrough. However, it started badly with the 'By The Light Of A Magical Moon' single flopping. The spring album, 'A Beard Of Stars', compensated somewhat for this, reaching a healthy chart position of 21 and selling steadily, if not spectacularly, over the following months.

By mid-1970 the duo were in something of a strange position. They appeared at many of the summer rock festivals held in Europe that year, where they usually commanded a mid-afternoon or early evening slot. They could also comfortably fill venues such as London's The Roundhouse or Lyceum, as well as command large audiences at clubs outside of the capital. However, they were in an underground limbo, where they had little hope of gaining a wider audience. However, signs of a sea change in the music audience's perceptions were imminent. Mungo Jerry's single 'In The Summertime' was a huge summer hit. On it, singer Ray Dorset was quite clearly influenced by Bolan's vocal style.

There was also a change in Marc's attitude, with commercial success seeming to have become a bigger priority. The waters were tested with a spoof single. 'Oh Baby' released under the alias of Dib Cochran And The Earwigs. It got nowhere. The breakthrough was provided by 'Ride A White Swan'. In truth the record was something of a freak hit. Bolan was still essentially playing the same music that he had been six months earlier. However, the record's success and the concurrent 'Top Of The Pops' appearances changed everything. Bolan was about to become the first post-Beatles idol. Audiences at concerts became progressively younger and predominantly female. The hippies began to be pushed aside and in the process became increasingly hostile to Bolan.

Thursday 1st January

BBC Paris Theatre, Regent Street, London, England
Set list: 'Hot Rod Mama' (1.26), 'Debora' (3.11), 'Pavilions Of Sun' (2.44), 'Dove' (2.12), 'By The Light Of A Magical Moon' (3.00), 'Elemental Child' (5.51), 'The Wizard' (8.13)
Recording date for a special radio concert for the new BBC Radio One programme 'John Peel's Sunday Show'. In addition to performing, brief interview segments were conducted by John Peel between songs. Originally Tyrannosaurus Rex were not scheduled to appear on the programme. However they were called in literally on the day to support Family who had to perform an instrumental set due to singer Roger Chapman's ill-health. The concert was broadcast on 4th January.

Sunday 4th January

Transmission date for 'John Peel's Sunday Show' on BBC Radio One. See entry for 1st January.

Tuesday 6th January

Marc went abroad somewhere! (Passport info).

Thursday 8th January

Trident Studios, St. Anne's Court, Soho, London, England

Recording session for a new David Bowie single produced by Tony Visconti. Marc guested on 'The Prettiest Star' and probably 'London Bye Ta-Ta', the two songs that were recorded that day. Recording personnel details in the booklet that accompanied the David Bowie 'Sound And Vision' box set are incorrect. According to Tony Visconti the correct line up is as follows: David Bowie – guitar and vocals; Marc Bolan – electric guitar; Tony Visconti – bass and string arrangement; Godfrey McClean – drums; Sue & Sunny and Lesley Duncan – backing vocals.

By all accounts the atmosphere at the session was tense with Bolan just doing his guitar parts and then leaving and June making sarcastic comments about Bowie's songs.

Friday 16th January

By The Light Of A Magical Moon / Find A Little Wood (Regal Zonophone RZ 3025)

The final single to be released under the Tyrannosaurus Rex moniker proved to be a commercial flop, failing to reach the charts.

"Marc Bolan with new sidekick Mickey Finn has another crack at the singles market with a typical Bolan Child vocal, but an untypical backing with some nice Beatley guitar sounds and unusual chord changes ... it will be nice to see them get a hit after all this time. Let's hope the DJs cough up with some plays."

Chris Welch, Melody Maker

"Never am too sure about this team. Sometimes they lose me – or I lose them. This is a gentle moody piece of lighthearted writing, with good vocal line and some intriguing guitar spasms. At least try it, please."

Unsourced

Wednesday 21st January

Winter Gardens, Bournemouth, Hampshire, England

Saturday 24th January

Van Dike Club, Devonport, Plymouth, Devon, England

Tyrannosaurus Rex were paid 70% of the door, which came to a total of £306.00.

Friday 30th January

Marc marries June Child at Kensington Registry Office, London. Guests include Mickey Finn and Sue Worth (Mickey's girl-friend), Jeff Dexter, Pete Sanders and Eric Clapton's girlfriend Alice.

January (?)

Trident Studios, St. Anne's Court, Soho, London, England

Probable month for the final recording sessions for the 'A Beard Of Stars' album.

Friday 13th February

The Lyceum, Strand, London, England

Support came from Taste, Edgar Broughton Band and Liverpool Scene.

Tuesday 17th February

Electric Garden, Glasgow, Lanarkshire, Scotland

Unconfirmed venue.

Wednesday 18th February

The Dome, Brighton, East Sussex, England

Support came from Rare Bird and Genesis.

Monday 23rd February

Civic Hall, Dunstable, Bedfordshire, England

Friday 13th March

A Beard Of Stars (Regal Zonophone SLRZ 1013)

'Prelude', 'A Day Laye', 'The Woodland Bop', 'Fist Heart Mighty Dawn Dart', 'Pavilions Of Sun', 'Organ Blues', 'By The Light Of A Magical Moon', 'Wind Cheetah', 'A Beard Of Stars', 'Great Horse', 'Dragon's Ear', 'Lofty Skies', 'Dove', 'Elemental Child'

Marc Bolan – vocals, acoustic guitar, electric guitar, bass guitar, percussion, chord organ;

concert programme

Mickey Finn – backing vocals, bass guitar, percussion; Tony Visconti – bass guitar; backing vocals.
Recorded at Trident Studios, London.
Produced by Tony Visconti; Engineered by Malcolm Toft. The album reached 21 in the charts.

"The fourth from T. Rex marks Mickey Finn's debut as sidekick and percussionist and young Mr. Bolan's emergence as guitar star extraordinaire. In fact, it's Marc's string bashing that makes this their most distinctive and perhaps most successful album so far.

The set opens with a strange guitar phrase sounding like a child picking notes at random and gains in momentum ... until on the instrumental tail off to the last track, 'Elemental Child', Marc proves his worth on a complex and lengthy run.

Of the 12 tracks, 'By The Light Of A Magical Moon' may be remembered as a good single; 'Wind Cheetah' has some nice gnashing guitar with an oriental flavour and 'Woodland Bop' has a cute set of lyrics.

All in all, a nice not too demanding album with the guitar and the electric embellishments a bonus to what we know the duo is already capable of."

Nick Logan, NME

Saturday 14th March
Great Hall, Devonshire House, University Of Exeter, Exeter, Devon, England

Saturday 29th March
Redcar Jazz Club, Coatham Hotel, Redcar, Cleveland, England

March (?)
CTS Studios, Wembley, Middlesex, England
Recording session for the spoof Dib Cochran And The Earwigs single. Two tracks, 'Oh Baby' (originally an 'A Beard Of Stars' outtake) and 'Universal Love', were recorded during a six hour

session. The track for 'Oh Baby' was built up on the original unreleased Tyrannosaurus Rex version. The group line up was Marc on guitar, Tony Visconti on bass, lead vocals and string arrangement, Rick Wakeman on keyboards and John Cambridge on drums. Mick Ronson who had recently joined David Bowie's band and moved into Haddon Hall in Beckenham was also present at the session though he did not appear on the disc. CTS Studios was used because David Platz, boss of Essex Music, had obtained some free time at the studio.

ROUNDHOUSE
(opposite Chalk Farm tube - London, N.W.1)
April 20-25
"POP PROMS"
Monday: ROY GUEST presents
TRAFFIC, MOTT THE HOOPLE, BRONCO, IF
Tuesday:
TYRANNOSAURUS REX
PRETTY THINGS, ELTON JOHN, HEAVY JELLY
Wednesday:
JOHNNY WINTER
JUICY LUCY
Thursday: QUINTESSENCE
FAIRPORT CONVENTION
FOTHERINGAY, MATTHEW'S SOUTHERN COMFORT
Friday:
FLEETWOOD MAC MIGHTY BABY HOOKFOOT
Saturday:
GINGER BAKER'S AIRFORCE
JODY GRIND, TOE FAT, SURPRISE GUEST ARTISTS!
HOST: JOHN PEEL
Admission on each night: 25/-
Tickets now on Sale! From Roundhouse; One Stop Records, Grand Central, 100 Charing Cross Road, W.C.2; or Hime and Addison, 37 John Dalton Street, Manchester. Restaurant, licensed bar, record shop, lights, events, heads, groupies, etc. Special "Pop Proms Pass" (£5) which admits you to ALL the shows obtainable by mail in advance only from Roy Guest, 39 Gloucester Avenue, London, N.W.1. These are limited in number and are not on sale at the door.
A NEMS Presentation
Don't miss at the Roundhouse this week the Incredible String Band and Stone Monkey in "U" (see display ad for times and prices)

Saturday 4th April
'Progressive Pop Festival 70
Köln', Sporthalle, Cologne,
West Germany
Among the other bands performing at the two day festival were Arthur Brown, Colosseum, Chicken Shack, Barclay James Harvest, Deep Purple, Procol Harum, Eire Apparent, Soft Machine, Spencer Davis and Yes. Tyrannosaurus Rex played on the second day.

Monday 6th April
Konzerthaus, Vienna, Austria
Set list: 'Hot Rod Mama', 'Debora', 'Wind Quartets', 'Pavilions Of Sun', 'One Inch Rock', 'By The Light Of A Magical Moon', 'Jewel', 'Organ Blues', 'Elemental Child', 'The Wizard'
This date was possibly as support to Deep Purple, who certainly played at the same venue on the same day. However, it's possible that the concert may well have been part of a festival similar to the event in Cologne two days earlier.

Saturday 11th April
The Blues Club, Village Roundhouse, Dagenham, Essex, England

Tuesday 21st April
'1970 Pop Proms', Roundhouse, Chalk Farm, London, England
Support came from The Pretty Things, Elton John and Heavy Jelly.

May

Trident Studios, St. Anne's Court, Soho, London, England
Probable month for the beginning of sessions for the 'T. Rex' album.

Saturday 9th May

Great Hall, College Block, Imperial College, Kensington, London, England
Support came from Taste, Kevin Ayers, Whole World, Mike Chapman, Wishbone Ash, Grail and Smile.

Saturday 16th May

'Pop Camp', Messehalle, Nuremburg, West Germany
Tyrannosaurus Rex played on a bill headlined by Colosseum and Chicken Shack.

Sunday 17th May

'Pop Camp 70', Circus Krone, Munich, West Germany
Like the previous night, Tyrannosaurus Rex played third on a bill headlined by Colosseum and Chicken Shack. Reports are confusing, but it is possible that all bands on the bill performed two sets; one series of performances beginning at 2 p.m. and a second beginning at 8 p.m.

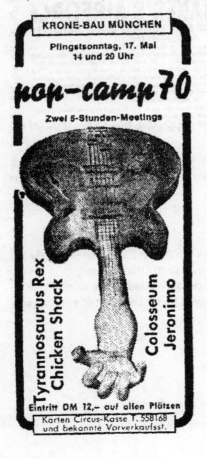

SCOTTISH TOUR

A series of dates at smaller halls, with a couple of appearances at larger venues as support to Ten Years After thrown in for good measure.

Wednesday 20th May

Adam Smith Hall, Kirkcaldy, Fife, Scotland

Thursday 21st May

Town Hall, Falkirk, Stirlingshire, Scotland
This concert was cancelled.

Friday 22nd May

Empire Theatre, Inverness, Invernesshire, Scotland

Saturday 23rd May

Town Hall, Motherwell, Lanarkshire, Scotland

Sunday 24th May

Caird Hall, Dundee, Angus, Scotland
Support to Ten Years After.

Monday 25th May

Electric Garden, Glasgow, Lanarkshire, Scotland

Tuesday 26th May

Usher Hall, Edinburgh, Lothian, Scotland

This concert was originally scheduled for 23rd May, but was re-arranged for the above date.

Saturday 30th May

'Festival Of Music And Fashion – Extravaganza 70', Empire Hall, Olympia, Kensington, London, England

Sunday 31st May

Gollum's Cave, Golden Torch Club, Stoke On Trent, Staffordshire, England

Tuesday 2nd June

Town Hall, Oxford, Oxfordshire, England

Friday 5th June

'Castle Rock', Dudley Zoo, Dudley, Bedfordshire, England

Set list: 'One Inch Rock', 'Debora', 'Hot Rod Mama', 'Wind Quartets', 'Pavilions Of Sun', 'King Of The Rumbling Spires', 'By The Light Of A Magical Moon', 'Organ Blues', 'Elemental Child', 'Conesuala', 'Salamanda Palaganda', 'Fist Heart Mighty Dawn Dart', 'The Wizard', 'Jewel' Tyrannosaurus Rex appeared third on the bill to The Faces and Edgar Broughton Band.

Saturday 6th June

Civic Hall, Dunstable, Bedfordshire, England

Sunday 7th June

Greyhound, Croydon, Surrey, England

Sunday 14th June

Redcar Jazz Club, Coatham Hotel, Redcar, Cleveland, England

Thursday 18th June

BBC Studio 2, Aeolian Hall, London, England

Recording date for a radio session for Sounds Of The 70's' with Stuart Henry on BBC Radio One. This was the first non-John Peel hosted programme that Tyranno-saurus Rex appeared on and was an indication that Bolan was beginning to cast his net a bit wider in his search for

concert programme

an audience. BBC records suggest that only three songs were recorded: 'One Inch Rock' (2.25), 'Jewel' (4.35) and 'Elemental Child' (7.45). The show was broadcast on 25th June. However, it's likely that one other song, a medley consisting of 'The Woodland Bop / Conesuala / The King Of The Mountain Cometh / The Woodland Bop' was also recorded at this session. This was not broadcast until 30th July.

Wednesday 24th June

Trident Studios, St. Anne's Court, Soho, London, England

Recording session that produced 'Seagull Woman'. While touring the U.K. with the Mothers Of Invention, Howard Kaylan and Mark Volman renewed their acquaintance with Marc, dropping into the session to add backing vocals. Can you hear them?!

Thursday 25th June

Broadcast date for the session recorded for the 'Stuart Henry Show'. See entry for 18th June.

Friday 26th June

Trident Studios, St. Anne's Court, Soho, London, England

A 1 inch tape containing 'Jewel', 'Summertime Blues' and 'Ride A White Swan' was produced on this date. However, this is unlikely to be the date of the recording session. The tape is more likely to have been compiled for purposes of the forthcoming single on the planned Octopus label.

Saturday 27th June

'The Holland Pop Festival', Kralingse Bos, Rotterdam, Netherlands

Tyrannosaurus Rex appeared Saturday afternoon, the second day of the three-day long 'The Holland Pop Festival'. Among the other acts appearing at the festival were Pink Floyd, Jefferson Airplane, Santana, Canned Heat and The Byrds.

The concert was shot for the film 'Stamping Ground'. The original German title was 'Love And Music'. The film is also known under the name of 'Rock Fever'. Only one Tyrannosaurus Rex song made the final edit of the film – 'By The Light Of A Magical Moon'. Among the other songs performed at the show was 'Pavilions Of Sun'. This appeared on a rare bootleg of the festival.

"Then comes a band that I have really loved for a long time: Tyrannosaurus Rex. Two beautiful guys, as beautiful as rural Gods and who have created their own unique style (which probably won't stay unique long as Roger Chapman and even Mungo Jerry are already imitating Marc Bolan's voice). Marc has an extraordinary way in quivering his voice and his compositions are lovely. Remember 'By The Light Of The Magical Moon' and 'Elemental Child' from the 'A Beard Of Stars' album? A band that deserves larger success and indeed were very welcome to the Rotterdam audience."

Michel Delorme, Rock et Folk

Saturday 4th July

The Eyre, Bedford Football Ground, Bedford, Bedfordshire, England

Among the other bands on the bill were Deep Purple.

Monday 6th July

Trident Studios, St. Anne's Court, Soho, London, England

Recording session for the forthcoming album. Three songs were recorded on this date: 'One Inch Rock', 'The Children Of Rarn' and 'The Wizard'.

Sunday 12th July

'Open Air Pop-Festival Aachen', Reiterstadion Soers, Aachen, West Germany

Among the other acts performing at the festival alongside Tyrannosaurus Rex were Deep Purple, Pink Floyd, King Crimson, Caravan, Fat Mattress, Can, Kraftwerk and others. Tyrannosaurus Rex played on the last day of the three day festival.

Sunday 19th July

The Lyceum, Strand, London, England

Set list: 'Debora', 'Suneye', 'By The Light Of A Magical Moon', 'The Children Of Rarn', 'Jewel', 'Organ Blues', 'The Wizard' (Not complete)

"Marc Bolan said it was good to be back in London again, and the Lyceum agreed ... (Bolan's) voice stabbed at the English language ... as (he) shattered syllables like stale cream crackers, Mickey's rhythm blew up into a frenzy, until the mood changed and 'Sunday' (sic), on the next album, relieved the tension ... Finally there was 'The Wizard' with Marc sitting cross-legged bawling like a child throwing a tantrum. Great!"

Andrew Means, Melody Maker

Thursday 30th July

Broadcast date on BBC Radio One for 'The Woodland Bop / Conesuala / The King Of The Mountain Cometh – Woodland Bop' medley on 'Sounds Of The Seventies' with Stuart Henry. See entry for 18th June.

Friday 21st August

Marc and Mickey enter Denmark for an appearance at the 'Copenhagen Beat Festival'.

Saturday 22nd August

'Copenhagen Beat Festival', KB Hallen, Frederiksberg, Copenhagen, Denmark

Sunday 30th August

Redcar Jazz Club, Coatham Hotel, Redcar, Cleveland, England

IMPLOSION
ROUNDHOUSE, CHALK FARM
SUNDAY, SEPTEMBER 6th, 3.30-11.30 p.m. 8/-
TYRANNOSAURUS REX
STEAMHAMMER
CURVED AIR
QUIVER
MANESHANDRA
JEFF DEXTER *
FIRST LIGHT
FILMS   STALLS   PHUN
AMPLIFICATION BY HI-WATT
* Records from MUSICLAND, 44 Berwick St., W.1

August

Oh Baby / Universal Love (Bell 1121)
Release date for the Dib Cochran And The Earwigs spoof project. Unsurprisingly the song failed to register on the charts.

Sunday 6th September

Roundhouse, Chalk Farm, London, England
Set list: 'Debora', 'One Inch Rock', 'By The Light Of A Magical Moon', 'Organ Blues' (Not complete)
Support came from Steamhammer, Curved Air, Quiver and Maneshandra.

"As usual they were greeted with a silent, but totally involved reverence ... Starting off acoustically ... they then ran through 'By The Light Of The Magical Moon', with Bolan whipping up frenzied passages on wah-wah that might have had Hendrix wondering where his vocation lay ...".

Chris Welch, Melody Maker

Friday 11th September

Caley Cinema, Edinburgh, Lothian, Scotland

Saturday 12th September

The Blues Club, Village Roundhouse, Dagenham, Essex, England

Saturday 19th September
Pilton Pop Festival, Glastonbury, Somerset, England
The band were paid £500 for the show in six instalments as the festival lost money. Marc later donated an acoustic demo of 'Sunken Rags' to bail out the 1971 festival. The band headlined by default when The Kinks, the original headline act, pulled out.

Friday 25th September / Saturday 26th September
Messehalle, Saarbrücken, West Germany

T. REX
October
Name of the band is officially shortened to T. Rex, though many concert promoters continued to bill them as Tyrannosaurus Rex for the next month or two. In the USA this went on into the following spring.

Friday 2nd October
Red Lion, Leytonstone, London, England

Friday 9th October
Ride A White Swan / Is It Love / Summertime Blues (Fly BUG 1)
Though its rise up the charts was far from meteoric, the single eventually peaked at number 2.

"Apparently because Tony Blackburn cannot say Tyrannosaurus, Marc and Mickey have become plain T. They also have the privilege of launching this new label with by far their most commercial song yet. The Bolan warble, to which I have been rather allergic to in the past, is not nearly so dominant ... An excellent sound. And there are TWO songs on the back, another Bolan song called 'Is It Love' and a unique 'Summertime Blues'. Fine stuff indeed."

NME

"'Ride A White Swan' is another 'Summertime Blues' ... A new label launch with the magic rock of Marc Bolan and his bongo beating partner Mickey Finn ... (They) cunningly recapture the drive and simplicity of late-fifties pop. 'Swan' is their most commercial sound to date. A great tune, with superb guitar sound from Marc."

Chris Welch, Melody Maker

"Jeez. Tyrannosaurus Rex was the subject of history's most unpleasant hype, a photograph of a promotion man humping a dinosaur skeleton. Their taste has improved and so have their singles. 'Ride A White Swan' is a good record, a clever record and a soon to be successful record (the last is no daring prediction, since the song's already gone top five in England) ... The initial impression that the record must be turning at the wrong speed is discounted by trying different speeds, making it sound more bizarre. The high notes, nonsense syllables and guttural noises are all Bolan and Finn's. There is no credit for the handclap that propels 'Swan', but one assumes it was at least their idea."

Paul Gambaccini, Rolling Stone

Albert Hall, Nottingham, Nottinghamshire, England

Sunday 11th October
King George's Hall, Blackburn, Lancashire, England

Wednesday 14th October
Town Hall, Birmingham, Warwickshire, England

Thursday 15th October
City Hall, Sheffield, Yorkshire, England

Tuesday 20th October
Guildhall, Southampton, Hampshire, England

Sunday 25th October
'3. Essener Pop Und Blues Festival', Grugahalle, Essen, West Germany
The band was billed as Tyrannosaurus Rex, not T. Rex. They played on the last day of a four-day festival.

Monday 26th October
BBC Studio Maida Vale 4, Maida Vale, London, England
The first radio session in a heavy autumn schedule. This session was the final one to be recorded for the John Peel hosted 'Top Gear' on BBC Radio One. It featured four songs: 'Ride A White Swan' (2.05), 'Jewel' (3.30), 'Suneye' (2.00) and 'Elemental Child' (7.40) and was broadcast on 7th November.

Thursday 29th October
Civic Hall, Dunstable, Bedfordshire, England

Friday 30th October
City Hall, Hull, Yorkshire, England
Set list: 'Debora', 'One Inch Rock', 'Elemental Child', 'Is It Love', 'By The Light Of A Magical Moon', 'Summertime Blues' (Not complete)
   "To begin with Messrs Bolan and

CITY HALL SHEFFIELD
THURSDAY 15th OCTOBER 1970

T. REX

TICKETS FROM LOCAL BOOKING OFFICES
PRICES 6/- 10/- 12/-

concert flyer

FOR REX FRIENDS
T. REX
IN CONCERT
Appearing: OCTOBER

THURS., 15th	CITY HALL,	**SHEFFIELD**
TUES., 20th	GUILDHALL,	**SOUTHAMPTON**
THURS., 29th	CIVIC HALL,	**DUNSTABLE***
FRI., 30th	CITY HALL,	**HULL**
TICKETS:	10/-, 8/-, 6/-	

* 12/-, 10/-, 8/-, 6/- ALL PERFORMANCES 8 p.m.

3. ESSENER POP-UND BLUES-FESTIVAL

Donnerstag: 21.10.: Jimi Hendrix, Mighty Baby, May Blitz, East of Eden, Gun, Brinsley Schwarz
Freitag, 23. 10.: Jack Bruce, Fotheringay, Quiver, Embryo u. a.
Samstag, 24. 10.: Moody Blues, Savoy Brown, Supertramp, Black Widow u. a.
Sonntag, 25. 10.: Taste, Chicken Shack, Tyrannosaurus Rex u. a.

22.~25. OKTOBER 1970 GRUGAHALLE

Veranstalter und Kartenvorverkauf
Mallison Managements GmbH. & Co
43 Essen, Zweigertstr. 32, Tel. 79 18 54

Finn went through a highly polished acoustic set ... Then they quickly switched over to electric guitars ... The duo have now changed their stage presentation completely ... Marc (doesn't) sit cross legged on the floor anymore. Instead, they both keep on the move ...

The atmosphere the duo creates is fascinating and the effect is startling, they really make you feel as though you were actually in on the act."

Ray Nortrop, NME

Saturday 31st October

Imperial College, Kensington, London, England
Support came from Quiver.

Wednesday 4th November

Mountford Hall, Liverpool, Lancashire, England

Thursday 5th November

BBC Studio Maida Vale 5, London, England
This radio session, recorded for BBC Radio One's 'Sounds Of The Seventies' programme saw Bolan and Finn joined by their record producer Tony Visconti, who played bass guitar, a duty he had occasionally performed live for David Bowie and to great effect on 'The Man Who Sold The World' album. A total of six songs were recorded, including two that have never officially been released on a T. Rex record: 'My Baby's Like A Cloud Form' (1.25), 'The Visit' (2.10), 'Elemental Child' (8.40), 'Ride A White Swan' (2.15), 'Is It Love' (2.15), 'Funk Music' (no BBC timing). The session was first broadcast on 18th November.

Saturday 7th November
Broadcast date for the final 'Top Gear' session'. See entry for 26th October.

Sunday 8th November
Greyhound, Croydon, Surrey, England
Support came from Status Quo.

Monday 9th November
Colston Hall, Bristol, Gloucestershire, England

Wednesday 11th November
BBC Television Centre, Wood Lane, Shepherd's Bush, London, England
With a surprise hit single on their hands T. Rex finally managed to obtain a slot on BBC 1's 'Top Of The Pops'. Bolan and Finn performed 'Ride A White Swan'. The programme was broadcast the following night, 12th November.

Thursday 12th November
Transmission date for the first 'Top Of The Pops' performance of 'Ride A White Swan', filmed the previous evening, 11th November.

Town Hall, Oxford, Oxfordshire, England
Tony Visconti augmented the band on bass guitar. It is possible that he also played bass at one or two other shows in late October/early November.

Monday 16th November
Transmission date on BBC Radio One for the 'Sounds Of The Seventies' radio session recorded on 5th November. Unusually, for a BBC session, all six songs were used. See earlier entry.

FOR REX FRIENDS

IN CONCERT Appearing: NOVEMBER
Tues., Nov. 24: **GUILDFORD**, Civic Hall
Fri., Nov. 27: **BOURNEMOUTH**, Winter Gardens

Tickets 10/-. 8/-, 6/-. Available from local Booking Agents

Tuesday 24th November
Civic Hall, Guildford, Surrey, England
After a few days of intense rehearsals, Steve Currie joined T. Rex as the permanent bass guitarist. He made his debut at this concert.

Wednesday 25th November
BBC Television Centre, Wood Lane,
Shepherd's Bush, London, England
A second performance of 'Ride A

FOR REX FRIENDS

Only London appearance at
DAGENHAM, ROUNDHOUSE
SATURDAY, NOVEMBER 28th

White Swan' was recorded for 'Top Of The Pops' (BBC 1) on this date. It was networked on the 26th November and also on 14th January the following year. Though Steve Currie had just joined the band he did not appear on this television performance; Bolan elected to perform the song as a duo.

Thursday 26th November
Broadcast date for the second 'Top Of The Pops' performance of 'Ride A White Swan' recorded on 25th November.

Friday 27th November
Winter Gardens, Bournemouth, Hampshire, England

Saturday 28th November
The Blues Club, Village Roundhouse, Dagenham, Essex, England
Howard Kaylan, back in town with the Mothers Of Invention, joined in backing vocals at this gig. Support came from Nick Pickett.

November (?)
Trident Studios, St. Anne's Court, Soho, London, England
Probable month for a session which saw 'The King Of The Mountain Cometh' committed to tape.

Thursday 3rd December
Green's Playhouse, Glasgow, Lanarkshire, Scotland

Friday 4th December
'Students Union Christmas Ball', Town Hall, High Wycombe, Buckinghamshire, England
Support came from The Groundhogs.

Saturday 5th December
Main Debating Hall, Manchester University, Manchester, Lancashire, England

Sunday 6th December
Civic Hall, Corby, Northamptonshire, England

Monday 7th December
Civic Hall, Wolverhampton, Staffordshire, England

Tuesday 8th December
BBC Studio Maida Vale 4, Maida Vale, London, England
In a special session for BBC radio's 'Top Gear' show, Marc was a featured member of 'The Top Gear Choir' – an ad hoc group of John Peel favourites – performing traditional Christmas carols. Other members of the choir were Rod Stewart, Ron Wood, Ronnie Lane, Kenny Jones, Ivor Cutler, Mike Ratledge, Robert Wyatt, Bridget St. John and Sonja Kristina (of Curved Air). Two

unknown Faces' roadies also sang. David Bedford played the piano. The session was broadcast on 26th December.

Wednesday 9th December

BBC Studio Maida Vale 5, Maida Vale, London, England

Another BBC radio session for Radio One was recorded on this date. Most of the songs were recorded for the Dave Lee Travis Show', but one was used for 'Radio One Club'.

A total of four songs were recorded: 'Summertime Blues' (3.30), 'Ride A White Swan' (2.05), 'Jewel' (3.15) and 'Hot Love' (3.10). The first three were included on 'The Dave Lee Travis Show' on the 19th December.

The session was then transmitted during the week 21st–25th December, with 'Hot Love' gaining its first transmission on the 22nd December. 'Ride A White Swan' was repeated on the 21st and 25th December. 'Summertime Blues' was repeated on the 22nd and 24th December. 'Jewel' was repeated on the 23rd December.

The session was also repeated during the week 18th January–22nd January on the 'Johnny Walker Show' and 15th March–19th March on the 'Tony Brandon Show'.

Thursday 10th December

BBC Paris Theatre, London, England

A second concert performance for the BBC was recorded for the Radio One show 'John Peel's In Concert'. The short set featured: 'Debora' (4.00), 'Elemental Child' (8.35), 'Woodland Bop' (6.40), 'Ride A White Swan' (2.30), 'Jewel' (6.55). The show was broadcast on 20th December. Most versions of this concert that have since been re-broadcast, and the version released on disc, feature 'Woodland Bop' edited out.

Friday 11th December

Community Centre, Welwyn Garden City, Hertfordshire, England

Saturday 12th December

Capitol Theatre, Cardiff, Glamorgan, Wales

Friday 18th December

Poporama, Devizes, Box, Wiltshire, England

T. Rex (Fly HIFLY 2)

'The Children Of Rarn', 'Jewel', 'The Visit', 'Childe', 'The Time Of Love Is Now', 'Diamond Meadows', 'Root Of Star', 'Beltane Walk', 'Is It Love', 'One Inch Rock', 'Summer Deep', 'Seagull Woman', 'Suneye', 'The Wizard', 'The Children Of Rarn'

The album peaked at number 13 in the UK Top Thirty and 188 in the US Top 200.

Marc Bolan – vocals, acoustic guitar, electric guitar, bass guitar, chord organ; Mickey Finn – backing vocals, bass guitar, bongos, drums. Howard Kaylan and Mark Volman – backing vocals on 'Seagull Woman'; Tony Visconti – string arrangements

Recorded at Trident Studios, London.

Produced by Tony Visconti. Engineered by Roy T. Baker.

A surviving Trident Studio acetate of the album with hand-written labels indicates that the original title of the album was to be 'The Wizard'. An even earlier article, from the time of the recording sessions, indicates that the original album title was to have been 'The Children Of Rarn'.

"'T. Rex' is at last here, and it's superb. Sweeping strings and lush backings suit this duo far better than one might have expected. The album starts with the theme of their new science-fiction story – 'The Children Of Rarn'... Then there's a smashing rock number – 'Jewel' – with Marc on organ and lead guitar. That, and 'Seagull Woman' on side two ... are most representative of T. Rex's new direction. And 'Beltane Walk' is a beautiful rocking semi-send up. But T. Rex haven't gone over to pure rock. There are still lovely peaceful numbers, with Marc's beautiful lyrics. A worthy album."

Disc And Music Echo

"'The Children Of Rarn' ... is possibly one of the most beautiful songs I've heard this year. It's a flying number, hovering over history and yet flying towards a scientific dream – spun by Bolan and executed with tact and mystery.

Bolan and Mickey Finn have come up with a valid rock album here ... It's a more electric Rex ... 'Seagull Woman', which features the playing (sic) of Howard Kaylan and Mark Volman of the Mothers Of Invention is the most complex thing I've heard from the unit. Even then, at the roots it's basically simple energy packed rock, basted with Bolan's poetic and imaginative vocals ... 'Suneye', another superb track, takes in chunky acoustic guitar and a relaxed drifting shifting mood. I can't help thinking that T. Rex, and Bolan especially, are going to be exceedingly big in 1971."

Ray Hollingworth, Melody Maker

"T. Rex started out with 'Debora' a long time ago. It was a strange sound – highly distinctive and ... very much a product of the emerging underground culture. The changes that have happened since then are clearly shown on the new album, 'T. Rex'. The acoustic, gentle approach has given way to a harsher, electric based music, and the influence of early rock and roll and r'n'b is very much to the fore. But through all the changes, T. Rex remain a very individual band.

The album starts with 'The Children Of Rarn'... The number is electric – emphasising the new T. Rex sound and setting the style for the rest of the tracks. 'Beltane Walk', the closing track on side one, shows the r'n'b influences on T. Rex's music – the riff is a straight lift from Jimmy Cracklin's 'The Walk' – but nevertheless it is all well assimilated and comes out as individual T. Rex.

Side two starts with 'Is It Love', also on the T. Rex 'Ride A White Swan' maxi-single, which has very simple rock and roll lyrics ... and then the two reminders of the past – 'One Inch Rock' and 'The Wizard'. The first track was one of T. Rex's early singles, this time electrically revamped and 'The Wizard' was Marc's solo single – even before T. Rex – now also re-recorded. In all, the best T. Rex album, showing at last that the duo have a lot more funk than many people gave them credit for.

Anonymous, Record Mirror

"T. Rex's first album, since their tentative sortie into more electronic sounds on 'Unicorn', produces a much more tangible and satisfying combination. This is a heavier, chunkier T. Rex than perhaps anyone who hasn't attended their recent concerts is used to. It works extremely well, both to give their overall sound much more solidity and to provide a perfect point for Bolan to bop his tonsils around.

Those tonsils undulate splendidly as usual ... but this time with Bolan's feet firmly on the

ground. The backing that he and Mickey Finn come up with actually keep that voice from sounding as though it's about to fly away.

People may argue that T. Rex's sound is no longer mystic and pure, but I for one am thankful it's not. The former was getting a little jaded around the edges and often became distinctly bad for the nerves – not to say boring. It is a happy situation that now leads to the fact that Marc, while still retaining a lot of typical Bolanesque, now has much more rhythmic appeal and firm attraction ... From this album it's not hard to see why T. Rex can draw mammoth audiences wherever they play."

Penny Valentine, Sounds

Poporama, Devizes, Box, Wiltshire, England

Saturday 19th December
Broadcast date for the session recorded for the 'Dave Lee Travis' show. Three songs were broadcast: 'Summertime Blues', 'Ride A White Swan' and 'Jewel'. See entry for 9th December.
'Big Apple', Regent Theatre Concert Hall, Brighton, East Sussex, England
Support came from Status Quo.

Sunday 20th December
Broadcast date on BBC Radio One of the special concert performance recorded for 'John Peel's In Concert'. See entry for 10th December.

Monday 21st December
Broadcast date on 'Radio One Club' for the version of 'Hot Love' which was recorded on 9th December. See entry for 9th December.

Tuesday 22nd December
Marc enters France on a short one-day trip, possibly to do TV work.
Roundhouse, Chalk Farm, London, England

Saturday 26th December

Transmission on BBC Radio One's 'Top Gear' for the special 'Top Gear Choir' session recorded on 8th December. See entry for 8th December.

Thursday 31st December

Town Hall, Birmingham, Warwickshire, England

December

Air Studios, 214 Oxford Street, London, England

Recording sessions for a new single. Bill Legend played drums on the session, though he was not officially added to the T. Rex line-up at the time. In addition to featuring Steve Currie's first studio outing as bass guitarist. Among the songs recorded were 'Hot Love' and 'Woodland Rock'. It's possible that an early version of 'Cosmic Dancer' was recorded at these sessions.

1971

1971 was the year of transformation for T. Rex from an underground cult band to teenage idols. By the end of the year, Marc Bolan was a superstar, at least in Britain and parts of Europe. The band also transformed into a full-blown hard rocking quartet. The old hippie audience which had sat and politely listened had largely disappeared, to be replaced by a younger audience, the majority of which were adolescent girls – a facet of Bolan's rise to fame that the smug underground counter-culture distinctly frowned upon.

Signs of the transition were apparent from the very beginning of the year, as indicated in Chris Welch's review of the January concert at London's Lyceum. And yet, musically, little had changed over the preceding twelve months. The addition of Steve Currie on bass guitar meant that the band had a fuller live sound, but that instrument had been part of the recorded sound for some time. Additionally, many of the songs played in concert had been staples of the T. Rex live set for several months.

Though concert reviews from early 1971 lack a detailed listing of the songs the band were performing at the time, it's possible to surmise that the band's live set was initially built around 'Debora', 'Elemental Child', 'Jewel', 'Ride A White Swan' and 'Summertime Blues'. 'One Inch Rock', 'Is It Love', 'Woodland Bop', 'Organ Blues' and 'The Children Of Rarn' also probably featured. The set list was thus a blend of the more up-tempo aspects of the old Tyrannosaurus Rex sound, combined with some of the more direct recent material as featured on the 'T. Rex' album.

If Bolan hadn't followed up 'Ride A White Swan' convincingly, T. Rex may nowadays be remembered as an underground group who managed to grab themselves one hit single. Bolan himself seemed to instinctively sense the change in his audience and cleverly seized the moment. It could however, have all gone wrong. Besides finding in 'Hot Love' the right song to follow 'Ride A White Swan', he also realised the band needed to be expanded to a full-blown rock quartet.

Following auditions, which were probably held at the end of February and the beginning of March, Bill Legend, who had previously worked with the band as a session drummer on 'Hot Love' and 'Woodland Rock', was chosen to occupy the drum stool. When he made his live debut is uncertain, but he was certainly in place for the North American concerts in April. It also seems possible that later that year Bolan may well have contemplated adding former King Crimson multi-instrumentalist Ian McDonald to the band. In addition to augmenting the band for a few live shows, he also appeared with the group that summer for the 'Top Of The Pops' performances of 'Get It On'.

Unfortunately very few T. Rex live recordings from this era have survived. Material taken from concerts in Wolverhampton (19th May), Stoke On Trent (22nd August) and possibly two other venues (one probably being Lewisham on 9th July) made up the Marc Bolan Fan Club's release 'T. Rextacy', currently available as 'Electric Boogie'. Radio sessions from New York in April 1971, currently available as the 'Spaceball' release, also survive. There's also an audience tape of the Weeley Festival performance. Unfortunately no tapes appear to survive neither from performances during the early part of the year nor from the 'Electric Warriors' tour at the end of 1971.

Saturday 2nd January
City Hall, Sheffield, Yorkshire, England

Sunday 3rd January
Guildhall, Preston, Lancashire, England

Monday 4th January
St. George's Hall, Bradford, Yorkshire, England

Thursday 7th January
New Theatre, Oxford, Oxfordshire, England

Thursday 14th January
Repeat transmission on BBC 1's 'Top Of The Pops' of the performance of 'Ride A White Swan' originally shown the 26th November edition.
Empire Theatre, Liverpool, Lancashire, England

Friday 15th January
Trentham Gardens, Stoke On Trent, Staffordshire, England

Saturday 16th January
King's Hall, Aberystwyth, Cardiganshire, Wales

Wednesday 20th January
Marc and T. Rex fly to Schiphol Airport, Amsterdam, possibly to do TV work.

Thursday 21st January
Gaumont Theatre, Southampton, Hampshire, England

Friday 22nd January
Trident Studios, St. Anne's Court, Soho, London, England
Studio session which saw a tape containing 'Hot Love', 'The King Of The Mountain Cometh' and 'Woodland Rock' produced. This may be a tape without the Kaylan and Volman overdubs.

Monday 25th January
The Lyceum, Strand, London, England
Set list: 'Elemental Child', 'Ride A White Swan' (incomplete)
Support group were America.

"Marc Bolan became a star and T. Rex a supergroup on Monday. Over 2,000 jammed London's Lyceum.

It was heart-warming for those who have followed the career of the unlikely duo down the years.

But several doubts arose during the almost unbelievable response ... there was something a little disturbing about the readiness to cheer what was frequently unmusical.

Marc whipped up incredible excitement with his minimal instrumentation and technique. While long sympathetic to the cause of Marc's cheerful pastiche of rock and poetry, when banging on top of a Woolworth's organ in loosely rhythmic fashion ... becomes the basis of a performance, one has to own up.

The best moments were during Marc's electric guitar freak-out on 'Elemental Child', where his fantasies of being a heavy rock star were fully played out. And 'Ride A White Swan' is a great riff and a lovely hit.

But the elements that make up the web of fantasy, fun and pop of Tyrannosaurus Rex are being uncomfortably stretched to the limits of credibility."

Chris Welch, Melody Maker

Thursday 28th January

Taverne de l'Olympia, Paris, France
Set list: 'Jewel', 'Ride A White Swan', 'Elemental Child', 'Summertime Blues' (incomplete)
This concert was filmed for the French programme 'Pop 2' and was broadcast on Antenne 2 sometime in late February/early March. A total of four songs were included in the final broadcast. These were 'Jewel', 'Ride A White Swan', 'Elemental Child' and 'Summertime Blues'. Unfortunately, in the final edit 'Jewel' was cut into two parts with Marc being interviewed in the gap between the two portions of the song.

Saturday 30th January

Broadcast date on French Television's First Channel (1re Chine) for 'Point Chaud' at 17.25 featuring a 'Pop Match' segment, Les Rotations contre T. Rex.

January

Trident Studios, St. Anne's Court, Soho, London, England
Further studio sessions working on 'Hot Love' and 'The King Of The Mountain Cometh'. This

included Mark Volman and Howard Kaylan recording their backing vocals. The session probably took place sometime around the week beginning 23rd January.

February (?)
Trident Studios, St. Anne's Court, Soho, London, England
Further studio sessions working on 'Hot Love' and other tracks.

February (?)
Radio Bremen Studios, Bremen, West Germany
For their first performance on Radio Bremen's TV show 'Beat Club' (networked on ARD), T. Rex performed two 'live' songs. A basic take of each song was filmed. Following this, a second take of Bolan singing and playing over the first take was filmed. These were then edited together to produce a composite performance. Two songs were completed: 'Ride A White Swan' and 'Jewel'. 'Ride A White Swan' remained pretty close to the record, but 'Jewel' was extended, as in concert, and indicated the increasingly heavier direction T. Rex were following. One song, 'Ride A White Swan' was broadcast on 13th February. 'Jewel' was shown on 20th March.

Thursday 4th February
Fairfield Halls, Croydon, Surrey, England

FAIRFIELD HALL, CROYDON
THURSDAY, FEBRUARY 4th, at 7.45
PETER BOWYER PRESENTS

T. REX

Tickets: 15/-, 13/-, 10/-, 8/-
From Fairfield Box Office, 01-688 9291

Saturday 6th February
University College, Gower Street, London, England

Monday 8th February
Top Rank, Cardiff, Glamorgan, Wales
Slade were to have been the original support at this concert, but there was a row over this leading to accusations in the music press that Bolan had prevented them from playing.

Saturday, 13th February
Broadcast date of episode 58 of 'Beat Club' which featured one of the performances, 'Ride A White Swan', recorded earlier in the month.
'Arts Festival', North East London Polytechnic, Barking, Essex, England
This concert was part of the North East London Polytechnic's 'Arts Festival', held between the 13th and 18th February.

Sunday 14th February
Essex University, Colchester, Essex, England

Monday 15th February
Civic Hall, Guildford, Surrey, England

Tuesday 16th February
Town Hall, Birmingham, Warwickshire, England

Wednesday 17th February
Caird Hall, Dundee, Angus, Scotland

UNIVERSITY COLLEGE, LONDON
Gower Street, W.C.1
The Entertainments Committee presents next term:

Jan. 16:	**NUCLEUS & MIGHTY BABY**
Jan. 23:	**BUDDY MILES EXPRESS**
Jan. 30:	**EVERY WHICH WAY & QUIVER**
Feb. 6:	**T. REX**
Feb. 13:	**URIAH HEEP & PALADIN**
Feb. 20:	**COLOSSEUM**

Students' Union Cards please
All groups booked through Nems — 629-6341
Advance tickets for Buddy Miles Express, Jan. 23.
Cheques & P.O.s to: U.C.L.U. Ents. Comm, 25
Gordon Street, W.C.1 (S.A.E.). 387-3611, Ext. 30

Friday 19th February

Hot Love / Woodland Rock / The King Of The Mountain Cometh (Fly BUG 6)

The first UK number one single, where it stayed for a total of six weeks. In the USA it peaked at 72 in the Top 100. The single was also a big hit in Germany, France, Italy, Belgium, Austria and Australia.

"Cosmic rock! Marc Bolan rushes back into the chart battle with a sound to appeal to all pop purists ... He has made this instantly commercial hit more in the spirit of nostalgia than in (an attempt) to recreate olde sounds. It's how we remember the hits of our youth. The "la la la" chorus will shortly be booming out of juke boxes where 'ere ten new pence will fit the slot."

Chris Welch, Melody Maker

"...Funny how the duo enjoyed only a minority appeal until the advent of its last single – then all hell broke loose! Presumably because "Swan" was the most commercial item the boys had then recorded.

Well, if anything, this is even more commercial! It's even got a repetitive la la chorus, in which Rex is joined by enthusiastic studio guests, and with which I'm sure you'll feel compelled to sing along. The very simplicity of the number is the key to its assured popularity...".

Derek Johnson, NME

"Marc Bolan's penchant for the records of his youth – all those jolly surfing/beach buggy tracks – comes leaping to the surface on this track that's absolutely bound to do as well, if not better than 'Ride A White Swan'. Lyrics like, "She's faster than most ..." are neatly tied up with leaping strings, easy handclapping and Bolan's unforgettable delivery, and to cap it all there's a real old bit of rock and roll gutsiness on the middle break ...".

Penny Valentine, Sounds

"'Hot Love' is built around a rolling slice of rhythmic development and the vocal side is both relaxed and urgent. Almost a cantering horse hoof backbeat – later on the odd yip and yell, and some beautiful use of violins etc. in boosting the sound level and that apart, it's plain centre, dead commercial. Do play it, and listen closely, before summing it up. Chart cert."

Peter Jones, Record Mirror

Saturday 20th February

University, Nottingham, Nottinghamshire, England

Monday 1st March

Unconfirmed venue, Cork, County Cork, Republic Of Ireland

If it took place, the concert was likely to have been held at the Savoy Theatre.

Tuesday 2nd March

Trident Studios, St. Anne's Court, Soho, London, England

Mixes were prepared of 'Seagull Woman', 'Hot Love', 'Beltane Walk' and 'Woodland Rock'. These were all without vocals and were made for 'Radio One Club'. As Marc may have been playing dates in Ireland at the time it's a possibility that these were entirely the work of Tony Visconti.

Queen's Hall, Belfast, County Antrim, Northern Ireland

The concert probably didn't take place.

READING UNIVERSITY
PRESENTS RAG WEEK

Saturday, February 27th, 8 p.m.
RAG QUEEN BALL

STRAWBS
plus BONEHEAD

50p in advance; 62½p on door

Wednesday, March 3rd, 7.30 p.m.
FOLK EVENING

STEFAN GROSSMAN
DECAMERON

30p in advance 37½p on door

Saturday, March 6th, 8 p.m.
RAG BALL

T. REX
STONE THE CROWS
MICK SOFTLEY
BOOZE DROOP
GRAPHITE

New Union Building, University of Reading
White Knights Park, Reading
Advance Tickets: G. Woodham, St. Patrick s Hall
Northcote Avenue, Reading. (S.A.E. please)

Wednesday 3rd March

Unconfirmed venue, Dublin, Republic Of Ireland

If it took place, the concert was likely to have been held at the National Stadium.

Saturday 6th March

New Union Building, Reading University, White Knights Park, Reading, Berkshire, England

Sunday 7th March

Marc and Jeff Dexter attend the Rolling Stones concert at The Marquee in London.

Tuesday 9th March

Playhouse Theatre, Northumberland Avenue, London, England

This special session for 'Radio One Club' featured the semi-playback versions of songs prepared on 2nd March. Three songs were featured in this session: 'Beltane Walk', 'Hot Love' and 'Seagull Woman'. 'Woodland Rock' was not used on British radio. They were broadcast during the week 29th March-2nd April. This was the first of many T. Rex semi-playback sessions. These usually featured a live vocal and additional guitar overdubs.

29th March – 'Beltane Walk' and 'Hot Love'; 30th March – 'Seagull Woman'; 31st March – 'Hot Love'; 2nd April – 'Hot Love'.

Wednesday 10th March

BBC Television Centre, Wood Lane, Shepherd's Bush, London, England

For their first performance of 'Hot Love' on BBC Television's 'Top Of The Pops', Mickey Finn mimed the drum part, though Bill Legend was the actual drummer on the record. Legend was still not officially a member of the band at this time. This performance was broadcast on 11th March and possibly also on the 18th March.

Thursday 11th March

Initial broadcast of the first performance of 'Hot Love' on BBC 1's 'Top Of The Pops'.

Fiesta Club, Sheffield, Yorkshire, England

This concert was abandoned after Marc discovered that the promoters had broached the concert contract and charged more than the permitted maximum price for a T. Rex concert.

Friday 12th March

Central Hall, University Of Lancaster, Bailrig, Lancaster, Lancashire, England

Thursday 18th March

Possible date for a second broadcast on 'Top Of The Pops' of the first performance of 'Hot Love'. However, it's possible that a promo film, made by the BBC, was used on this date.

Friday 19th March

Lanchester Polytechnic, Coventry, Warwickshire, England

Saturday 20th March

Broadcast date for episode 59 of 'Beat Club' featuring the performances of 'Jewel', which had been recorded back in early February.

'Saturday Dance Date', Winter Gardens Pavilion, Weston-Super-Mare, Somerset, England

Wednesday 24th March

BBC Television Centre, Wood Lane, Shepherd's Bush, London, England

The second BBC Television 'Top Of The Pops' performance of 'Hot Love', recorded on this date, was used more extensively than the first. It was broadcast on the 25th March, 1st April, 8th April and 15th April editions and possibly also on the 22nd April edition of the show.

Thursday 25th March

First broadcast date for the second performance of 'Hot Love' recorded for 'Top Of The Pops' (BBC 1).

Friday 26th March

The Best Of T. Rex (Fly TON 2)

'Debora', 'Child Star', 'Cat Black (The Wizard's Hat)', 'Conesuala', 'Strange Orchestras', 'Find A Little Wood', 'Once Upon The Seas Of Abyssinia', 'One Inch Rock', 'Salamanda Palaganda', 'Lofty Skies', 'Stacey Grove', 'King Of The Rumbling Spires', 'Blessed Wild Apple Girl', 'Elemental Child' The album reached number 21 in the charts.

This album was a budget priced compilation of Tyrannosaurus Rex material, which was issued as part of the Flyback retrospective series of albums. All the material had been previously released apart from 'Once Upon The Seas Of Abyssinia' and 'Blessed Wild Apple Girl' which had been recorded during or just after the 'Unicorn' sessions.

Monday 29th March

Broadcast date on BBC Radio One for the session recorded for 'Radio One Club'. See entry for 10th March.

Wednesday 31st March

Trident Studios, St. Anne's Court, Soho, London, England

Recording session which produced basic tracks for 'Mambo Sun' and a version of 'Cosmic Dancer'.

March (?)

Gooseberry Studios, 19 Gerrard Street, London, England

Recording session which saw a demo of 'Monolith', 'Bolan's Blues', 'Honey Don't' and an instrumental jam committed to tape.

Thursday 1st April

Repeat broadcast of the second performance of 'Hot Love' on 'Top Of The Pops' (BBC 1). See entry for 24th March.

US TOUR

While T. Rex were swiftly becoming huge stars in Britain, in America they continued to mean little outside of a small coterie of supporters. The disastrous 1969 tour had not been completely forgotten. The band had switched record labels, from Blue Thumb to the significantly more heavyweight Reprise, but nobody there seemed to know how to promote them. Dates with bands like Emerson, Lake And Palmer and Mountain were unlikely to find sympathetic audiences.

T. Rex appeared low on the bill (usually third) at concerts in large halls. At bigger clubs, those with a capacity of 500 to 1,000, their status improved to that of support band. Headline status was restricted to small venues like the Whiskey A Go Go in Los Angeles. All this took place against the backdrop of 'Hot Love' enjoying a six-week run in the top spot in the British singles chart.

Originally the band were due to tour the USA from 25th February to 26th March, with another UK tour to begin on 2nd April. However, everything was delayed for several weeks. The visit to the US did have some compensations. Tony Visconti was also visiting the US at the time, so between gigs in New York and Los Angeles, six of the basic tracks for 'Electric Warrior' were put down on tape.

Tuesday 6th April

Marc and T. Rex fly to New York to undertake the US tour.

Thursday 8th April

Repeat broadcast of the second performance of 'Hot Love' on 'Top Of The Pops' (BBC 1). See entry for 24th March.

WBAI Studios, New York, New York, USA

The likely date for a radio session to help promote the American tour. This appearance was probably broadcast live. Prior to the session Marc was interviewed. The songs performed were 'Cosmic Dancer', 'Planet Queen', 'Elemental Child', 'Jewel', and 'Hot Love'. The first two songs were acoustic solo performances. Mickey Finn and Steve Currie joined in for 'Elemental Child' and Bill Legend joined in half way through 'Jewel'. The session is likely to give a fair indication of the T. Rex live set at that time.

Friday 9th April

Eastown Theatre, Detroit, Michigan, USA

Supporting Paul Butterfield Blues Band. Tower Of Power were also on the bill.

Saturday 10th April

Eastown Theatre, Detroit, Michigan, USA

Supporting Paul Butterfield Blues Band. Tower Of Power were also on the bill.

Monday 12th April

Fillmore East, Manhattan, New York, New York, USA

Third on the bill to Mountain.

Tuesday 13th April

Fillmore East, Manhattan, New York, New York, USA
Third on the bill to Mountain.

Wednesday 14th April

Fillmore East, Manhattan, New York, New York, USA
Third on the bill to Mountain.

Thursday 15th April

Fillmore East, Manhattan, New York, New York, USA
Third on the bill to Mountain.

"Very strange indeed and very loud ... (T. Rex) started the show with a most original set of numbers, explosive and jogging at the same time, burstingly full of decibels.

T. Rex's music is built on the contrast between Marc Bolan's expressive stylised unreal vocals, his inhumanly electronic guitar technique and the adamantly idiotic rhythms of the percussion section

The great mystery of the group is how they can create a head-splitting wall of sound, with no appreciable melody, and simultaneously maintain that there is a certain order ... even an obscure kind of beauty. At the same time they can do a 'Hot Love' or a 'Ride A White Swan', commercial pop à la T. Rex ... Musical value of paradox may be debatable, but T. Rex are as intriguing as a jigsaw puzzle."

Nancy Erlich, Billboard

WPLJ Studios, New York, New York, USA
The probable date for a second New York radio session. This was broadcast live and was an acoustic set featuring only Bolan and Finn. Four songs were performed: 'Cosmic Dancer', 'Honey Don't', 'Planet Queen' and 'Get It On Blues'.

In England there was another repeat broadcast of the second performance of 'Hot Love' on 'Top Of The Pops' (BBC 1). See entry for 24th March.

Friday 16th April

Unconfirmed hotel, New York, New York, USA
Marc was interviewed by Keith Altham for the BBC Radio One programme 'Scene And Heard'. The interview was broadcast the next day, 17th April and lasted just under six and a half minutes.

Saturday 17th April

Broadcast date for the interview recorded for BBC Radio One's 'Scene And Heard' programme.

Sunday 18th April – Tuesday 20th April (?)

Wally Heider Studios, Los Angeles, California, USA
The likely dates for three days of recording sessions. These produced the basic tracks for 'Get It On', 'Monolith', and 'The Motivator'. They probably recorded in the daytime, prior to the evening shows. It's possible that 'Planet Queen' and not 'The Motivator' was recorded at these sessions, however two reliable sources indicate that the latter was recorded. Mark Volman and Howard Kaylan were in attendance for at least one day of the sessions, contributing backing vocals.

Monday 19th April
Whiskey A Go Go, Sunset Strip, Los Angeles, California, USA
Howard Kaylan and Mark Volman may have sung backing vocals on some songs at this show. The band was still billed as Tyrannosaurus Rex for both nights.

Tuesday 20th April
Whiskey A Go Go, Sunset Strip, Los Angeles, California, USA
Howard Kaylan and Mark Volman may also have added backing vocals on this date.

Wednesday 21st April
Sarve Auditorium, Montreal, Quebec, Canada
Though scheduled, this concert, as support to Johnny and Edgar Winter, was cancelled at the last minute.

Thursday 22nd April
Possible repeat broadcast of the second performance of 'Hot Love' on 'Top Of The Pops' (BBC 1). See entry for 24th March. However, it's unclear from BBC records just what was transmitted that day. It's possible that the 17th March performance was used or possibly a BBC produced promo film which included neither Bolan nor the band.

Friday 23rd April
State University Of New York, Albany, New York, USA
This date was probably as support to Johnny Winter and the Edgar Broughton Band.

Saturday 24th April
Washington And Lee High School, Arlington, Virginia, USA

Sunday 25th April
The Spectrum, Philadelphia, Pennsylvania, USA
Support to Emerson Lake And Palmer and Procol Harum.

Tuesday 27th April (?)

Media Sound Studios, New York, New York, USA

The probable first day of a two day recording session which produced the basic tracks for 'Jeepster', 'Lean Woman Blues' and 'Girl'.

Wednesday 28th April

Media Sound Studios, New York, New York, USA

The probable second day of recording at the above studio. The basic track for 'Jeepster' was recorded on this date.

Saturday 29th April

Pines Hotel, South Fallsburg, New York, USA

Friday 30th April

The Rock Pile, Long Island, New York, USA
Support to Humble Pie.

Saturday 1st May

The Rock Pile, Long Island, New York, USA
Support to Humble Pie.

Monday 3rd May

T. Rex return to the UK.

Air Studios, 214 Oxford Street, London, England

A tape was produced on this date containing 'Planet Queen', 'Monolith', 'Get It On', 'Girl', 'Jeepster' and 'Lean Woman Blues'. The title 'Girl' has been crossed out on the track sheet, and Marc had written 'Electric Witch' in its place. 'Jeepster' and 'Monolith' have "cello" written next to them and 'Get It On' has "sax" written next to it. It's likely that this tape is a composite of the songs recorded in America, however see the above entry for 18th – 20th April regarding this.

May (?)

Trident Studios, St. Anne's Court, Soho, London, England
Recording sessions which saw 'Planet Queen', 'Life's A Gas' and possibly the album version of 'Cosmic Dancer' recorded.

BRITISH TOUR

From this point onwards, the choice of songs performed in concert increasingly began to reflect Bolan's changing audience and the material that audience was familiar with. 'Hot Love' had been added to the live set for the North American dates. The May British tour now featured a fixed acoustic interlude in the middle of the show, largely consisting of songs from the then forthcoming 'Electric Warrior' album. The Tyrannosaurus Rex past wasn't totally forgotten. Concerts began with Bolan appearing unaccompanied on stage performing 'Elemental Child'. 'Debora' still made frequent appearances during the acoustic portion of the set. Another feature of the set was that songs started to be extensively lengthened in performance. 'Jewel' was lasting anything up to a reputed thirty minutes. 'Ride A White Swan' was clocking in at just under ten. 'Get It On' also made its debut as part of the live set on this tour.

JOHN & TONY SMITH present

T
REX
IN CONCERT

appearing at

BOURNEMOUTH	WINTER GARDENS	SUNDAY	MAY 9th	7.45
PORTSMOUTH	GUILDHALL	TUESDAY	MAY 11th	7.45
NOTTINGHAM	ALBERT HALL	FRIDAY	MAY 14th	7.30
MANCHESTER	FREE TRADE HALL	SUNDAY	MAY 16th	7.30
SHEFFIELD	CITY HALL (40p)	MONDAY	MAY 17th	7.30
WOLVERHAMPTON	CIVIC HALL	WEDNESDAY	MAY 19th	7.30
NEWCASTLE	CITY HALL	THURSDAY	MAY 20th	7.30
GLASGOW	GREENS PLAYHOUSE	FRIDAY	MAY 21st	8 p.m.
CROYDON	FAIRFIELD HALL	SUNDAY	MAY 23rd	8 p.m.
BRISTOL	COLSTON HALL	MONDAY	MAY 24th	7.30
LEICESTER	DE MONTFORT HALL	TUESDAY	MAY 25th	7.30
BRADFORD	ST. GEORGE'S HALL	THURSDAY	MAY 27th	7.30
LIVERPOOL	PHILHARMONIC	FRIDAY	MAY 28th	7.30

All seats 60p, with the exception of Sheffield City Hall, which is 40p

All seats bookable in advance from Local Box Offices and usual Ticket Agencies

Sunday 9th May

Winter Gardens, Bournemouth, Hampshire, England

Tuesday 11th May

Guildhall, Portsmouth, Hampshire, England
Set list: 'Debora', 'Summertime Blues' (incomplete)

"Bob Dawbarn in his Sounds column appealed for excitement to return to rock. Well it would have warmed the kernels of his heart to have seen T. Rex in concert at Portsmouth Guildhall. When the group launched into 'Hot Love' midway through their act, it was the signal for most of the capacity audience to besiege the stage area. And there they stayed for the remainder of the concert, dancing and jostling all the while ... it was the sort of warm atmosphere you expect to find at a friend's party.

As Marc Bolan gyrated around the stage like the new Elvis Presley, girls clambered on the stage to kiss him. Others, with a touch of hero worship ... reached their arms across the stage to grab him as he hopscotched around. The few to remain seated jumped up and down like dervishes as T. Rex pounded their exciting message home. Most of the music was good driving rock, like the encore number 'Summertime Blues', though the group did include 'Debora', for old time's sake Bolan told me afterwards."

Barry Dillon, Sounds

Friday 14th May

Albert Hall, Nottingham, Nottinghamshire, England
The photo which went on to become the basis for the 'Electric Warrior' cover was taken at this concert.

Sunday 16th May

Free Trade Hall, Manchester, Lancashire, England

Monday 17th May

City Hall, Sheffield, Yorkshire, England

Wednesday 19th May

Civic Hall, Wolverhampton, Staffordshire, England
Set list: 'Elemental Child', 'Beltane Walk', 'One Inch Rock', 'Girl', 'Rip Off', 'Debora', 'Ride A White Swan', 'Instrumental Jam', 'Hot Love', 'Get It On', 'Jewel', 'Summertime Blues'.
Material from this concert has appeared on various live T. Rex releases.

Thursday 20th May

City Hall, Newcastle, Northumberland, England

Friday 21st May

Green's Playhouse, Glasgow, Lanarkshire, Scotland

Sunday 23rd May

Fairfield Halls, Croydon, Surrey, England

Ian McDonald guested on saxophone at this concert.

Monday 24th May

Colston Hall, Bristol, Gloucestershire, England

Tuesday 25th May

De Montford Hall, Leicester, Leicestershire, England

Thursday 27th May

St George's Hall, Bradford, Yorkshire, England

Friday 28th May

Philharmonic Hall, Liverpool, Lancashire, England

Sunday 30th May

Roundhouse, Chalk Farm, London, England

Ian McDonald guested on saxophone at this concert.

Tuesday 1st June

Advision Studios, 23 Gosfield Street, London, England

A song with the title, on the tape box, 'String Thing' was recorded on this date. This may well be something more familiar under another title.

June (?)

Advision Studios, 23 Gosfield Street, London, England

Studio session which saw 'Rip Off' and possibly 'Raw Ramp' and 'Electric Boogie' put down on tape.

Tuesday 22nd June

Marc enters The Netherlands at Rotterdam. It's likely that the band recorded the promo films of 'Get It On' and 'Jeepster' at some point during the next few days.

Friday 25th June

Air Studios, 214 Oxford Street, London, England

The master mix of 'The Motivator' was produced.

Saturday 26th June

Amsterdam Free Concert, Amsterdamse Bos, Amsterdam, Netherlands

T. Rex perform at the above festival, though it's possible they may have appeared the previous day.

Sunday 27th June
Unconfirmed venue, Erbach im Odenwald, West Germany

Television recording for the SDF produced programme 'Hits A Go Go'. This performance of 'Hot Love' was a mimed version and also featured B. P. Fallon, Bolan's publicist of the time, along with Mickey Finn pretending to play congas. The show was probably broadcast in early July.

Monday 28th June
Unconfirmed television studio, Milan, Italy

Television recording for an unknown Italian TV show. Though no details are available, this recording probably featured another mimed performance of 'Hot Love'.

Friday 2nd July
Get It On / There Was A Time / Raw Ramp (Fly BUG 10)

The second number one for T. Rex to reach the top of the UK singles chart. It remained there for a total of four weeks. In America the single was released in the first week of August, but it took nearly eight months to reach its peak position of 10 in the US Top 100. The song was also a big hit in Germany, France, Japan and Italy.

The basic track had been recorded in Los Angeles. After the tapes were brought back to London, Tony Visconti added further overdubs, including Ian McDonald's sax part and Rick Wakeman on piano. Strings were also added in London.

"It's an understated shuffle beat, monotonous, but compulsive. Marc sings mysteriously and is backed by stomping drums and grumbling guitar. Perhaps not as instantly hit worthy as 'Hot Love', but positive and likeable. Typical of the new Rex, with its roots in classic pop."

Chris Welch, Melody Maker

"I'm sure a lot of Rex aficionados have found themselves wavering recently in the face of all the anti-Rex sniping. But there is a simple cure... listen to the music. Of course T. Rex is now commercial, but they... are playing today in a different context as well as they have ever done.

'Get It On' is another instant number one and none the worse for it. Tony Visconti's strings provide a link between this and 'Hot Love', but if anything, 'Get It On' is nearer the old Tyrannosaurus Rex – treated in the modern manner.

...the thudding drum bass work that evokes memories of Sun, and the raspy, rooty-tooty and fruity guitar of Bolan. With the Mothers' vocalists again in tow, Ian McDonald a-blowing on sax, there's a lot more to this multi-textured single than space here permits me to go into. Just listen."

Nick Logan, NME

"Boley does it again. I don't care a damn if people think he's sold out or any other tommy-rot ... To say this is going to streak off to the top of the charts is unnecessary. It follows on the 'Hot Love' feel, all sneaky and suggestive."

Penny Valentine, Sounds

"This is an absolute cert for the top – it would be even if T. Rex changed their name to protect the innocent. It's just instantly commercial, with an excellent sense of rhythm and power and an insistent basic riff which clicks even after a couple of bars. Good guitar figures worked into the patchwork rock and roll setting. No point in getting detailed about it – it's instant and it's a giant hit. Chart cert."

Peter Jones, Record Mirror

Odeon, Birmingham, Warwickshire, England
Set list: 'Elemental Child', 'Beltane Walk', 'One Inch Rock', 'Ride A White Swan', 'Girl', 'Cosmic Dancer', 'Debora', 'Is It Love', 'Hot Love', 'Get It On', 'Summertime Blues' (Both shows)
Two shows.
Support came from Bronco.

"By sticking to a predictable pro-gramme, T. Rex scotched suggestions that they are changing their musical direction ... Their stage set got under way with Marc occupying the stage alone to sing 'Elemental Child'. It developed into a really rocking affair when he was joined by Mickey Finn ... and bassist Steve Currie. Drummer Bill Legend completed the line-up for 'Beltane Walk' and 'One Inch Rock' ... The rest of their perform-ance was confined to single material – 'Debora', 'Ride A White Swan', 'Hot Love' and their new release, 'Get It On'."

Dennis Detheridge, Melody Maker (First show)

JOHN & TONY SMITH

present

T. REX

in concert

with SPECIAL GUESTS

BRONCO

TWO SHOWS at 6.30 p.m. and 9 p.m.

FRIDAY, 2nd JULY
ODEON
BIRMINGHAM Tel. 021-643 0815

FRIDAY, 9th JULY
ODEON
LEWISHAM Tel. 852 1331

All Seats: 60p. Bookable in Advance from:
ODEON BOX OFFICES

"Apart from four acoustic numbers (sic) halfway through the T. Rex set ... it was mostly hard rock all the time, with Marc Bolan skipping around the stage trying to pierce everybody's head with those too-loud guitar licks ...

Bolan opened the set alone, giving the audience a good copy of Hendrix's wild guitar style ... then on came Mickey Finn and off the music went.

I always found T. Rex music a bit monotonous ... but there are a lot of things I do like such as the poetic song called 'Girl', due to be on their next album ...

Running over time, Bolan told the audience he wanted to feel some vibes and brought them to their feet with 'Ride A White Swan', 'Hot Love' and the new boogie single 'Get It On'."

Tony Stewart, Sounds

"Quite a nice balance has been reached in the T. Rex set... Marc Bolan opens things with his screeching guitar effects, the rest of the band join in for some solid rock, and then we have the acoustic set, followed by the T. Rex hit parade.

And what the band lack in musical ability, they certainly make up in enthusiasm, bringing the whole of the audience down to the front of the stage at the end of the night. Whatever Rex you prefer you should be satisfied with some of what they're doing at the moment.

★★★★★★★★★★★★★★★★★★★★
★ **STARLIGHT ROOMS** BOSTON
Tel. (0205) 3579 ★

Saturday, 3rd July

T. REX

SUPER TRAMP   **D.J. RICKY TEE**

7 to 12   BARS, etc.   **50p**
★★★★★★★★★★★★★★★★★★★★

Mickey Finn lays down some fast conga playing that seems to have an infectious beat about it, with heavy driving bass and drum work...

Surprisingly enough his vocals were clear and crisp, especially on the acoustic numbers which included 'Debora' and a new one called 'Girl'.

Throughout the set Bolan insisted on the audience joining in with stamping and clapping. To me this is what their music is all about, a wild sort of party with a short relief period. 'Ride A White Swan', 'Hot Love' and then the new single 'Get It On' finish their well-appreciated act."

Tony McNally, NME

Saturday 3rd July

Starlight Rooms, Boston, Lincolnshire, England
Support was Supertramp.

Wednesday 7th July

BBC Television Centre, Wood Lane, Shepherd's Bush, London, England
Recording date for the first television slot of 'Get It On' for BBC 1's 'Top Of The Pops'. In total, this performance was broadcast a total of four times; on the 8th July, 22nd July, 29th July and 12th August. The band was augmented by former King Crimson member Ian McDonald on saxophone.

Thursday 8th July

Transmission date on BBC 1's 'Top Of The Pops' of the first performance of 'Get It On'. See previous entry.

Friday 9th July

Odeon, Lewisham, London, England
Set list: 'Elemental Child', 'One Inch Rock', 'Girl', 'Debora', 'Ride A White Swan', 'Hot Love', 'Get It On', 'Summertime Blues' (Second show) (Possibly incomplete)
Two shows. One at 6.30 p.m., the other at 9.00 p.m.
Support came from Bronco.

"The mood in the dressing room was subdued and Marc had just heard that the news of Jim Morrison's death had been confirmed ...

Marc opened the set with an amazing solo electric guitar number using pedals and feedback and a remarkable sense of time and dynamics ... I got strong memory flashes of Hendrix as he stood alone on that stage ... The band joined him for 'One Inch Rock' and then Marc did a solo song called 'Girl' with Spanish guitar, sitting cross-legged on the floor in a blue spotlight ...

There are very few rock musicians around who have that understanding of an audience, combined with the feel and understanding of rock music that allows them to reach such a wide audience ... I can't imagine anyone who could remain unmoved by it all ... and while I wouldn't want rock music to be solely T. Rex, I wouldn't like to be without them."

Steve Peacock, Sounds (Second show)

"It's really heartening to see a T. Rex concert. The excitement's there, effervescent and loose, as Marc would say, reminiscent of days when pop really was a volatile medium.

Though the thousands strong crowd listened and joined in with the music, they exploded after each number. The lone figure of Marc Bolan opened, but he suffered from overamplification and lack of guitar control. But when Mickey Finn and Steve Currie joined him the hall erupted to the sounds of pounding bass and interesting congas. 'One Inch Rock' was a belter, with the balance sounding better ... Before singing 'Girl' from his forthcoming album Marc explained how people are troubled by the direction they've taken, but how he understood. Sitting cross legged on stage, Marc produced some lovely vocals – his strongest feature throughout the set – on 'Debora' which had everyone clapping along, and squealing with glee when he arose to reveal a large gash down his trouser leg seam.

After the hour long set – which flew by – the four musicians were brought back for an exciting encore of 'Summertime Blues'. They're a good instrumental unit and Marc's notable vocals add power throughout."

Val Mabbs, Record Mirror

Thursday 15th July

Possible second transmission of the first performance of 'Get It On' recorded for 'Top Of The Pops' (BBC 1). However, it's more likely that a promo film was broadcast on this date.

Saturday 17th July

The Pavilion, Bath, Avon, England

Tuesday 20th July

Unconfirmed BBC Radio Studio, London, England

This radio session, transmitted on BBC Radio One's 'Radio One Club' programme, was broadcast during the week of 9th to 13th August. One song was broadcast each day, with the session version of 'Get It On' being broadcast twice. The session was a semi-playback affair. Bolan added vocal and the occasional guitar overdub to the basic tracks of the following songs: 'Electric Boogie' (1.35), 'Raw Ramp' (2.15), 'Get It On' (4.35) and 'Jeepster' (3.45).

9th August – 'Electric Boogie' 10th August – 'Raw Ramp' 11th August – 'Get It On' 12th August – 'Jeepster' 13th August – 'Get It On'.

Some of the songs were also broadcast on the Johnny Walker Show between the 23rd August to 27th August and 4th October to 8th October.

23rd August – 'Get It On' 25th August – 'Jeepster' 26th August – 'Raw Ramp'. No information for 4th to 8th October.

Wednesday 21st July

Trident Studios, St. Anne's Court, Soho, London, England

A master tape of the 'Electric Warrior' album was compiled on this date. The track listing was slightly different from the final album:

T. REX
THE FACES KING CRIMSON
COLOSSEUM CURVED AIR EDGAR BROUGHTON
GREASEBAND GROUNDHOGS MUNGO JERRY
RORY GALLAGHER QUINTESSENCE
STONE THE CROWS VAN DER GRAAF GENERATOR
CARAVAN LINDISFARNE
AL STEWART ARTHUR BROWN'S KINGDOM COME
BARCLAY JAMES HARVEST & SYMPHONY ORCHESTRA
HEAD, HANDS AND FEET JUICY LUCY STATUS QUO STRAY
ANNE BRIGGS ASSAGAI BEING BELL AND ARK COMUS COUNTRY JUG
CROW FAIRFIELD PARLOUR FUSION ORCHESTRA GERRY LOUGHRAN
GHIDROLOG GRINGO HACKENSACK LOUSIE MIKE MARAN
NATURAL ACOUSTIC BAND ON PAUL BRETT'S SAGE
PRINCIPAL EDWARDS MAGIC THEATRE PICOTTE AND ALBEQUERQUE
TIR NA NOG TUDOR LODGE STEVE TILSTON VECCHIO
HOME CASTLE MIKE SAUNDERS
Sunday's special guest   Saturday's special guest
JULIE FELIX   MOTT THE HOOPLE

Side One: 'Mambo Sun', 'Cosmic Dancer', 'The Motivator', 'Monolith', 'Lean Woman Blues'

Side Two: 'Get It On', 'Girl', 'Planet Queen', 'Jeepster', 'Life's A Gas', 'Rip Off'

Thursday 22nd July

Repeat broadcast on BBC 1's 'Top Of The Pops' of the first performance of 'Get It On'. See entry for 7th July.

Thursday 29th July

Repeat broadcast on BBC 1's 'Top Of The Pops' of the first performance of 'Get It On'. See entry for 7th July.

July (?)

Tony Visconti's flat, Courtfield Road, South Kensington, London, England

An acoustic demo session was recorded at Tony Visconti's home. 'Cadilac' and 'Truck On (Tyke)', were put down on tape. Mary Hopkin, Visconti's wife of the time, sang backing vocals on 'Truck On (Tyke)'. The songs also featured contributions from Visconti.

Tuesday 3rd August

BBC Studio T1, Shepherd's Bush, London, England

Recording date for the final true radio session for the BBC, i.e. one fully recorded in their studios. The session was recorded for the 'Bob Harris Show'. It was broadcast on 23rd August. T. Rex recorded five songs for transmission: 'Sailors Of The Highway', 'Girl', 'Cadilac', 'Jeepster' and 'Life's A Gas'. To date this is the only T. Rex studio version of 'Sailors Of The Highway' to have been made public.

Wednesday 4th August

BBC Television Centre, Wood Lane, Shepherd's Bush, London, England

A second television performance of 'Get It On' was recorded for 'Top Of The Pops' on this date. It was used just the one time, on the following day's edition.

Thursday 5th August

Transmission of the second performance of 'Get It On' recorded for BBC 1's 'Top Of The Pops'. See entry for 4th August.

Monday 9th August

First day of broadcast for the songs recorded at the radio session for 'Radio One Club' on 20th July. One song was broadcast each day and the songs were broadcast throughout the week. Some of the material was to be transmitted again at various dates and on differing shows throughout the next few years.

Thursday 12th August

Another repeat broadcast on BBC 1's 'Top Of The Pops' of the first performance of 'Get It On'. See entry for 7th July.

Starker's Club, Royal Ballrooms, Bournemouth, Hampshire, England

Saturday 14th August

Broadcast in West Germany of 'Disco 71' featuring a film segment on T. Rex. This included footage of T. Rex on a stage in England, but not during a concert. It was probably filmed during a soundcheck. Audience sequences were then mixed in to playback versions of 'Hot Love' and 'Get It On'. Also included in the programme an interview and film of Marc and wife June recorded at home in London.

Sunday 22nd August

Trentham Gardens, Stoke On Trent, Staffordshire, England

Set list: 'Cadilac', 'Beltane Walk', 'One Inch Rock', 'Spaceball Ricochet', 'Debora', 'Ride A White Swan', 'Hot Love', 'Get It On'.
Support from Gentle Giant.
A large portion of the material performed has since been released.

Monday 23rd August

Broadcast date for the session recorded for the 'Bob Harris Show' (BBC Radio One). See entry for 3rd August.

Saturday 28th August

Clifton Park, Rotherham, Yorkshire, England

Support came from Marmalade, Atomic Rooster and The Crazy World Of Arthur Brown.
This open-air concert was primarily a rehearsal for the following night's performance at the Weeley Festival.

Sunday 29th August

'Weeley Festival', Clacton On Sea, Essex, England

Set list: 'Cadilac', 'Beltane Walk', 'One Inch Rock', 'Spaceball Ricochet', 'Debora', 'Ride A White Swan', 'Get It On'

T. Rex headlined a day which saw Rory Gallagher, Mott The Hoople, Caravan, Quintessence, Head Hands And Feet, Lindisfarne, Julie Felix and The Faces play.
Initially there were problems between Bolan's management and that of The Faces as to who should headline that night. In the end Bolan's camp prevailed.

"As if following the Faces' incredible show stopping performance wasn't more than enough... T. Rex had to contend with... hang-ups like equipment failure and a barrage of abuse from certain sections of the crowd whose feelings towards Mr. Bolan's band had been aroused by Mr. Uncool himself, Colin King.

It would appear to some that T. Rex have committed the unforgivable and cardinal sin of becoming popular. With his tongue planted firmly in cheek, Marc stated "I'm Marc Bolan – you've seen me on 'Top Of The Pops' – I'm a big star." Unfortunately, some took this as gospel and gave him some lip to which Marc retorted "Why don't you fuck off." Eventually his dissenters were silenced by Marc threatening to leave the stage, "If you don't want to listen, then I'll leave." ...they kicked off with a lengthy as yet unrecorded rocker 'Cadilac' followed by 'One Inch Rock' which paved the way for an acoustic interlude... 'Spaceball Ricochet' led into 'Girl' and their well received 'Debora', then it was back to high wattage with 'Ride A White Swan', 'Hot Love and 'Get It On' amongst others.

T. Rex are a strange band. When electrified they encompass the basic rudiments of rock music... They emit a naïve enthusiasm one would expect from a bunch of blokes who had just acquired their first instruments and were having a good old blow down the local church hall or in someone's front room.

Bolan seems to be the 20th Century schizoid rock man, for as he draws on all the traditional mechanics of rock he's suddenly transformed into a reincarnation of that person. Chuck Berry as he duck walks across the stage... Eddie Cochran as he belts out a repetitive riff... Pete Townshend playing at human windmills. Hendrix doing his sexual symbolism sequence... Indeed, Bolan did just about everything except smash his guitar and take off into space.

You can't compare either Bolan or T. Rex to other bands, they are a power unto themselves and an essence that needs savouring on more than one hearing and under far better conditions than at Weeley."

Roy Carr, NME

Wednesday 1st September

Marc flies to New York on business. The British success of T. Rex took Reprise by total surprise. Originally they wanted the band back in the States for a tour in October/November of that year. The demands of the British market put paid to that idea. A tour with Alice Cooper was then mooted for December. Bolan seemingly holding out for a tour with full headline status.

Friday 24th September

Electric Warrior (Fly HIFLY 6)

'Mambo Sun', 'Cosmic Dancer', 'Jeepster', 'Monolith', 'Lean Woman Blues', 'Get It On', 'Planet Queen', 'Girl', 'The Motivator', 'Life's A Gas', 'Rip Off'.

Marc Bolan – guitar, vocals; Mickey Finn – percussion; Steve Currie – bass; Bill Legend – drums; Ian McDonald – saxophone on 'Get It On' 'The Motivator' and 'Rip Off'; Burt Collins – flugel horn; Rick Wakeman – piano on 'Get It On'; Howard Kaylan and Mark Volman backing vocals on 'Mambo Sun', 'Cosmic Dancer', 'Monolith', 'Get It On', and 'Planet Queen'.

Recorded at Trident Studios, London; Advision Studios, London; Wally Heider Studios, Los Angeles; Media Sound Studios, New York.

Produced by Tony Visconti; Engineered by Rik Pekkonen (Wally Heider Studios), Malcolm Cecil (Media Sound Studios), Roy T. Baker (Trident Studios), Martin Rushent (Advision Studios).

The album was a huge success spending over six months in the UK Top Thirty and reaching number 1. In America the album spent nearly eight months in the Top 200 reaching a high point of number 32.

"In the face of all the slanging, not only does he refuse to duck and run for the obscurity that seems the only sacrifice the knockers will accept, but damn it if he doesn't further pause to spit blithely in their eyes.

But whether or not you feel you have a legitimate grievance that Bolan has butchered the spirit of Tyrannosaurus Rex, you must admire his composure and concede his sincerity.

What Marc has done here is... draw upon the range of rock and roll influences that is the diet of any child of rock, impress them with his own individual penchant for lyrics and a finely attuned producer's ear, and drag them kicking and screaming into '71 ...

What you get is songs that Marc could easily have written for 'My People Were Fair ...' ... but given the whole blitzkrieg treatment of '71 T. Rex.

But I'm not sure that he hasn't been a little too clever ... I began to feel towards the end, that the diligent pursuit after the quintessence of rock and roll had robbed a lot of the songs of their initial funk.

Much as I can admire Marc for refusing to be swayed by the critics, it would be damaging if he reacted by cutting himself off and trusting only his own head. For all the satisfaction of 'Electric Warrior', the tightrope could turn into a plank."

Nick Logan, NME

"Marc Bolan and friends seem to be causing a great deal of upset and confusion lately. "Boo, rubbish," is the cry, which is a shame because Marc's music is getting better all the time.

He has developed the knack for writing good, original pop, and with the aid of producer Tony Visconti is developing an amazing studio sound with its roots in the fifties. It's not exactly rock and roll, but New York juvenile delinquency, hubcap stealing rumble music.

'Warrior' is a quaint and curious twisting of the skeins of pop, a gathering and weaving, which makes it not in the least significant, but decidedly enjoyable ... Marc's Clapton influenced (literally) guitar wails and the studio echoes. The lyrics are nonsense ...

They're not even good-bad ... Yet the three minutes 30 of 'Rip Off' are striking, and this odd piece has a strange quality of despair which maybe even Marc doesn't notice ... There's also a good six months worth of complaining ahead for Bolan dissidents. And that's how long it should stay in the charts."

Chris Welch, Melody Maker

"T. Rex have never been one of my favourites, and until "Get It On' I had more or less ignored them, but I was entirely converted when I heard the tapes of their new album at Mickey Finn's flat (August 1971). It's all down to the new, dynamic T. Rex of their recent single releases, with a much fuller, stronger sound than before...

Marc Bolan's voice cavorts and gasps, and his guitar playing has improved immeasurably since his switch to an electronic instrument. Seven of the tracks were recorded in the States during their tour, and their experience of America seems to have affected them... It's tougher and funkier, more energetic than I imagined.

Tracks like 'Jeepster' and 'Rip Off' ... are very present statements... They are not afraid to use other people's things where it suits them, but they convert them into a totally T. Rex sound, as on 'Jeepster' which becomes almost Motown at the end.

'Monolith' which has an old time rock and roll sound; reminds me of going to local group hops, rushing home from school to take out your favourite chick and trying to get it together to Johnny Kidd and The Pirates' 'Duke Of Earl'.

Said Mickey, to quote, of this (album), he says that he was very pleasantly surprised to hear the finished product after the final mixes of so many different sessions, and so am I."

Martin Hayman, Sounds

"Bolan has so cunningly utilised a panorama of influences... that anyone who has travelled a similar path will find his head spinning from one nostalgia to the next. On 'Monolith' you might be listening to a '71 remake of 'Duke of Earl'. 'Cosmic Dancer' has strings which could have been scored by Bert Berns. 'Jeepster' might have been cut in Sam Phillips's midget Sun Studios,... 'Lean Woman Blues' could be an unused Bob Dylan tape from 'Bringing It All Back Home'. On top of that Bolan has added a spicy icing and a cultured producer's ear to produce a finished product very much '71 and very much his own. 'Electric Warrior' is certainly a major achievement in Bolan's career, both as a performer and producer."

Uncredited, Sounds

Thursday 30th September

Stadthalle, Bremen, West Germany

A mimed performance, firmly in the realms of kitsch, for the ZDF networked programme 'Starparade'. T. Rex performed two songs 'Hot Love' and 'Get It On', both of which were shorter versions, faded out early. In addition to the musical spots, there was a short chat which included congratulating Marc on his twenty-fourth birthday. The show was broadcast live.

Hotel "Zur Post", Bremen, West Germany

The band stayed at this hotel, where several photo sessions took place on this and the following day.

Friday 1st October

Radio Bremen Studios, Bremen, West Germany

In contrast to the previous days filming, this appearance for 'Beat Club' was 'live'. The same procedure as on the previous appearance back in January was followed. The TV crew filmed a first take and then a second take of Bolan was recorded and the two sets of pictures were mixed together.

Three songs were recorded, but only two were completed and transmitted: 'Jeepster' and 'Life's A Gas' were networked in West Germany on 13th November. 'Jeepster' was kept tight and concise, while 'Life's A Gas' showed marked differences from the studio version on 'Electric Warrior'. Marc chose to play the song totally on electric guitar, rather than make use of his acoustic guitar and then adding electric overdubs.

An early and slightly shaky version of 'Baby Strange', featuring a different arrangement, was also filmed, but the filming was left incomplete and the song not broadcast.

Saturday 2nd October (?)

Unconfirmed BBC Studio, London, England (?)

Interview with Keith Altham.

Sunday 3rd October

Broadcast date for an interview with Keith Altham on BBC Radio One's 'Scene And Heard'. The segment lasted six minutes.

Thursday 7th October

T. Rex fly to Schiphol Airport, Amsterdam for a couple of dates in The Netherlands.

Friday 8th October

Grote Zaal, De Doelen, Rotterdam, Netherlands

Saturday 9th October

Concertgebouw, Amsterdam, Netherlands

John & Tony Smith
in association with E.G. Management present:

Electric Warriors

T.REX in concert

October Dates:

Tuesday	19th	Guildhall Portsmouth
Wednesday	20th	ABC Cinema. Plymouth
Thursday	21st	Capitol. Cardiff
Saturday	23rd	City Hall Sheffield
Sunday	24th	Fairfield. Croydon
Monday	25th	St. Georges Hall. Bradford
Wednesday	27th	The Dome. Brighton
Friday	29th	Greens Playhouse. Glasgow
Sunday	31st	City Hall. Newcastle

November Dates

Thursday	4th	ABC Stockton
Friday	5th	Town Hall. Birmingham
Saturday	6th	Free Trade Hall Manchester
Monday	8th	De Montfort Hall Leicester
Tuesday	9th	ABC Lincoln
Wednesday	10th	ABC Wigan

October 1971 (?)

Unknown house, London, England

Another acoustic demo session which saw 'Thunderwing', 'Spaceball Ricochet' and 'Telegram Sam' all put down on tape.

'ELECTRIC WARRIORS' BRITISH TOUR

As in the case of The Beatles before them, it was debatable as to how much music you could actually hear at a T. Rex concert. The noise from the predominately young audience was enough to smother anything being produced on stage. What's apparent from surviving live material (the Weeley Festival for example) and contemporary concert reviews is that T. Rex were a rather ramshackle live band. When it was good, it was very good, but when it was bad, well ...

Marc's guitar playing was inconsistent, while Legend and Currie were still learning to play together and Mickey Finn was largely redundant. If Bolan played poorly, there were just not enough instrumentation there to cover up. An incredible amount of work was being left to Steve Currie. Additionally, the increasingly lengthy guitar solos being taken by Marc left huge holes in the sound. T. Rex records were driven by Marc's original rhythm guitar playing, and featured a complex web of guitar overdubs. The absence of another guitar player on stage meant that this aspect of the T. Rex sound failed to translate into live performance.

T. Rex were not in the same league as a power group like The Who or Led Zeppelin. Bolan's guitar abilities didn't match those of Jimmy Page or Pete Townshend, for example. In retrospect the failure to fully incorporate Ian McDonald into the band's line-up was a major error. Besides being a talented multi-instrumentalist, whose sax playing was one of the highlights of 'Electric Warrior', the addition of sax would have made a nice counterpart to Bolan's guitar, and given much needed colour to the group's live sound.

Tuesday 19th October

Guildhall, Portsmouth, Hampshire, England

Wednesday 20th October
ABC, Plymouth, Devon, England

Thursday 21st October
Capitol, Cardiff, Glamorgan, Wales

Saturday 23rd October
City Hall, Sheffield, Yorkshire, England

Sunday 24th October
Fairfield Halls, Croydon, Surrey, England
Set list: 'Cadilac', 'Jeepster', 'Spaceball Ricochet', 'Cosmic Dancer', 'Ride A White Swan', 'Hot Love', 'Get It On', 'Summertime Blues' (First show)
Set list: 'Cadilac', 'Jeepster', 'Debora', 'Cosmic Dancer', 'Spaceball Ricochet', 'Ride A White Swan', 'Hot Love', 'Get It On', 'Summertime Blues' (Second show)
Two shows.

"Magic is a hard thing to summon up on a Sunday after lunch afternoon audience. So, if anyone deserves the award of the month, it's Marc Bolan ... who did his damnedest to keep rock and roll alive and well at the Fairfield Halls Croydon at the weekend. That he didn't quite manage, it wasn't for the want of trying ...

Midway through T. Rex's second number, 'Jeepster', a majority of the audience had left their seats and crowded dancing and clapping around the front of the stage, five deep. Admittedly when it came to Marc's acoustic numbers ... there were a few people whose view ... was blocked. But the ensuing hustling that went on to get people back into their seats was the reason that later, when the band really got their music off the ground, the seated audience freaked and were warned off getting to their feet ...

Musically and visually T. Rex can't go wrong and Bolan is an ace at giving a crowd of kids who were in nappies during the original rock era all that knee-trembling hot-panted feel that Presley, Holly, Chuck Berry and others brought to that age."

Penny Valentine, Sounds (First show)

"In days past when a group found themselves with an audience of ravers and dancing fans, the music very often suffered. But not so in the case of T. Rex ...

At the second house, the bewildered bouncers found themselves engulfed in a sea of stomping, ear splitting young ladies, trying to get as close to their idols as possible.

T. Rex opened with 'Cadilac', a wild rocker, and from then, until the 'Summertime Blues' encore, a happy madness reigned. Led by princeling Bolan, T. Rex gave a fine example of contemporary rock, coupled with gentle acoustic songs.

Bolan's electric guitaring is moving away from its former Jimi Hendrix orientation, and is relaxed yet forceful, with an emotional style of his own ... the hits 'Swan', 'Hot Love' and 'Get It On' (were) extended and funkier than the recordings.

During 'Summertime Blues' it all ended, the fans finally stormed the stage and T. Rex retreated having played some excellent music under very strange circumstances."

Martin Marriott, Disc

Monday 25th October
St. George's Hall, Bradford, Yorkshire, England

Wednesday 27th October
The Dome, Brighton, East Sussex, England
According to Mickey Marmalade, the band's gear arrived late for this concert after the equipment truck, driven by Mick O Halloran and his friend Charlie, caught fire.

Friday 29th October
Green's Playhouse, Glasgow, Lanarkshire, Scotland

Saturday 30th October
Empire Theatre, Edinburgh, Lothian, Scotland

Sunday 31st October
City Hall, Newcastle, Northumberland, England

Monday 1st November–Wednesday 3rd November
Rosenberg Studios, Vanloese, Copenhagen, Denmark
Studio sessions which produced at least four tracks: 'Cadillac', 'Telegram Sam', 'Baby Strange' and 'Thunderwing'. It's possible that one or two further tracks were put down.

Thursday 4th November
ABC, Stockton On Tees, County Durham, England

Friday 5th November
Jeepster / Life's A Gas (Fly BUG 16)
This single was released against Marc's wishes after his contract with Fly had expired, not that Fly had to get Marc's agreement regarding the release of material. Despite the huge success of the 'Electric Warrior' album, the single still reached number 2 in the Top Thirty and was probably only kept from the number one slot by popular comedian Benny Hill's Christmas novelty disc 'Ernie'.

"While Marc Bolan can come up with instant no nonsense success the merry pundits are in for a nail biting session – and 'Jeepster' is just one of those tracks destined to be huge. The fact that it's a single taken from a new album – 'Electric Warrior' – when the other number ones weren't may slow it down a little. Though, on reflection, compared to the singles' releases lately I doubt it. It is, as T. Rex addicts will know, a highlight of their live act."

Penny Valentine, Sounds

Town Hall, Birmingham, Warwickshire, England

Saturday 6th November
Free Trade Hall, Manchester, Lancashire, England

Monday 8th November
De Montford Hall, Leicester, Leicestershire, England

Tuesday 9th November

ABC, Lincoln, Lincolnshire, England

Wednesday 10th November

ABC, Wigan, Yorkshire, England

Thursday 11th November

Liverpool Stadium, Liverpool, Lancashire, England

Set list: 'Cadilac', 'Jeepster', 'Spaceball Ricochet', 'Cosmic Dancer', 'Debora', 'Ride A White Swan', 'Hot Love', 'Get It On', 'Summertime Blues' (Both shows)

Two shows.

The finale of the second show featured Marc's speaker stack falling on Bob Harris's gear and destroying it. This happened as a result of vibrations on the stage which was actually a boxing ring.

"Marc Bolan grins and says hello, but he looks tired. In fact, all the band and travelling entourage do, but then it's the last night of a long tour and there are two shows to do that night.

The audience for the first house are filling in. They look very young (it's a 6 p.m. show) and are a bit edgy... There's the feeling in the air of school kids on an organised outing who aren't quite sure how to behave; quick backward glances to see if someone is going to push them back in their seats if they get up and rave.

Down the front there's a band of dedicated screamers – some close to tears at the frustration of being ten feet from Marc, Mickey, Steve and Bill, yet knowing that's as close as they're likely to get ...

The whole thing's a bit tense in the first house, but it loosens up with the last few numbers. The band's warmer then, punching out the hits and the 'Summertime Blues' encore, and standing out in the audience you can feel the energy flowing. They've got a lot to get out these kids and it's beginning to come now, but there's still a block somewhere and you feel as the set ends neither they nor the band quite made it.

Back in the dressing room everyone's a bit more lively. It's warmer in a physical sense, and in atmosphere...

The feeling's different out in the hall too. The people coming in are still young, but a bit older than the last lot, and there's more of them. They seem more at ease, noisier, more alive. The girls gather in groups and chatter excitedly – there's a lot of giggling – the blokes move in gangs, swaggering a bit, shouting to each other over the hall ...

Bob Harris announces the band and they bound on stage, Bill Legend, Steve Currie and Mickey Finn first, pause, then Marc. The place erupts with screams and cheers and clapping and shouts. Rock on. The joint was rocking. The band's playing well from the start, a lot better than the first house, the people are stomping and around the stage – at the front and at the side – girls are leaning forward as far as they can arms outstretched, trying to touch.

Will he notice me? Some of them scream a name, over and over again, some of them throw rings, pendants, anything ... Fingernails painted bright red, bright green. Will I stand out? From the stage it's a sea of faces and arms waving, pleading, pushing forward. It's rare to see a couple – at the back maybe, but near the stage it's mostly girls, with groups of blokes dancing in the aisles or standing on their seats shaking shoulders and heads, arms up, flashing peace signs with the beat.

The band retire and Marc sits crossed legged to sing 'Spaceball Ricochet', 'Cosmic Dancer' and 'Debora', with Mickey. Three or four times ... girls make it over the edge of the stage and lurch towards Marc, grab him by the neck, hang on for dear life until they're dragged off and gently, but firmly, pushed back into the crowds.

The band come back for the final push up. 'Ride A White Swan', 'Hot Love', 'Get It On'. I'm beginning to get a bit scared. The bass cabinets had already been pushed over once, a spotlight has been toppled from the p.a. cabinets, and I've got visions of them tipping over on top of people. It doesn't happen. "You want more?" asks Beep and they come back. 'Summertime Blues' it is. It's a good way to end – hard rocking but loose enough. You think back over the music, separate it in your mind from the whole thing, and you realise without thinking about it you've been hearing some great playing.

Marc's still out front, but his guitar playing is much less flash, much more part of the band than it used to be, and the rhythm section is really strong. Steve Currie, particularly, had been playing some excellent bass, and the combination of Bill and Mickey's just right."

Steve Peacock, Sounds

Saturday 13th November
Broadcast date on ARD in Germany for the performances of 'Jeepster' and 'Life's A Gas' recorded for Radio Bremen's 'Beat Club' programme. The songs appeared in episode 64. See entry for 1st October.

Monday 15th November
Trident Studios, St. Anne's Court, Soho, London, England
A studio session which involved further production work on 'Telegram Sam', 'Baby Strange' and 'Cadilac'.

Thursday 18th November
Marc's home, Little Venice, London W2, England
Television interview for the ATV programme documentary programme 'Whatever Happened To Tin Pan Alley'. The documentary was broadcast on 28th March the following year.
A promo film for 'Jeepster' was broadcast on BBC One's 'Top Of The Pops'.

Monday 29th November
Unconfirmed BBC Radio Studios, London, England
Another semi-playback radio session, this time for the 'Jimmy Young Show' and the 'Johnnie Walker Show'. Six songs were recorded. These were: 'Jeepster' (4.05), 'Raw Ramp' (2.18), 'Cadilac' (3.52), 'Baby Strange' (3.00), 'Electric Boogie' (1.45) and 'Telegram Sam' (3.35). Four songs were broadcast on the 'Johnnie Walker Show': 13th December – 'Jeepster', 14th December – 'Raw Ramp' 16th December – 'Cadilac' 17th December – 'Baby Strange'.
Two were broadcast on the 'Jimmy Young Show': 13th December – 'Electric Boogie', 14th December – 'Jeepster', 15th December – 'Jeepster'.
'Telegram Sam' was not broadcast until 29th January 1972 on the 'Peter Powell Show'.

November (?)
Trident Studios, St. Anne's Court, Soho, London, England
An undated tape was produced at the above studio containing two takes of 'Telegram Sam'. These were presumably the single version and an outtake.

November (?)
London Weekend Television Studios, Kent House, Southbank London, England
Recording of an interview for the programme 'Pop And The Media'.

Friday 3rd December
Planned starting date for a three-week tour of the USA supporting Alice Cooper. In the event the tour never happened. Though such a tour would have exposed T. Rex to a much wider (and probably more sympathetic) audience than they had previously found in the USA, it seems that the Bolan ego demanded that any tour was going to be done as the headline act.
Unconfirmed BBC Radio Studio, London, England
Interview for Radio One's 'Scene And Heard' programme which was broadcast on 4th December.

Saturday 4th December
Broadcast date for the interview recorded the previous day for BBC Radio One's 'Scene And Heard'. The broadcast segment lasted 10 minutes.

Wednesday 8th December
Cockpit Theatre, Marylebone, London, England
Date for television recordings for a special documentary produced by London Weekend Television entitled 'Music In The Round'. The programme was subtitled 'Rock Of Ages'. The show was broadcast on 23rd April the following year. The show was based around T. Rex.

Four songs were filmed 'live' in performance: 'Jeepster', 'Cadilac', 'Spaceball Ricochet' and 'Telegram Sam'. Of these only 'Spaceball Ricochet' was a genuine live version. The other songs performed consisted of the original studio recordings stripped down to the basic track with an "open mike" for Marc to sing into. In addition Marc was interviewed between songs by a sceptical Humphrey Burton, then London Weekend Television's head honcho in the Arts department. Marc sensing he was being sent up responded in kind, with more than a fair amount of bullshit.

After the filming was over, T. Rex performed a short live set for the studio audience. Among the songs performed was 'Baby Strange'.

Thursday 9th December
Marc and June, together with Tony Secunda fly to New York for media and business meetings regarding the first T. Rex headlining tour of the USA and Canada. Visits were also made to Boston, Philadelphia, Detroit, Cleveland, Los Angeles and San Francisco. Marc did a series of radio interviews and some acoustic sessions to promote 'Electric Warrior'.

December
WRUW-FM Studios, Cleveland, Ohio, USA
During Marc's tour of US radio stations, an acoustic set was performed on WRUW-FM in Cleveland. The set consisted of 'Ballrooms Of Mars', 'Spaceball Ricochet', 'Please Rearrange My Nose', 'The Slider', an interview and concluded with 'The Children Of Rarn'. 'Please Rearrange My Nose' utilised the melody of 'My Baby's Like A Cloudform'.

December
WGLD Studios, Oak Park, Chicago, Illinois, USA
Another acoustic radio session was performed on the above station. Among the songs per-

formed were an improvised one and a rough version of 'Main Man'. It's possible that 'Life's A Gas', 'Spaceball Ricochet' and 'Sunken Rags' were also part of the session.

Sunday 12th December
Broadcast date on London Weekend Television of the programme 'Pop And The Media', on which Marc was a guest. See earlier entry. While this was taking place in Britain, across the Atlantic, Marc and June were visiting Canada. The programme was part of the 'Freedom Roadshow' series.

Monday 13th December
First day of broadcast of the radio session recorded for the 'Jimmy Young Show' (BBC Radio One). For details see entry for 29th November.

Wednesday 15th December
Marc and June return to London from the USA.

Monday 20th December
BBC Television Centre, Wood Lane, Shepherd's Bush, London, England
Television recordings for the two Christmas 'Top Of The Pops' specials. T. Rex filmed two songs: 'Hot Love' which was broadcast on the 25th December edition and 'Get It On', featuring Elton John guesting on piano, which was broadcast on the 27th December edition. Neither song was performed live in the studio, both being straight mimes to slightly different mixes of the original singles.

Saturday 25th December
Broadcast date of the first 'Top Of The Pops' Christmas Special on BBC 1. 'Hot Love' was transmitted during this edition. See entry for 20th December.

Monday 27th December
Broadcast date of the second 'Top Of The Pops' Christmas Special on BBC 1. On this day the show's producer included the performance of 'Get It On' in the programme.
Fairfield Halls, Croydon, Surrey, England
Marc joined Elton John and his band on stage for the encore at the latter's concert. Among the songs performed were 'Whole Lotta Shakin', 'Get It On' and others.

Wednesday 29th December
BBC Television Centre, Wood Lane, Shepherd's Bush, London, England
Bolan was interviewed about the year's success by Bob Wellings for BBC1's 'Nationwide' evening magazine programme. The interview was broadcast later that day.

Friday 31st December
Trident Studios, St. Anne's Court, Soho, London, England
A slightly different version of 'Telegram Sam', with a longer fade, was produced on this date.

1972

1972 was probably the busiest year in T. Rex's history. It began with a special concert, which was recorded by British television, though little actual footage was used in the final programme. Then, following a short series of dates in Europe, the band went to North America for their first tour of the continent as a headlining act.

The tour was generally a success, allowing for audience's probable lack of familiarity with much of the material. Mickey Marmalade rates the concert at the Spectrum in Philadelphia as one of the two best T. Rex concerts he witnessed (the other being at Wembley). However, the tour seemed to end badly in New York.

At the time T. Rex were playing a short fifty-minute set. Most songs were played fairly straight, with their length kept relatively short. Only a couple of songs, 'Get It On' among them, were extended beyond their natural length.

By the time of the second tour, in September and October, the musical policy had shifted. The T. Rex live set was now longer, with most songs clocking in at more than twice the length they were on disc. Some, 'Chariot Choogle', 'Buick Mackane' and 'Get It On' were frequently reaching ten minutes or more. Sadly Marc's guitar skills were not good enough to sustain this throughout a concert, and once again the absence of a second guitar player from the group's line-up was strongly felt.

A large part of the year was also spent recording. Most of 'The Slider' was recorded in the early part of 1972 (not in three days as has erroneously been portrayed elsewhere). In addition to this, the complete 'Tanx' album, the attendant singles and the reworked soundtrack to 'Born To Boogie' were also put down on tape.

Tuesday 4th January
Studio Wandsbeck, Hamburg, West Germany

T. Rex gave a mimed performance of 'Jeepster' on the ZDF networked 'Disco 72'. The programme was networked on 15th January. In addition to performing 'Jeepster', a number of other songs were also performed. However, these were left unused and further details regarding the songs are not available.

Wednesday 5th January
Unconfirmed television studio, Baden Baden, West Germany

To promote 'Electric Warrior' in West Germany and Switzerland, Marc and T. Rex appeared on the Schweizer Fernsehen/SWF Baden Baden co-production 'Hits A Go Go'. T. Rex played two songs on the show: 'Jeepster' and 'Mambo Sun'. Unfortunately both were lip-synch efforts. A very short 10 second interview with Marc and Mickey was held purely to announce the forthcoming gigs in Hamburg and Münster. The show was broadcast on the ARD network in West Germany on 14th January.

Friday 14th January
Initial broadcast date on the ARD networked SWF3 channel for the 'Hits A Go Go' performance. See entry for 5th January.

Saturday 15th January
Broadcast date for the 'Disco 72' performance recorded on 4th January. See entry for that day.
Starlight Rooms, Boston, Lincolnshire, England
Set list: 'Cadilac', 'Jeepster', 'Thunderwing', 'Baby Strange', 'Spaceball Ricochet', 'Girl', 'Cosmic Dancer', 'Hot Love', 'Get It On'
'Telegram Sam' made its concert debut at this gig. Steve Took was present at the show, having been brought along by underground magazine 'Frendz' whose agenda involved causing trouble for Marc. After trying to join the band on stage Marc ordered Mickey Marmalade to throw him off the stage.

The concert was a one off performance filmed by ATV for the 'Whatever Happened To Tin Pan Alley?' documentary. No footage with the actual sound recorded that night was used in the final programme.

Wednesday 19th January
BBC Television Centre, Wood Lane, Shepherd's Bush, London, England
To promote 'Telegram Sam' on BBC Television's 'Top Of The Pops', T. Rex recorded one slot performing the song. Correspondence indicates that two takes were filmed. The song appeared on the 20th January, 27th January, 3rd February and 10th February editions of the show.

Thursday 20th January
Initial broadcast of 'Telegram Sam' on 'Top Of The Pops' (BBC 1). See entry for 19th January.

Friday 21st January
Telegram Sam / Cadilac / Baby Strange (EMI T. Rex 101)
Release date for the first single on Bolan's own label. It peaked at number 1 and was a top 10 hit in several European countries. In the USA it reached 68 in the Top 100.

"Like all T. Rex singles, on a third play you Get It On. At first one tends to say, "Gosh chaps, Marc's newie sounds a bit of an oldie." But press the headphones a little closer and one begins to convulse in a not altogether unpleasant fashion. Boley piles on the guitar riff and the strings top around him, rocking menace."
Chris Charlesworth, Melody Maker

"'Cadilac' ... opens with heavy yelling, a lot of overlain conga work from Mickey Finn and Bolan a little more down pace than usual. 'Baby Strange' has some effective dark string passages on the chorus and Bolan's light sly horniness coming over much clearer than usual. 'Sam' has a really raunchy feel about it ... Aside from the usual heavy rhythm section and Boley's 'Get It On' guitar riff, there's a great gritty Boots Randolph kind of sax player who burps in on cue ... Bolan's multi-tracked voice gives out the hook line ... plus the usual grinning lyrics ... that always sound like he's sending himself up. Much less breathy than usual, if of need of a few plays, unless your aged enough to remember some of those good time real rock and roll records of the past."

Penny Valentine, Sounds

Thursday 27th January

A repeat broadcast of 'Telegram Sam' on BBC 1's 'Top Of The Pops'. It's possible that the second take filmed on the 19th January was shown.

EUROPEAN TOUR

Just prior to their first headlining tour of the USA, T. Rex performed a short series of live dates in Scandinavia and West Germany. One surviving tape, of a concert in Oslo, reveals the band to be especially tight, with all the excesses tightly reigned in.

Friday 28th January

T. Rex flew from London at 10.25 in the morning and arrived in Oslo at 1.30 in the afternoon.

Chateau Neuf, Oslo, Norway

Set list: 'Cadilac', 'Jeepster', 'Baby Strange', 'Spaceball Ricochet', 'Girl', 'Cosmic Dancer', 'Hot Love', 'Get It On'

After the concert the band stayed at the Grand Hotel in Oslo.

Saturday 29th January

Konserthuset, Gothenburg, Sweden

"Along with the increasing popularity of T Rex – breaking in the USA seems to be a fact … it has been said that their music in a way is the 70s version of classic Rock and Roll.

There might be a lot of truth in this. Yesterday evening it was straight on with 3 chords and a hard hitting drummer and a heavy pumping bass. Simple and functional, but also not very inspiring. To really like the stuff T. Rex do, you shouldn't have heard too much similar music before and rather be of a different sex than me. And probably younger too.

Even though they have enjoyed some success with albums, T Rex is a typical singles band in the respect that the records sound very much better than the versions presented on stage. But, that could be said of the early Beatles too. Marc Bolan is a good composer with a feeling for simple and striking tunes and will surely develop with time."

Bert Gren, Göteborgsposten

After the concert the band stayed at the Park Avenue Hotel.

Sunday 30th January

Tivolis Konsertsal, Copenhagen, Denmark

The band's hotel for this evening was the Palace Hotel.

Monday 31st January

T. Rex exit Denmark.

Originally the band were supposed to do an autograph session at the record shop Schallplatte am Mönckebergbrunnen in Hamburg. About two thousand fans were waiting for the band's

concert programme

arrival. Unfortunately because of a delayed arrival on the flight from Denmark, there was no time left and the band went straight on to the concert venue for the sound check.

Grosser Saal, Musikhalle, Hamburg, West Germany

Mickey Finn missed part of the concert due to suffering from diarrhoea.

After the show, the band stayed the night at the Intercontinental Hotel.

Tuesday 1st February

Münsterlandhalle, Münster, West Germany

Status Quo were support.

The band's hotel for this evening was the Wald Hotel in Kreurkresser, Münster.

Wednesday 2nd February

The band were driven from Münster to Düsseldorf airport where they flew to Orly Airport in Paris.

Strawberry Studios, Chateau d'Herouville, Pontoise, Paris, France

The band arrived at the Chateau after 10 in the evening after travelling from Münster. They stayed at the Chateau overnight. No work was done on this day.

Thursday 3rd February

Date for the third showing of 'Telegram Sam' on BBC 1's 'Top Of The Pops'. See entry for 19th January.

Strawberry Studios, Chateau d'Herouville, Pontoise, Paris, France

In a busy day at Strawberry Studios, Bolan and T. Rex recorded the basic track of 'Ballrooms Of Mars' for their next album, as well as doing overdubs on 'Thunderwing'.

They were also filmed by French television for the programme 'Rockenstock'. This was shown on Antenne 1 on 12th February. T. Rex performed a special live set in the studio consisting of 'Telegram Sam', 'Cadilac', 'Hot Love' and 'Jeepster'. Prior to the live set, Marc was interviewed for the twenty five-minute programme.

Unlike with other European television programmes, this performance was authentically live in the studio. All songs were extended versions, with 'Cadilac' being the longest, running for more than twice the length of the version released on disc.

The band flew back to England in the evening.

Friday 4th February (?)
Unconfirmed BBC Studio, London, England (?)
Interview with Keith Altham for BBC Radio.

Saturday 5th February
Interview with Keith Altham broadcast on BBC Radio One's 'Scene And Heard'.

Thursday 10th February
Final transmission of 'Telegram Sam' on 'Top Of The Pops' (BBC 1). See entry for 19th January.

Saturday 12th February
Transmission date on Antenne 1 in France for the special T. Rex edition of 'Rockenstock' recorded at Strawberry Studios. See entry for 3rd February.

Sunday 13th February
Broadcast date for a Danish radio programme on which Marc and Mickey appeared as guest DJ's. The show had been recorded at an earlier date, probably in London.

NORTH AMERICAN TOUR

The first tour as a headline act was a short series of dates designed to promote the 'Electric Warrior' album and 'Get It On' single (retitled in America 'Bang A Gong'). The tour could not be described as an all out assault on America, but was instead a carefully selected series of dates in the major cities, playing moderate size venues. Given its limited aims, to introduce T. Rex to a wider audience, the tour succeeded. Both the album and the single it was designed to promote were successful. Critical reaction was more mixed, and the tour ended disastrously with a poor first show at New York's Carnegie Hall. As fate would have it, this was the show that most critics caught.

Sunday 13th February
T. Rex and entourage depart London for Los Angeles.

Monday 14th February
T. Rex fly into Los Angeles
KDAY Radio Studios, Los Angeles, California, USA
To promote the concert at the Hollywood Palladium Marc performed a special acoustic radio session featuring renditions of 'Spaceball Ricochet', 'Jeepster', 'Cosmic Dancer', 'Main Man', 'Ballrooms Of Mars', 'Mystic Lady', 'Girl' and 'Baby Strange'. It's likely that the performance was syndicated to other radio stations by Warner Brothers.

Tuesday 15th February

Hollywood Palladium, Hollywood,
California, USA

Support from Ballin' Jack and Doobie
Brothers.

"More than 5,000 people, including Mick Jagger and one of the
largest contingents of reviewers/writ-
ers to see a rock show here in
months, jammed the Hollywood Palladium Tuesday night to see if T. Rex can generate ... some
of the extraordinary excitement in this country that it's achieved in ... England.

The answer was quite possibly, but probably not overnight. T. Rex had to be satisfied with a
split decision at the Palladium.

As Jagger watched, hidden from the audience by amplifiers, T. Rex ... showed several reasons for its success, part of them musical, part of them in the glamour surrounding the lead
singer/writer/guitarist Marc Bolan.

In its best numbers, T. Rex has an enormously accessible, driving rock and roll sound, one
which is firmly rooted in the roots of rock music rather than dependent on one or more of the
current trends (in orchestral rock to jazz rock).

'Jeepster' for instance, has a direct link with the guitar style of Scotty Moore (who backed
Elvis Presley on his early recordings) and the general spirit of the old Sun records product.

Though the area in front of the stage was jammed so tight that people could barely move,
much less dance, there was a lot of dancing – a good test of a music's ability to stir an audience – in the less crowded areas at the side of the stage even Jagger moved to such upbeat
numbers as 'Jeepster' and 'Bang A Gong'.

In addition to the music's accessibility, Bolan ... has a certain star quality about him. He's
fun to watch as he goes quite gracefully through such manoeuvres as a Chuck Berry duckwalk
or some Eddie Cochran twists and turns.

Despite these strengths, however, Tuesday's concert didn't generate anything like the hysteria that apparently occurs at the group's English concerts. There wasn't the overwhelming
audience/performer electricity, the final test of the group's claim to superstar status in rock.

There was clearly some room for improvement in T. Rex's performance particularly in the
area of pacing, but the Palladium concert was the first stop on the US tour. Perhaps things will
get smoother before the tour ends...

While T. Rex didn't bring its English hysteria with it to the Palladium Tuesday night, the
response was enthusiastic and the group's strengths ... suggest the hysteria may just be a matter of time. The ingredients are there."

Robert Hillburn, Los Angeles Times

Following the concert there was an aftershow party at the Universal Sheraton Hotel.

Wednesday 16th February

Marc, accompanied by Tony Secunda and photographer Keith Morris, flys to Detroit to give radio
interviews.

WABX-FM, Detroit, Michigan, USA

Marc is interviewed by DJ Mark Parenteau at 5 p.m.

KDAY PRESENTS
TUES. FEB. 15 8 PM
HOLLYWOOD PALLADIUM

T. REX
BALLIN' JACK
DOOBIE BROS

FRIDAY FEB. 18 8 PM
LONG BEACH AUDITORIUM

JOHN MAYALL
TAJ MAHAL
ERIC MERCURY
TICKETS $3.50, $4.50, $5.50

SUNDAY FEB. 27 8 PM
HOLLYWOOD PALLADIUM
FRIDAY MAR. 3 8 PM
SWING AUDITORIUM SAN BERNARDINO

SAVOY BROWN
FLEETWOOD
MAC
JOHN BALDRY

TICKETS ALL WALLICHS STORES,
LIBERTY AND MUTUAL AGENCIES, AT THE DOOR

PACIFIC PRESENTATIONS

Detroit Hilton Hotel, Detroit, Michigan, USA

An interview with Bolan was scheduled to be recorded at 7 p.m. at the above hotel for use on the radio station CKLW-AM.

Following this interview Marc travels to Windsor in Canada.

CJOM-FM, Windsor, Ontario, Canada

Marc is interviewed by DJ's Dave Loncao and Larry Himmel.

After the show, in the early hours of the morning, the party returned to the USA for overnight accommodation at the Detroit Hilton.

Thursday 17th February

CKLW-AM, Detroit, Michigan, USA

Marc had a 9.30 meeting with Rosalie Trombalie, Managing Director of the station. Following this Bolan travelled to Canada by road to give a short interview before returning to Detroit to catch the midday flight from Detroit to Washington, arriving at the latter just after 1 p.m.

WHFS-FM, Bethesda, Maryland, USA

Marc went straight from the airport to the above radio station for a 2.30 p.m. interview with DJ Damian.

WMAL-FM, Washington D.C., USA

From Bethesda Marc went to Washington for a 4 p.m. interview with Ray Freeman at WMAL-FM.

WHMC-FM, Gaithesburg, Maryland, USA

Marc went to this station for a 5.30 interview with Barry Richards.

WKTK-FM, Baltimore, Pennsylvania, USA

For the fourth interview in a busy day, Marc went to the above station for a 7 p.m. interview with Joe Buccheri.

After this interview Marc and his party flew from Baltimore to Philadelphia.

WMMR-FM, Philadelphia, Pennsylvania, USA

Marc was interviewed at 11 p.m. by Michael Tearson.

Following this interview Marc and party went on to the Bellvere Stratford hotel for this, and the following, night. The band and road crew had travelled directly from Los Angeles to Philadelphia.

Friday 18th February

Bellvere Stratford, Philadelphia, Pennsylvania, USA

Press interviews were held from 10.30 a.m. at the hotel.

WFIL-AM, Philadelphia, Pennsylvania, USA

Marc went to this radio station for a meeting with Managing Director Jay Cook.

WIBG-AM, Philadelphia, USA
Following the meeting at WFIL, Marc went on to the above station for a meeting with Managing Director Sandy Metzelof and Programme Director Don Cannon.

Spectrum Theatre, Philadelphia, Pennsylvania, USA
A soundcheck was held at 5 p.m.

Saturday 19th February

The tour entourage flew from Philadelphia to Detroit at just after 11 in the morning, arriving at just after 12.30. No press or radio interviews were scheduled for that day. A soundcheck was held at 5 p.m. The band checked in to the Holiday Inn hotel.

Memorial Hall, University Of Detroit, Detroit, Michigan, USA
Set list: 'Cadilac', 'Jeepster', 'Spaceball Ricochet', 'Girl', 'Cosmic Dancer', 'Get It On' (incomplete)
Support from Brave Belt (they later became Bachman Turner Overdrive).

"In the auditorium, 9,100 frenzied teenies started chanting "T. Rex-T. Rex-T. Rex". The guards, backed by a crew of flashlight flicking ushers, awaited a riot.

By the time the houselights went out, pandemonium had already begun to set in. Several DJs began a rumour (true) that Alice Cooper was in the house. The crowd began moving off the bleachers and onto the floor. When the special lavender spotlight hit Marc, the cheers began. They didn't stop for an hour.

Bolan ... had the audience in the palm of his hand from the very first.

By the second number, 'Jeepster', they were dancing in the aisles and in the back of the hall. Two teenies, rosebud nipples ecstatically erect, dragged a guard away from his post by the sound console and danced with him.

Then the band left the stage. Bolan grabbed an acoustic guitar and sat on the floor. Unbelievably, the house shut up. Usually when someone plays in Detroit, they don't play acoustically. Detroit audiences ... throw things – like firecrackers and bottles – at the stage. Not this time.

Bolan had them and he knew it. He played 'Spaceball Ricochet' and they screamed. He played 'Girl' and they screamed. When he played 'Cosmic Dancer' they screamed and whistled and screamed for more.

By the time the more-than-an-hour set drew to a close with 'Bang A Gong', the house had gone absolutely bananas.

It was, in one critic's words, a killer concert. Detroit had been primed for T. Rex ... The concert couldn't just be a good one. It had to be a masterpiece. It was."

John Wiesman, Melody Maker

Sunday 20th February

The whole entourage fly from Detroit to Washington, leaving at noon and arriving shortly after 1 p.m. They checked in to the Holiday Inn and had the customary 5 p.m. soundcheck.

Roller Rink, Alexandria, Virginia, USA
Set list: 'Cadilac', 'Jeepster', 'Spaceball Ricochet', 'Girl', 'Cosmic Dancer', 'Get It On', 'Summertime Blues' (incomplete)
Support from Grin.

"It was a night for Big Noise – well played but loud – Sunday at the Alexandria Roller Rink as Britain's T. Rex and Washington's Grin gave an oversold crowd just what it wanted: loud, loud rock music.

T. Rex, one of Britain's most successful groups … has only recently begun to expand what was a small cult following in this country.

Singer, guitarist, songwriter Marc Bolan leads the group, strutting, prancing and dancing Sunday in blue silk trousers, a bright silver jacket and orange high heel shoes, singing and screaming while the band brought the fans to their feet with several long and loud instrumental jams. Bolan displayed a skill on the guitar that none of the group's six albums had shown.

After opening with a few songs from the current T. Rex album 'Electric Warrior', Bolan settled on the stage, Donovan style, for an acoustic set with percussionist Mickey Finn … Three acoustic songs, musically the highlight of the evening, and an unfulfilled attempt to get the audience to join in rhythmic clapping drew silence and convinced Bolan that the crowd wanted it loud.

So that's what Bolan and T. Rex gave them, launching into 'Hot Love', one of their biggest hits in Britain, never released here, followed by their current American single called 'Bang A Gong' here, but 'Get It On' in Britain. The set closed with another long jam, with Bolan moving about the stage so wildly that twice he accidentally unplugged his guitar from the amplifier.

Called back for an encore Bolan excitedly announced Eddie Cochran's 'Summertime Blues' the best known hit of Bolan's own favourite rock and roll guitarist, another T. Rex release not available in America."

John Allen, Washington Post

Post concert accommodation is arranged at the Holiday Inn in Alexandria.

Monday 21st February
Marc, Secunda and Morris fly from Washington to La Guardia airport in New York. Radio and press interviews were planned for the day. No further information is available. They stay at the Sherry Netherlands Hotel.

Tuesday 22nd February
Marc, Secunda and Morris fly from New York to Boston for live radio interviews in the morning.
WBCN-FM, Boston, Massachusetts, USA
Marc is interviewed at 10.30 by Jim Perry.
WMEX-AM, Boston, Massachusetts, USA
Marc has a 12 noon meeting with Programme Director Mark Ratner.
WRKO-AM, Boston, Massachusetts, USA
Marc has a 12.30 appointment with Managing Director Scotty Power and Programme Director Scotty Brink.
Following this meeting the party fly from Boston to Cleveland, checking in to the Hollenden House hotel.
WIXY-AM, Cleveland, Ohio, USA
Marc has a 4.30 meeting with the Programme Director Chuck Dunway and Managing Director Marge Bush.
WMMS-FM, Cleveland, Ohio, USA
Marc was scheduled to have a 5.30 interview with Martin Perlich at this radio station.
WNCR-FM, Cleveland, Ohio, USA
An interview was set-up for 9 p.m. with DJ Jeff Gelb.

Hollenden House, Cleveland, Ohio, USA
A final interview with an unidentified promo man was arranged to be recorded at the hotel for use by Cleveland station WRUW-FM. The interview was set for 10 p.m.
In the meantime the band travel from Washington to Chicago.

Wednesday 23rd February

Marc, Secunda and Morris fly from Cleveland to Chicago for interviews and meetings.
WDAI-FM, Chicago, Illinois, USA
A meeting is arranged for 11 a.m. with Managing Director Maggie Flank. Programme Director Steve Staffold tapes an interview.
WLS-AM, Chicago, Illinois, USA
A 12.30 lunch date is arranged with Chuck Buell and Fred Winson, the station's Programme Director and Managing Director, respectively.
WCFL-AM, Chicago, Illinois, USA
A brief 2.30 meeting is arranged with Programme Director Nick Acerenza.
Continental Plaza, Chicago, Illinois, USA
The period from 3 p.m. to 6 p.m. is left free for press interviews at this hotel.
WGLD, Oak Park, Illinois, USA
A 7 p.m. interview with Morgan Moore is scheduled at this station.
Overnight accommodation is arranged for the Holiday Inn.

Thursday 24th February

The day is left open for press interviews at the Holiday Inn. A soundcheck is scheduled at, yes, you guessed it, 5 p.m.
Auditorium, Chicago, Illinois, USA
Support from Uriah Heep
   "When I left the auditorium last night at 11.30, the T. Rex concert wasn't over, but Marc Bolan's mic had just zonked out completely for what probably would be the first of many times and I decided to call it the end of a perfect evening. Perfect, that is, if you groove on mismanagement, forty-minute delays between sets, general screw-ups and noise, noise, noise.
   Bolan, the fey lead singer/composer of T. Rex – the biggest thing in England since The Beatles, they say – once wrote rather literate songs with poetic aspersions; now he's gone in for rock and roll with a few acoustic numbers thrown in. Admittedly, the sound system was terrible, but Bolan's not all that hot either. The sequins he had pasted on his cheekbones sparkled more than his music."

Lynn Van Matre, Chicago Tribune

Friday 25th February

The entourage travel from Chicago to Cleveland. Tony Secunda was arrested at the airport for causing a disturbance on the inbound flight.
Yorktown Theatre, Cleveland, Ohio, USA
Two shows.
Overnight accommodation was arranged for the Holiday Inn.

Saturday 26th February

The entourage fly from Cleveland to Boston.

Holiday Inn, Cambridge, Massachusetts, USA
From 1.30 p.m. Marc gave press interviews at the above hotel.

Fenway Theatre, Boston, Massachusetts, USA
The original schedule indicates that two shows were planned for this venue. In the event, the concerts were cancelled. Overnight accommodation was at the Holiday Inn.

Sunday 27th February
The band fly from Boston to New York. Tony Secunda rejoined the party after spending the previous day in jail.

Carnegie Hall, New York, New York, USA
Set list: 'Cadilac', 'Jeepster', 'Spaceball Ricochet', 'Cosmic Dancer', 'Get It On', 'Summertime Blues' (second show) (incomplete)
Two shows.

80th ANNIVERSARY SEASON

Sunday Evening, February 27, 1972, at 7:30

Ron Delsener presents

T. Rex

Jackie Lomax

concert programme

"Headlining for the first time in New York, Britain's T. Rex showed why they are causing more commotion in England than any band since the heyday of The Beatles ...

Bolan's a true showman. Resplendent in silver suit and sequins pasted around his eyes ... (he) proved an excellent musician and a capable singer.

The group opened with three fast rock numbers before Bolan took the stage alone. Accompanying himself on acoustic guitar, he ran through 'Girl' and 'Cosmic Dancer' ... When the group returned, things started getting hectic ... As (they) moved into a frenetic ten-minute version of their hit 'Get It On', the crowd left their seats and filled all available standing room. By the time a frenzied 'Summertime Blues' encore ended, (T. Rex) had treated New York to one of its most uninhibited and enjoyable evenings in a long time."

Bob Kirsch, Billboard

"Smoking spotlights on 57th Street, virtually non-stop radio announcements, heavy newspaper advertising – the aura surrounding T. Rex's first Carnegie Hall concerts

Sunday night had all the elements of hyped superstardom. Too bad the results couldn't justify the means.

T. Rex is England's most popular rock group at the moment, and the lead singer, Marc Bolan, has been touted from all sides as the new Mick Jagger. On the evidence of the Carnegie Hall performance, the popularity and the reputation would have to be based on something a bit more intangible – a notable absence of other new talent, for example or a desperate need to hang on to the vestiges of the rock and roll dream.

Mr. Bolan is a performer who builds an illusion of style with an almost total lack of substance. He struts back and forth in Mick Jagger's patented drum major routine, he tries the hand on hip bisexual mimicry of Alice Cooper and Iggy Stooge. He keeps trying to find a distinctive sound like Rod Stewart's.

But it's all for nought. One is constantly aware of the mannerism rather than the music, of the self-consciousness rather than the total, energetic performance. And the ego behind it all – underneath his white satin and lamé suit Mr. Bolan wore a t-shirt with a picture of himself printed on the front – was first of all humorous and then simply disturbing.

When T. Rex played its current hit 'Get It On', a shadow of the band's potential talent slipped through, but it was never anything more than that. T. Rex, by the way, started out as Tyrannosaurus Rex – that monstrous carnivorous creature from the distant past; the change to the current blander name may have been a more accurate reflection of the real capacities of the group than it realised."

Don Heckman, New York Times

Overnight accommodation is arranged at the St. Moritz Hotel.

Monday 28th February
The band members of T. Rex return to London. Marc, June Bolan and Mickey Marmalade remain in the USA.

Friday 3rd March
Marc, June Bolan and Mickey Marmalade return to the UK. Their flight is temporarily diverted to Frankfurt because of bad weather at Heathrow.

Wednesday 8th March – Sunday 12th March
Strawberry Studios, Chateau d'Herouville, Pontoise, Paris, France
The bulk of 'The Slider' was recorded in five days at Strawberry Studios. Basic tracks for the following songs were recorded between these dates: 'Metal Guru', 'Lady', 'Rabbit Fighter', 'Mystic Lady', 'Rock On', 'The Slider', 'Baby Boomerang', 'Spaceball Ricochet', 'Main Man' and 'Buick Mackane'.

Friday 10th March
Strawberry Studios, Chateau d'Herouville, Pontoise, Paris, France
Recording work was done on 'Buick Mackane', 'The Slider', 'Metal Guru', 'Lady' and 'Main Man' on this day. This may have included some overdubs, as well as recording basic tracks. The version of 'Buick Mackane' recorded on this date is not the album version, but the track more familiarly known as 'Buick Mackane And The Babe Shadow'. This is not written on the tape box and is probably a later concoction, though handwritten lyrics do exist of a song with this title.

Saturday 18th March

Empire Pool, Wembley, Middlesex, England

Set list: 'Cadilac', 'Jeepster', 'Baby Strange', 'Spaceball Ricochet', 'Cosmic Dancer', 'Telegram Sam', 'Hot Love', 'Get It On', 'Summertime Blues' (Both shows)

Two shows

These concerts were filmed by a film crew under the direction of Ringo Starr for Apple Films. The material became the core of the film 'Born To Boogie'. No film recorded at the first show made the final cut, though parts of it can be seen throughout the credits at the end of the film.

"Musically it took a while to get going, but for the teenage girls, all Marc had to do was to smile to receive the kind of ovation that any artist in the world would envy. For Ringo Starr, who was filming the concert from the front of the stage, it must have been a nostalgic occasion.

Each song was greeted by a roar ... He finished with 'Get It On', which involved some Hendrix style guitar work using a broken tambourine to ring out the feedback from his Stratocaster in that phallic position all the girlies love ...

The outfit is really little more than a good rhythm section. Bolan relies mainly on chords / lead work, but the effect is very funky ... Mickey Finn bashes the bongos, but is definitely second billing ... Steve Currie has more responsibility in keeping the action going ... he played some really good bass and contributed a great deal to the overall sound. But it's Bolan who's the star ... Every move brings a scream ... and when he grins and shakes his head, the din is deafening. In (the audience's) eyes he's the equivalent of a John, Paul, George and Ringo."

Chris Charlesworth, Melody Maker

Friday 24th March

Debora / One Inch Rock / The Seal Of Seasons / Woodland Bop (Fly Magnifly ECHO 101)

In an attempt to continue benefiting from Bolan's success and also to satisfy an undoubted public demand, Fly Records began to reissue old material beginning with this EP of Tyrannosaurus Rex material. The disc reached number 7 in the Top 30.

Tuesday 28th March

Broadcast date on the British ITV network of the 'Whatever Happened To Tin Pan Alley' documentary. The final edit of the programme featured a short interview with Marc and a snippet of film recorded at Starlight Rooms in Boston, Lincolnshire. See entries for 18th November 1971 and 15th January 1972.

Jahrhunderthalle, Höchst, Frankfurt, West Germany

A one-off concert was announced for the above hall on this date. Posters were printed, though it's not certain whether the concert took place.

Thursday 30th March

Sheraton Hotel, Munich, West Germany

Marc, Mickey Finn and B.P. Fallon attend the 'Bravo' magazine awards ceremony in Munich. At 3.30 in the afternoon a photo-session was held in the hotel's fitness rooms. The awards ceremony was preceded by a gala dinner at 8.30 in the evening. Marc and Mickey collected the 'Otto' award on behalf of the band.

Friday 31st March

Marc, Mickey Finn and B.P. Fallon fly to Copenhagen via Frankfurt for recording sessions.

JOHN & TONY SMITH PRESENT···

T REX

`LIVE' AT EMPIRE POOL

WEMBLEY

SAT. 18th. MARCH 8-30 pm.

SOLD OUT!

ADDITIONAL SHOW at 5.30 pm. TICKETS 75p.

D.J. and COMPERE

EMPEROR `ROSKO'

PLUS SUPPORTING PROGRAMME

TICKETS AVAILABLE FROM ALL HARLEQUIN RECORD SHOPS.
POSTAL APPLICATION TO HARLEQUIN RECORDS. 67 GT. TITCHFIELD ST. W.1.

Postal Orders & S.A.E. ONLY.

Friday 31st March – Sunday 2nd April
Rosenberg Studios, Vanloese, Copenhagen, Denmark

A second block of sessions for 'The Slider' saw T. Rex coming away with the basic tracks for the following material: 'Chariot Choogle', 'Sunken Rags' and the album version of 'Buick Mackane'. Additionally a 12-minute jam based around an early version of 'Children Of The Revolution' was also committed to tape.

Friday 7th April
Marc flies into Los Angeles.

April
KMET, Pasadena, California, USA

Marc appears on the above radio station reading the news and giving an interview.

April
Continental Hyatt House, Hollywood, California, USA

Marc gives an impromptu press conference in his hotel room at the above hotel.

April
Elektra Studios, Los Angeles, California, USA

While visiting Los Angeles Marc and Tony Visconti spent time at Elektra Studios overdubbing Howard Kaylan and Mark Volman's backing vocals on 'Metal Guru', 'Lady', 'Mystic Lady', 'Rock On', 'Baby Boomerang' 'Buick Mackane', 'Rabbit Fighter', 'Chariot Choogle', 'Main Man' and 'Sunken Rags'. They also spent time mixing songs for the forthcoming album.

Friday 14th April
My People Were Fair And Had Sky In Their Hair... But Now They're Content To Wear Stars On Their Brows / Prophets, Seers And Sages (Fly TOOFA 3/4)

Fly's repackaging of Bolan's old material didn't just rest with the single's market. In a special two for the price of one package they reissued the first two Tyrannosaurus Rex albums. Their efforts were rewarded with a number 1 album.

"And here at last you have it. For people who missed out on them the first time around or for people who, like me, wore out the original copies, two of the early Tyrannosaurus Rex album with Marc Bolan and Steve Peregrine Took ... it's quite a nostalgic thing listening to the two albums ... At the same time, these aren't merely collector's items. There are some of Marc's best songs here ... and don't forget the voice of John Peel."

Steve Peacock, Sounds

Sunday 16th April
Broadcast date for 'Music In The Round – Rock Of Ages' programme on ITV networks, excluding LWT.

Sunday 23rd April
Broadcast date on London Weekend Television for the 'Music In The Round' special recorded the previous year. See entry for 8th December 1971.

Friday 5th May
Metal Guru / Lady / Thunderwing (EMI T. Rex MARC 1)

The fourth T. Rex British number 1 spent four weeks in the top slot. Though the single was a huge hit in Europe, Australia and Japan, the single surprisingly failed to dent the US top 100.

"I like it, I like it, I like it and if any of you fleshy thirty year olds snigger and snarl at that, I'll put me boots through yer ... Moody Blues albums.

Bolan is ace cat ... king groove and master of ... swing back boogie. This is the fattest sound he's obtained as yet ... (Metal Guru) is instantly attractive, beautifully monotonous ... with those swollen rising rushes which Marc Bolan is so rightly famous. Yes, swishy, dizzy and full on. What's more, it's 1972 and there's an idol there for the idolising."

Ray Hollinghurst, Melody Maker

"If there was any doubt in anyone's mind that Rex's passage to success has been very much based on the simplicity, repetition and overall feel of original untutored rock and roll, then one listen to this track should iron it out once and for all. 'Metal Guru' is ... a real throwback to those naive "oop-da doop-da" days of Danny And The Juniors, Frankie Avalon and Bobby Vee ... the number gains impetus ... with a tongue in cheek flourish and lunacy, noisy and crass and totally unsubtle and although the non-Bolan honkies in the office shouted "'orrible" throughout ... I have no doubt in forecasting a number one success for the clever Mr. Bolan."

Penny Valentine, Sounds

"The whole T. Rex thing has been really a gas, but on 'Guru' the accent on simplicity is taken a bit too far. The song is quite catchy – but lacks any depth in the music or lyrics to keep bringing you back to it. Marc is just scratching the surface of his talents here ... I think it's time for T. Rex to alter or accentuate their musical spectrum."

Danny Holloway, NME

Bolan Boogie (Fly HIFLY 8)

'Get It On', 'Beltane Walk', 'King Of The Mountain Cometh', 'Jewel', 'She Was Born To Be My Unicorn', 'Dove', 'Woodland Rock', 'Ride A White Swan', 'There Was A Time', 'Raw Ramp', 'Jeepster', 'Fist Heart Mighty Dawn Dart', 'By The Light Of A Magical Moon', 'Summertime Blues', 'Hot Love'

Issued "accidentally-on-purpose" to coincide with the release date of 'Metal Guru', this cash-in disc issued by Fly also hit number 1 in the album charts. Without a doubt its appearance harmed the sales of 'The Slider'.

Saturday 6th May
London Weekend Television Studios, Kent House, Southbank, London, England

Transmission date for the LWT programme 'Russell Harty Plus' on which Marc was interviewed by Russell Harty. The programme may have been recorded at a slightly earlier date.

Monday 8th May
Air Studios, 214 Oxford Street, London, England

Mixes were made of 'Rabbit Fighter', 'The Slider' and 'Buick Mackane' on this day. The version of 'Buick Mackane' mixed on this date did not feature the string arrangement.

Tuesday 9th May

Air Studios, 214 Oxford Street, London W1, England
A master mix of 'Rock On' was completed on this date. Strings and additional instruments may also have been recorded. However, there are no backing vocals at the end of the song and where they are included, the backing vocals are less prominent than on the mix used on the album.

Wednesday 10th May

BBC Television Centre, Wood Lane, Shepherd's Bush, London, England
The first television performance of 'Metal Guru' for BBC Television's 'Top Of The Pops' was recorded on the above date and broadcast on the 11th May, 18th May and 1st June editions of the show.

Thursday 11th May

First broadcast on BBC 1's 'Top Of The Pops' of the performance of 'Metal Guru' recorded on 10th May.

Friday 12th May

Unconfirmed BBC Radio Studio, London, England
Marc was interviewed by Andrew Salkey for the BBC Radio One magazine programme 'Scene And Heard'. The interview was broadcast the following day, the 13th May.

Saturday 13th May

Transmission on 'Scene And Heard' (BBC Radio One) of the interview with Marc recorded the previous day. The segment lasted just over eight minutes.

Thursday 18th May

Repeat performance of the first version of 'Metal Guru' recorded for 'Top Of The Pops'. See entry for 10th May.

Wednesday 24th May

BBC Television Centre, Wood Lane, Shepherd's Bush, London, England
A second 'Top Of The Pops' performance of 'Metal Guru' was recorded on this date and broadcast on the 25th May and 8th June shows.

Thursday 25th May

First broadcast of the second 'Top Of The Pops' performance of 'Metal Guru'. See entry for 24th May.

May

Radio Luxembourg Studios, London, England
Marc was interviewed by Marc Wesley for his show on Radio Luxembourg.

May

Marc and June go on holiday to Cannes in the south of France with Ringo Starr, George Harrison, Cilla Black and others. On return the band go into rehearsal for the forthcoming tour. Further work on 'Born To Boogie' is undertaken.

May (?)

Tittenhurst Park, Ascot, Surrey, England

Additional filming for 'Born To Boogie' at John Lennon's country estate. The garden scenes were filmed here. This included the 'Mad Hatter's Tea Party' scene with Mickey Finn, Ringo Starr, June Feld, Chelita Secunda and actor Geoffrey Bayldon reciting Marc's poetry.

Marc also played an acoustic medley, accompanied by a string quartet conducted by Tony Visconti, consisting of 'Jeepster', 'Hot Love', 'Get It On' and 'The Slider'.

May (?)

Apple Studios, London, England

Film was made of a special studio session for 'Born To Boogie'. T. Rex were joined by Elton John on piano and Ringo Starr on occasional second drum kit. Two songs were used in the final film: 'Tutti Frutti' and 'Children Of The Revolution'. A preliminary running order for the film, written by Bolan, suggests that a Bolan and Elton John version of 'The Slider' was also filmed and recorded. Finally, in a radio interview Marc said that 'Long Tall Sally' had also been played.

June

Marc and June move to 47 Bilton Towers, Great Cumberland Place, London.

Thursday 1st June

Final transmission date on 'Top Of The Pops' (BBC 1) for the first recording of 'Metal Guru'. See entry for 10th May.

Thursday 8th June

The second 'Top Of The Pops' performance of 'Metal Guru', recorded 24th May, was networked on this date.

Trident Studios, St. Anne's Court, Soho, London, England

The production master of 'The Slider' album was completed on this date.

Friday 9th June

Odeon, Birmingham, Warwickshire, England

Set list: 'Jeepster', 'Telegram Sam', 'Spaceball Ricochet', 'Cosmic Dancer', 'Debora', 'Thunderwing', 'Metal Guru', 'Hot Love', 'Get It On', 'Summertime Blues'

Two shows

Support from Quiver

"… at the end of their set, an hour of actions and sounds designed to produce the maximum audience reaction, it was clear that the T. Rex phenomenon is no longer about music. It's an act. A circus music hall or a primitive tribal ceremony and like such ritualised events, the fans contributed, but were essentially irrelevant … when the musical offering is a succession of identikit songs, performed in a flat unenterprising manner, it becomes clear that the music is merely the medium for Bolan's self expression.

What he's doing up there is two things. Going through the motions demanded of him by his audience … Secondly he's enjoying the experience and finding it gratifying. But, there's a lack of conviction to the smile. A hint of boredom in the hip shaking … Just an indication he's being used by the fans for their purposes and is beginning to feel constricted.

There's no musical progress, so nowhere new to go on stage. That can't last too long before the performer or the performed grow tired of it ... With luck, when this phase is over, Bolan will find something new and, with luck, it might just be music."

Howard Fielding, Sounds

Saturday 10th June

Capitol Theatre, Cardiff, Wales

Two shows.

Set list: 'Jeepster', 'Cadilac', 'Baby Strange', 'Debora', 'Spaceball Ricochet', 'Telegram Sam', 'Metal Guru', 'Hot Love', 'Get It On', 'Summertime Blues'

Support from Quiver.

Friday 16th June

Jasper C. Debussy / Hippy Gumbo / The Perfumed Garden Of Gulliver Smith (Track 2094 013)

This was the original release date for the 'Jasper C. Debussy' single. Within a matter of days it had been withdrawn, but not before several copies had reached the shops.

Belle Vue, Manchester, Lancashire, England

Support from Quiver.

Monday 19th June

EMI Factory, Hayes, Middlesex, England

Marc attends the opening of EMI's new pressing plant.

Friday 23rd June

The original scheduled release date for 'Hard On Love' on Track Records. The release was stopped by court order and the material was eventually released two years later under the title of 'The Beginning Of Doves'. According to the late Malcolm Jones, Simon Napier-Bell had originally offered the material to Fly Records who had passed on the offer.

Saturday 24th June

City Hall, Newcastle, Northumberland, England

Two shows.

Support from Quiver.

Saturday 8th July

Marc returns from the USA.

Friday 21st July

The Slider (EMI T. Rex BLN 5001)

'Metal Guru', 'Mystic Lady', 'Rock On', 'The Slider', 'Baby Boomerang', 'Spaceball Ricochet', 'Buick Mackane', 'Telegram Sam', 'Rabbit Fighter', 'Baby Strange', 'Ballrooms Of Mars', 'Chariot Choogle', 'Main Man'

Marc Bolan – guitars and vocals; Mickey Finn – percussion; Steve Currie – bass; Bill Legend – drums; Howard Kaylan, Mark Volman – backing vocals on 'Metal Guru', 'Mystic Lady', 'Rock On', 'Baby Boomerang' 'Buick Mackane', 'Rabbit Fighter', 'Chariot Choogle' and 'Main Man'; Tony Visconti – backing vocals on 'The Slider', 'Spaceball Ricochet, 'Telegram Sam' and 'Baby Strange'; Howie Casey – tenor sax; unknown session man – baritone sax; Fiachra Trench – piano.

JUNE 1972

PRICE 15p.

UK summer tour programme 1972

Produced by Tony Visconti; Engineered by Freddie Hanson and Dominique
Recorded at Rosenberg Studios, Copenhagen; Strawberry Studios, Paris; Elektra Studios, Los Angeles.

'The Slider' peaked at number 4 in the UK album charts, a sign that Fly's cash-in efforts were beginning to have an effect on Bolan's fortunes. In the USA the album peaked at 17 in the charts.

"To change or not to change, that is the question ... This time (Bolan's) played to the gallery ... and produced an album in which the winning formula is jiggled around enough to make a thoroughly enjoyable, and exceptionally good, album.

What's not there (i.e. something different) is just about the only fault anyone who likes T. Rex could find with 'The Slider'. Those with experience of albums containing two hit singles ... will know what rubbish is usually dredged up to pad them out ... There are no dud tracks on 'The Slider'. And it says a lot for (Bolan) that he is prepared to put himself out rather than rest on his laurels ... More than anything, this is an album for T. Rex fans ... All the familiar ingredients are here: loud, raucous rock; softer, more melodic, acoustic numbers; mystical lyrics, rich in imagery. It's music to listen to, not to analyse ...".

Michael Oldfield, Melody Maker

"Looking like a sultry dark-eyed Theda Bara on the front and Oliver Twist's mate Fagin on the back, courtesy of Ringo Starr, who took the pics, Mr. Marc Bolan presents his hottest album yet in the context of timing and content ... In its way, it's a much more important album than Warrior, which tended to be a bridge between the old and new Bolan ... The Slider is a very precisely thought out set of thirteen tracks directed totally towards T. Rex's audience. Each track ... is a solid piece of chart appeal, a whole string of commercial enterprises, many of which could be whipped off as a single at anytime ... Each number is a careful conglomeration of everything that the audience have come to expect.

The songs themselves, aside from the well known 'Telegram Sam', 'Spaceball Ricochet' and 'Metal Guru', have been kept clean edged, far sharper than the 'Warrior' tracks, all tied up by Bolan's frugal repetitive lyrics that are simply a series of images and twists."

Penny Valentine, Sounds

"If you're a frequenter of T. Rex concerts you'll recognise most of the tracks on this album ... However, unlike the concerts, which possibly come over sounding a bit rougher if the acoustics aren't just right, the quality is much higher. 'Spaceball Ricochet' is probably the best number here. It leaves the standard Bolan rhythm for more unconventional timing and has clearer lyrics.

Other numbers are of the usual heavy bass type ... I don't know why 'The Slider' was chosen as the title track, because there doesn't seem to be anything extra-special about it ... 'Ballrooms Of Mars' has a John Lennon feel about it, as was probably intended, as the song mentions him ...".

Rosalind Russell, Disc

July
Twickenham Film Studios, Twickenham, Middlesex, England

Post-production work on 'Born To Boogie' was done here.

Late July (?)
Denham Sound Stage, Denham, Berkshire, England (?)

Date for the re-recording of the 'Born To Boogie' soundtrack. Marc had played most of the concert out of tune, which required the re-recording of his guitar parts. Some backing vocals were also added. Mickey Finn, Steve Currie and Bill Legend's original concert parts were left intact. It's possible that some of this was done at another studio.

Tuesday 1st August – Friday 4th August
Strawberry Studios, Chateau d'Herouville, Pontoise, Paris, France
Dates for studio sessions that produced backing tracks for the following songs: 'Jitterbug Love', 'Life Is Strange', 'Easy Action', 'Rapids', 'Free Angel', 'Mad Donna', 'Highway Knees Blues', 'Children Of The Revolution'. This information comes from a note from Tony Visconti to Wizards Artists. However it seems certain that this is not 100 % accurate. 'Rapids' as featured on 'Tanx', certainly dates from the later October sessions. If the song were recorded at this time, then it would appear to be a previously unknown version.

Wednesday 2nd August
Strawberry Studios, Chateau d'Herouville, Pontoise, Paris, France
Basic tracks for 'Jitterbug Love', 'Life Is Strange' and two takes of 'Fast Blues (Easy Action)' were recorded on this day.

Friday 11th August
Air Studios, 214 Oxford Street, London, England
Further work was done on 'Jitterbug Love' and 'Children Of The Revolution' at this session.

August
Correspondence indicates that by the 11th August an early working print of 'Born To Boogie' was in existence and this had been sent to America for viewing by Warner Brothers.

Tuesday 15th August
Air Studios, 214 Oxford Street, London, England
Yet more work was done on 'Jitterbug Love and 'Children Of The Revolution'.

Friday 25th August (?)
Unconfirmed BBC Radio Studio, London, England (?)
Interview with Johnny Moran.

Saturday 26th August
Broadcast on BBC Radio One's 'Scene And Heard' of the interview with Johnny Moran. The segment lasted ten and a half minutes.

Wednesday 30th August
Air Studios, 214 Oxford Street, London, England
The backing track of 'Children Of The Revolution' was prepared for broadcast purposes on the BBC.
BBC Television Centre, Wood Lane, Shepherd's Bush, London, England
Prior to the band's forthcoming tour of North America, T. Rex entered the BBC television studios to record a performance of 'Children Of The Revolution' for 'Top Of The Pops'. The slot was broadcast on 14th September, 21st September and 28th September. The 21st September edition may have featured a special promo film.

Saturday 2nd September
Radio London Studios, London, England
Radio interview.

NORTH AMERICAN TOUR

In many ways this was the first and only serious attempt to break the T. Rex in America. Sadly, it turned into something of a disaster. Though 'The Slider' was doing well, if not spectacularly on the US albums chart, the critical reaction to the live T. Rex was nearly totally negative. Support act The Doobie Brothers proved to be far more in tune with the American audience, receiving a far better reception, both from critics and audiences.

In many ways the failure was partly one of marketing. Unlike in Britain and Europe, outside of certain large urban areas on the West Coast, the East Coast and around the Great Lakes, there was no natural audience for T. Rex in North America. Secondly audiences were confused by what they were getting. Was it pop music? Was it hard rock? You were either one or the other and T. Rex, being a hybrid, just didn't fit in.

The failure to break America was also a musical one. Surviving live tapes of the tour indicate T. Rex to be extremely ramshackle in concert. In fact, the band sound tired and jaded. There was a huge contrast between the live T. Rex sound and that on disc. In retrospect it seems that Marc may have misjudged the audience, seeming to think they wanted long guitar jams, rather than the tight punchy anthems from the records.

The original tour schedule was significantly different from that which took place. See the appendix for the planned schedule.

Tuesday 5th September
T. Rex fly to Montreal in Canada, departing from Heathrow just before 11 in the morning and arriving just before 1 p.m. local time. The band are located in the Bonaventure Hotel for this night and for the rest of their stay in Montreal.

Wednesday 6th September
Pierre Fondes Arena, Montreal, Quebec, Canada
Rehearsal from midday at the above venue.
CHOM-FM, Montreal, Quebec, Canada
Marc gave a long interview to DJ Dougie Pringle between 8 and 10 p.m. at the above radio station.

Thursday 7th September
Pierre Fondes Arena, Montreal, Quebec, Canada
All day rehearsal at the above venue.

Friday 8th September
Children Of The Revolution / Jitterbug Love / Sunken Rags (EMI T. Rex Marc 2)
The single reached number 2 in the British single charts and was a large hit in West Germany, Austria and Japan amongst other countries.

"I didn't like the last single much at all and felt even before then that (Bolan) was becoming a bit trapped in his own image. This, however, is an excellent single, possibly the best he's ever done ... (a) solid dogmatic feel against lovely dark Visconti strings. A nice heavy bite to it all ...".

Penny Valentine, Sounds

"While scarcely revolutionary in concept, it's a different sound from Marc that should ensure that the phenomenal flow of hits is maintained."

NME

"... it will be interesting to see if T. Rex can continue their incredible trail of success... ('Children') is much heavier than anything the band have done singles-wise before. The familiar riffs and refrains are there alongside some string arrangements to make this a fuller sounding T. Rex release than previous songs. In its own right, it's a good song with plenty of attack ... but will it capture the imagination of the record buying public who are for ever looking for new heroes?"

Chris Welch, Melody Maker

Pierre Fondes Arena, Montreal, Quebec, Canada
"... Bolan and his band literally barnstormed their way through the set ... It was a rough gig to start with ... sound resembling honey blown through a lawn sprinkler ... (He mistook) domestic troubles in the audience as evidence of T. Rex's failure to dazzle the fans. But it wasn't that way at all. In Montreal he pulled out every stop and then some, leaving few doubting that Bolan's time to conquer America has come."

Ritchie Yorke, NME

The band grossed $7,000 from the show.

Saturday 9th September
The band flies from Montreal to Toronto, leaving at noon and arriving in Toronto at 1.05 p.m. They stay at the Holiday Inn. June Bolan arrives in Toronto.

Massey Hall, Toronto, Ontario, Canada
Set list: 'Jeepster', 'Baby Strange', 'Telegram Sam', 'Spaceball Ricochet', 'Cosmic Dancer', 'Honey Don't', 'Hot Love', 'Chariot Choogle', 'Get It On'

"Zinc Alloy took over the stage in a blaze of glory ... and without letting the audience recover from the visual onslaught, he burst straight into 'Jeepster' ... 'Baby Strange' and 'Telegram

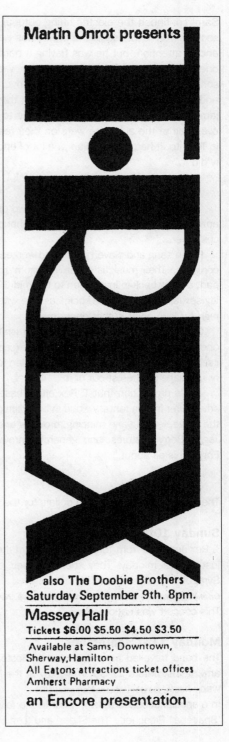

Sam' continued the electric riffing outpour, with Bolan's guitar screaming like a bleating sax section. The response of the crowd was warm, but reserved ... Bolan had aroused the audience's attention, but he was having a hard time in winning them over ... 'Hot Love' was the one that finally converted the audience, with its sheer rock and roll splendour. It was the first song to receive screeches of recognition ... the sheer noise and energy of it brought the noise and excitement to a new pitch, and in they went for 'Chariot Choogle' and a twenty minute jam on 'Get It On', still their biggest hit to date here, to close ... By the time the song was over, half of the audience were on their feet, clapping and dancing in the aisles, a rare sight in Toronto. It had taken Bolan ... a lot of effort to get the audience on their side, but they finally did it."

Marco Livingstone, NME

"(T. Rex) brought a near sell-out crowd on Saturday night to Massey Hall where Marc Bolan arrived on stage painted in lots of eye-shadow and sparkly make-up and wearing a shiny green costume ...

Bolan sang and played guitar and worked with a band made up of another guitar, drums and congas ... Their music is dynamic rock 'n' roll in style, straight-ahead fireball stuff for the most part, a throwback in inspiration to the mid-1950s. And there's also a heavy emphasis on explicitly sexual material, "rape rock," as one writer describe it. A song called 'Get It On' ... was the high (or low) point in that department.

On any strictly musical terms, Bolan isn't awfully impressive. He sang a couple of tunes at one point during the show with nothing except unamplified accompaniment ... his voice revealed itself as a thin, harsh, nervous thing. Bolan forced it and twisted it, but never wrung much music or message or interest out of it.

... it's production that T. Rex offers best of all, visual stuff ... Bolan looked like a cheerful adventurer from a fantasy world in his ridiculous costume. And he never stopped moving around the stage, leaping and mincing, prowling and scissor-kicking, working his variations on all those Jagger-Berry postures, and generally throwing out some hints on what the T. Rex frenzy in England is all about."

Jack Batton, The Globe And Mail, Toronto

The concert grossed $5,500 dollars for the band.

Sunday 10th September
T. Rex departed from Toronto at 11.15 in the morning and arrived at Rochester, NY in the USA just before midday. They then travelled on to their hotel, the Holiday Inn-Downtown in Syracuse.
Onandaga War Memorial Auditorium, Syracuse, New York, USA
This concert was cancelled.

Monday 11th September
The band travelled from Syracuse to Boston, departing just after 11.30 in the morning and arriving just before 12.30. They stay at the Fenway Commonwealth Motor Hotel.
WBCN Radio, Boston, Massachusetts, USA
In a special acoustic session prior to the following day's concert, Marc performed three songs: 'Spaceball Ricochet', 'The Slider' and 'Left Hand Luke'. He was also interviewed.

Tuesday 12th September

The Orpheum / Aquarius Theatre, Boston, Massachusetts, USA

Set list: 'Jeepster', 'Baby Strange', 'Telegram Sam', 'Spaceball Ricochet', 'Cosmic Dancer', 'Chariot Choogle', 'Hot Love', 'Get It On'

The band received a mere $1,639 for the concert.

Wednesday 13th September

The band travelled left Boston for New York City at 12.30 in the afternoon and arrived some 45 minutes later. They are housed at the City Squire Inn for this day and the rest of their time in New York.

ABC Television Studios, New York, New York, USA

The original tour schedule included an appearance on the 'Dick Cavett Show'. It's highly unlikely that this took place, however see the next date entry.

Thursday 14th September

Initial transmission in the UK of the performance of 'Children Of The Revolution' recorded for 'Top Of The Pops' (BBC 1). See entry for 30th August.

City Squire Inn, New York, New York, USA

Prior to that evening's concert, Marc gave interviews at the above hotel.

Unconfirmed Television Studio, New York, New York, USA

Marc was featured in a short segment on an unconfirmed television programme broadcast on Channel Eleven. The segment featured him performing 'The Slider'. This was possibly a pre-produced commercial for the tour, which was also shown on CBS News. It's also possible that this performance was for the 'Dick Cavett Show'.

Academy Of Music, New York, New York, USA

Set list: 'Telegram Sam', 'Jeepster', 'Cosmic Dancer', 'Get It On' (incomplete)

Two shows, one at 8 p.m. and one at 11 p.m. Gloria Jones, Julia Tillman and Stephanie Spruill sang backing vocals.

Argent were also on the bill.

"It is to Marc Bolan's credit that he did take what started out to be a lethargic audience and bring them to their feet by the end of the set – after 'Telegram Sam', 'Jeepster' and 'Get It On', replete with swirling mirrored lights in the hall, blue lights flashing on and off the ramp, up and down, with Marc racing around the ramp – so much so that they were screaming for more."

Lisa Robinson, Disc

"Finally, light's down, curtain back, and twin beams probing through the forbidden (sic) smoke to ignite twin icons of Marc Bolan, twenty-foot black and white elves frozen in mid-squeal and framing the stage like bookends... then Bolan's first full exposure as he walks deftly to the front..."

"Hello, New York," said the warrior, and he was answered by a rough blend of squeals, laughter, applause. Still the folks were seated...

Hmmm. America hasn't exactly been propelled into action, transported in to the electrified mysticism of The Slider. 'Telegram Sam' inspires some energy, but even during that, the brotherhood of the faithful has yet to truly boogie. At least their interest ... is not diminished by a brief acoustic set, capped with a freer, slightly funky 'Cosmic Dancer'.

But the set never really lifts off. And those weary cries for 'Bang A Gong', when finally answered, do not a riot make. When Bolan finally gets it on, blocking out those beloved wedges of rhythm, the hall finally rises to its feet, but... the arms waving above the faithful's heads are somehow languid in their commitment.

In short, the performance itself offered little evidence of the mystique that has galvanised European audiences. Bolan was lithe, energetic, charming in his openness, admirable in his determination to win the audience... But he did not cauterise that open wound, that need for high energy, with anything beyond pure sonic pressure.

So, the first wave met with mixed resistance, some ground gained, but slowly.

Will Bolan finally win them over? We can only stay tuned."

Sam Sutherland, Record Mirror

The two shows grossed $10,000 for the band.

'The Factory', Manhattan, New York, New York, USA

After the concert Marc and June visited Andy Warhol's studio, where Marc was interviewed by Glen O'Brien for the Warhol published magazine 'Inter/view'. Warhol also took Polaroids of Bolan.

Friday 15th September

The band travelled to Providence, Rhode Island, leaving just before 6.30 in the evening and arriving just after 7.00 p.m.

Palace Theatre, Providence, Rhode Island, USA

Originally the concert was slotted in for the Providence Civic Centre. The concert was probably cancelled.

Saturday 16th September

Capitol Theatre, Passaic, New Jersey, USA

The show grossed $3,500 for the band.

Sunday 17th September

Constitution Hall, Washington DC, USA

This concert was cancelled. The band were due to stay overnight at the Holiday Inn-Downtown before flying on to Miami. It's not clear if this actually happened.

Monday 18th September

The original schedule indicated that the band were due to depart from Washington at 11.30 a.m. and arriving in Miami at 1.40 p.m. However, it's more likely that they flew from either New York or Washington. They were housed in the Holiday Inn at Miami Beach for this day and the next.

WSUS Studios, Miami, Florida, USA

Marc gives an interview at the above radio station to promote the forthcoming concert.

Tuesday 19th September

Jai-Aloi Fronton, Pirate's World, Miami, Florida, USA

Billy Preston played as extra support.

T. Rex received $4,000 for the show.

Wednesday 20th September

The band left Miami at just before 2 p.m. to fly to St. Petersburg – a forty-minute flight. Accommodation was arranged at the Holiday Inn-South in the city.

Bayfront Centre, St. Petersburg, Florida, USA

Set list: 'Chariot Choogle', 'Baby Strange', 'Telegram Sam', 'Spaceball Ricochet', 'Cosmic Dancer', 'Buick Mackane', 'Jeepster', 'Get It On'

T. Rex received $4,000 for the performance.

Thursday 21st September

Repeat broadcast in the UK of the performance of 'Children Of The Revolution' recorded for 'Top Of The Pops' (BBC 1). However, it's possible that a promo film may have been shown in this edition. See entry for 30th August.

The band flew from St. Petersburg to New Orleans, leaving at 11.40 a.m. and arriving at 11.55 a.m. Presumably they crossed a time zone. Accommodation was arranged at the Royal Sonesta Hotel.

Friday 22nd September

The Warehouse, New Orleans, Louisiana, USA

The band stayed a second night in New Orleans.

T. Rex received $5,500 for their performance.

Saturday 23rd September

The band took a two hour twenty minute-flight from New Orleans to Atlanta, departing at noon.

Municipal Auditorium, Atlanta, Georgia, USA

The band received $4,000 for the performance.

Sunday 24th September

The band were originally due to fly to Charleston. However, as the show was cancelled, it's unlikely that this happened. The band probably continued to stay in Atlanta.

Municipal Auditorium, Charleston, South Carolina, USA

This show was cancelled.

Monday 25th September

Day off.

Tuesday 26th September

Day off.

Wednesday 27th September

The original schedule indicated that the band were due to fly from Charleston to Pittsburgh and stay at the Holiday Inn-Green Tea. However, it's unclear if this actually happened.

Syria Mosque, Pittsburgh, Pennsylvania, USA

This show was cancelled.

Thursday 28th September

The band were due to fly from Pittsburgh to Cleveland. However, bearing in mind the previous cancellations, it is unlikely that this schedule was adhered to. The band stayed at the Statler Hilton.

Final transmission in the UK of the performance of 'Children Of The Revolution' recorded for 'Top Of The Pops' (BBC 1). See entry for 30th August.

Allen Theatre, Cleveland, Ohio, USA
T. Rex received $3,250 for the performance.

Friday 29th September
Prior to travelling from Cleveland to Detroit, Marc made another trip to Canada via Windsor to give an interview. No further details are available.

Ford Auditorium, Detroit, Michigan, USA
The band received $7,500 for the performance.

Saturday 30th September
The band flew from Detroit to Chicago. They stayed at the Playboy Towers hotel for this night and the following two.

Auditorium Theatre, Chicago, Illinois, USA
The band got another $7,500 for that night's show.

Sunday 1st October
Day off in Chicago.

Monday 2nd October
Day off in Chicago.

Tuesday 3rd October
The band travelled from Chicago to St. Louis, leaving the former at just after midday and arriving in St. Louis one hour later. They were accommodated at the Holiday Inn.

Kiel Auditorium, St. Louis, Missouri, USA
The band received $5,000 for the show.

Wednesday 4th October
The band left St. Louis on a flight to Kansas City in the early afternoon. They stayed at the Holiday Inn-Downtown.

Memorial Auditorium, Kansas City, Missouri, USA
The band's fee for the night was $4,250.

Thursday 5th October
Civic Centre Music Hall, Oklahoma City, Oklahoma, USA
T. Rex received $4,000 for their performance that night.

Friday 6th October
Civic Auditorium, Shreveport, Louisiana, USA
The show for this date was originally scheduled to be held at the Lauri Auditorium, Trinity College, San Antonio, Texas. It was then switched to the Community Centre, before being cancelled in favour of the above.

The band received $4,000 for the performance.

Saturday 7th October

Music Hall, Houston, Texas, USA
The gross for that night's performance came to $7,000.

Sunday 8th October

Texas Hall, Arlington, Texas, USA
T. Rex grossed $7,000 for their performance that night. The band stayed at the Hyatt House in Dallas for this night and the following two.

Monday 9th October

This date was suggested for a possible broadcast/recording on the 'Dick Clark – American Bandstand' TV programme.

Wednesday 11th October

Prior to the concert, the band were scheduled to fly from Dallas to Salt Lake City. It's uncertain if this actually happened in view of the cancellation of the planned concert.
Terrace Ballroom, Salt Lake City, Utah, USA
This concert was cancelled.

Thursday 12th October

The band were originally scheduled to fly from Salt Lake City to San Francisco. It's more likely that they flew from Dallas. The entourage was booked into the Miyako Hotel for this night and the following one.

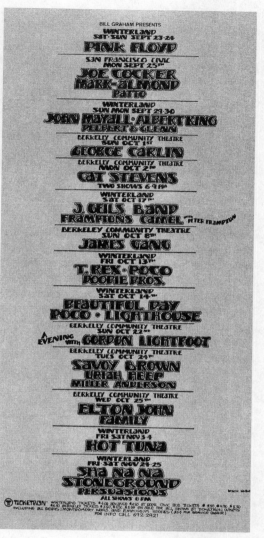

postcard – flyer

Friday 13th October

Winterland, San Francisco, California, USA
Gloria Jones, Julia Tillman and Stephanie Spruill joined T. Rex on backing vocals for this concert and the following shows at the Santa Monica Civic and Long Beach Arena.
The band grossed a total of $6,311.25 for their show that night.

Saturday 14th October

The band flew from San Francisco at noon and arrived in Los Angeles just over an hour later. Marc and June were booked into the Beverley Hills Hotel.
Civic Auditorium, Santa Monica, California, USA
"This was supposed to be the tour that would plant T. Rextasy into a previously resistant

America, but that hasn't quite been the way it's worked out ... Marc's equation is unbalanced ... There's too much missing and too many visible flaws glaring straight at you. I love the albums. The live T. Rex is a terrific disappointment.

There are obvious things. Marc and his band do manage to build an intensity during some of his long, boring guitar solos, but then – snap! – the song ends, they dawdle and tune and wait for the energy to fade away before starting on the next one. Pacing is an elementary requirement of a good rock 'n' roll show, but T. Rex indicate no consciousness of its necessity or existence ... On stage his movements are repetitive, empty and forced. He's trying much too hard and the result is a total lack of spontaneity. He deflates the illusion instead of giving it additional substance."

Richard Cromelin, Melody Maker

The band received $7,500 for their performance that night.

Sunday 15th October
Long Beach Auditorium, Long Beach, California, USA
The highest grossing single concert of the tour brought in a total of $9,554.08 for the group.

Saturday 21st October–Wednesday 25th October (?)
Strawberry Studios, Chateau d'Herouville, Pontoise, Paris, France
Backing tracks for the following songs were cut at these sessions: 'Tenement Lady', 'Rapids', 'Mister Mister', 'Broken Hearted Blues', 'Darling', 'Country Honey', 'Born To Boogie', 'The Street And Babe Shadow', 'Left Hand Luke' and 'Solid Gold Easy Action'.

Monday 23rd October
Strawberry Studios, Chateau d'Herouville, Pontoise, Paris, France
Basic tracks for 'County Honey', 'The Street And Babe Shadow', 'Rapids' and 'Born To Boogie' were recorded on this date.

Wednesday 25th October
Strawberry Studios, Chateau d'Herouville, Pontoise, Paris, France
Overdubs and additional work was done on 'Tenement Lady', 'Broken Hearted Blues', 'Born To Boogie', 'Solid Gold', 'Easy Action', 'Left Hand Luke', 'Mister Mister' and 'Darling'.

October

Unconfirmed BBC Television Studio, London, England

Marc was interview for BBC2's 'Old Grey Whistle Test'. The interview was included on the 31st October edition of the programme.

Friday 27th October

Air Studios, 214 Oxford Street, London, England

Studio session which produced demos of '20th Century', 'Mr. Motion', 'Down Home Lady' and 'You're So Fine' plus the 'Top Of The Pops' mix of 'Solid Gold Easy Action'.

Tuesday 31st October

Broadcast date for the interview filmed for 'Old Grey Whistle Test' (BBC 2).

Thursday 2nd November – Thursday 9th November

Morgan Studios, 169–171 High Road, Willesden, London, England

Marc, in the company of Harry Nillson, Keith Moon, Donovan and others, attended Alice Cooper's 'Billion Dollar Babies' sessions on one day between these dates. Cooper himself has indicated on at least one occasion that Bolan played guitar on 'Hello Hooray' and 'Slick Black Limousine'. Other sources close to the sessions disagree with this. It's likely that they jammed around 'Jailhouse Rock' and Harry Nillson's song 'Coconuts'. Unfortunately the results were of poor quality as everyone became progressively drunker.

Friday 10th November

Unicorn / A Beard Of Stars (Fly TOOFA 9)

Another re-issue by Fly of two early Tyrannosaurus Rex albums. See earlier track listings for further details.

Wednesday 22nd November

BBC Television Centre, Wood Lane, Shepherd's Bush, London, England

T. Rex recorded one performance of 'Solid Gold Easy Action' for BBC Television's 'Top Of The Pops'. The band was augmented by a trio of female backing singers for filming purposes; they still mimed to a slightly remixed record version. The clip was shown on 7th December, 14th December, 21st December and 4th January 1973 editions of the programme.

November

Air Studios, 214 Oxford Street, London, England

Overdubbing and mixing sessions for the 'Tanx' album.

November

Tony Visconti's flat, Courtfield Road, Earl's Court, London, England

The material for the Fan Club flexi-disc was recorded here. All the band members apart from Bill Legend were present for the recordings. Mickey Marmalade and Alphi O'Leary were also present and contributed backing vocals to 'Christmas, It's A T. Rexmas'.

FAR EAST TOUR

Originally T. Rex were scheduled to play concerts in Japan, Australia, New Zealand and Hong

Kong. Eventually only the Japanese concerts took place. The planned Australian dates can be found in the Appendix. Contracts were signed and a fee of $60,000 had been agreed for the tour.

Saturday 25th November
The T. Rex tour party departed Heathrow for Tokyo just before midday.

Sunday 26th November
T. Rex fly into Haneda Airport, Tokyo and go on to their hotel, the Tokyo Hilton.

Monday 27th November
Hilton Hotel, Tokyo, Japan
A press reception was scheduled for 1 p.m. at the above hotel.

Tuesday 28th November
Budokan Hall, Tokyo, Japan
Set list: 'Chariot Choogle', 'Baby Strange', 'Telegram Sam', 'Metal Guru', 'Spaceball Ricochet', 'Buick Mackane', 'Jeepster', 'Hot Love', 'Get It On'
Due to equipment problems Mickey Finn took a rare conga solo just after 'Baby Strange'.

Wednesday 29th November
The band travelled to Nagoya by Tokaido Line. Their accommodation for this night and the following was at the Nagoya International hotel.
Aichikenritu Taiikukan, Nagoya, Japan

Thursday 30th November
The band have a day off in Nagoya.

Friday 1st December
Solid Gold Easy Action / Born To Boogie (EMI T. Rex MARC 3)
Release date for the above single. Though the record progressed to number 2 in the charts, in comparison with previous releases, its rise to that position was less dynamic.

concert poster

The band travel from Nagoya to Osaka by Tokaido Line, staying overnight at the Osaka Royal.
Furitu Taiikukan, Osaka, Japan

Saturday 2nd December
The band travel by plane from Osaka to Tokyo.

Sunday 3rd December
EMI Toshiba Studios, Akasaka, Tokyo, Japan
Studio session which produced the basic tracks for '20th Century Boy', "Electric Slim And The Factory Hen' and 'Street Back'. 'Street Back' was later retitled 'Shock Rock'.

Monday 4th December
Budokan Hall, Tokyo, Japan

Tuesday 5th December
Interview with Nobuyuki Yoshinari for EMI Japan promo single.

Wednesday 6th December
T. Rex leave Japan from Haneda Airport, Tokyo and arrive back in London in the late morning.

Thursday 7th December
Initial broadcast in the UK of the performance of 'Solid Gold Easy Action' recorded for 'Top Of The Pops' (BBC 1). See entry for 22nd November.

Friday 8th December
Air Studios, 214 Oxford Street, London, England
Master reductions of 'Country Honey', 'Rapids' and 'Tenement Lady' were made.

Thursday 14th December
Second broadcast on BBC 1 of the performance of 'Solid Gold Easy Action' recorded for 'Top Of The Pops'. See entry for 22nd November.

Oscar One, Soho, London, England

'Born To Boogie' was premiered at the above cinema. In addition to Marc and T. Rex, Elton John and Ringo Starr were also in attendance. The film received the predictable bad reviews.

"As a rock 'n' roll film, it's one of those total-personality efforts – As opposed to the pain-in-the-ass 'Mad Dogs And Englishmen' / 'Stomping Ground' syndrome of boring documentary.

'Boogie's' only saving grace is the viewers a chance to see Bolan as he wants us to view him. Half the film is taken up with the T. Rex show at Wembley. The camera, naturally, fixes itself almost exclusively on Bolan. We occasionally get a chance to watch Mickey Finn ... while members Currie and Legend are seen only when they happen to accidentally find themselves next to where Marc is being filmed.

The music is fuzzy, primal and repetitive but that's OK. There's a good version of 'Jeepster' sounding like it's being played in the middle of a swamp.

The most embarrassing part of the film ... is when Marc decides to play acoustic. New heights of fey precociousness are reached as Bolan strums the most blatantly out-of-tune guitar I've possibly ever heard, and whines obnoxiously for over five minutes ...

There actually is one really good scene in this film. T. Rex perform 'Tutti Frutti' with Ringo Starr on the drums and Elton John playing great piano. Here the band really do rock, and just when you think it's too good to be true they move into a fine, fine version of 'Children Of The Revolution', which cuts the single to pieces. Ah, if only the film had ended there, but no ... it's time for more Wembley Pool histrionics."

NME, Nick Kent

"Even in the undistinguished annals of pop documentaries, the latest offering – Born To Boogie – must be regarded as a failure.

Starring and dominated by Marc Bolan, it is merely a collection of shots from T. Rex's recent Wembley concert alternating with meaningless indulgent sketches which only underline the complete lack of purpose of it all.

... but surely in a 65-minute spectacular one can expect more than the incomplete visual catalogue of a concert interspersed with major events like T. Rex gorging hamburgers or Bolan emerging from the distance in an aged Cadilac and spluttering a few inane phrases.

Musically the highlight is a sequence when T. Rex join forces with Ringo Starr and Elton John which is a rock revelation. Otherwise it's fairly predictable with Bolan convincing one of the hard work involved in projecting and preserving the image of sexual mystique.

One is forced to the conclusion, however, that T. Rex should in future stick firmly to their limited field."

Robert Whittaker Music Week

Saturday 16th December

Air Studios, 214 Oxford Street, London, England

Mixes of 'Tenement Lady', 'Free Angel' and 'Mister Mister' were completed.

Thursday 21st December

Transmission date for another repeat of the performance of 'Solid Gold Easy Action' recorded for 'Top Of The Pops' (BBC 1). See entry for 22nd November.

BBC Television Centre, Wood Lane, Shepherd's Bush, London, England

Recording date for the Christmas editions of 'Top Of The Pops'. T. Rex performed two songs for

flyer

the shows. 'Metal Guru' was broadcast on the 25th December and 'Telegram Sam' was broadcast on 27th December.

Friday 22nd December

Sundown, Edmonton, London, England
Set list: 'Baby Strange', 'Telegram Sam', 'Jeepster', 'Spaceball Ricochet', 'Buick Mackane', 'Metal Guru', 'Get It On' (incomplete)
The concert was filmed by an unknown film crew.

"... there's all those weird little people jumping around ... and I can't see or hear a thing ... Despite the melee, it seems to these ears that T. Rex are playing more proficiently than they were earlier this year at Wembley. But ... it's impossible to say that they're really a kickass hot-action destructo band. It rattles along okay ... Okay, I'm being snide, again. What happened on Friday is that Marc Bolan played a gig to around 5,000 people, and he gave them a really fine time. Which I can dig, despite the rather low-grade music."

Charles Shaar Murray, NME

Saturday 23rd December

Sundown, Brixton, London, England
Two shows.

Monday 25th December

Broadcast date on BBC 1 for the performance of 'Metal Guru' recorded for the Christmas edition of 'Top Of The Pops'. See entry for 21st December.

Wednesday 27th December

The second 'Top Of The Pops' Christmas special, featuring the version of 'Telegram Sam' recorded on the 21st December was networked on this date.

Friday 29th December

BBC Television Studios, Pebble Mill, Birmingham, Warwickshire, England

To promote the general release of 'Born To Boogie', Marc was interviewed by Tom Gyne for BBC television's 'Pebble Mill At One'. The interview was broadcast live and included an extract of 'Children Of The Revolution' from 'Born To Boogie'.

Sunday 31st December

Air Studios, 214 Oxford Street, London, England

A tape containing the 'Tanx' versions of 'Born To Boogie', 'Life Is Strange', 'The Street And Babe Shadow', 'Highway Knees', and 'Left Hand Luke' was produced on this date. In other words, the second side of the album apart from the opening cut, 'Mad Donna'.

1973

1973 saw Bolan and T. Rex perform a considerable number of tour dates – none of them in the United Kingdom. Marc turned his attention to other territories and made a second attempt to make substantial inroads in America (the February tour of 1972 can be seen more as a case of introducing T. Rex to America). In addition T. Rex spent a great deal of time in recording studios in the USA, Denmark, Germany and Britain recording material for the follow up album to 'Tanx'.

It was during the early part of the year that Bolan first began to show signs of discontent with the "traditional" T. Rex sound. While touring America he had been listening mainly to soul and black music stations on the radio. The music he heard obviously connected to some of the music of his youth which lead to the idea of incorporating elements of that style of music into the T. Rex sound. Some of this had been put into practice on the 'Tanx' track 'Left Hand Luke', but the full plunge was not taken until the spring of 1973.

The first move in a "soul" direction was the employment of Gloria Jones and Stephanie Spruill for an American TV concert. Both had previously appeared as backing vocalists at T. Rex performances in New York and in California the previous year. Spruill was later replaced by Sister Pat Hall.

Before that the band had toured Europe for the final time as a four piece. Again the tour was something of a mixed bag performance-wise. An excellent concert in Essen would be followed by a complete disaster in Vienna. Part of the reason for this could have been that, again the band was tired from the punishing touring and recording schedule. The alcohol and drugs were also beginning to have a telling effect.

For the summer tour Bolan sensibly decided to bolster the band's line-up with the addition of guitarist Jack Green, who not only fitted in well, but also gave Marc more freedom on stage. This resulted in some of the best T. Rex live music ever. Unfortunately the tour, supporting AOR veterans Three Dog Night, was a complete farce. The pairing of T. Rex and Three Dog Night was a complete mismatch, with audiences largely bemused by T. Rex. If anything, it was even worse than going out on the road with The Doobie Brothers.

Thursday 4th January
Final repeat of 'Solid Gold Easy Action' on 'Top Of The Pops' (BBC 1). See entry for 22nd November.

Saturday 6th January
Marc and June go on holiday to Barbados.

Monday 8th January

Air Studios, 214 Oxford Street, London, England

The master tape of the 'Tanx' album was completed, probably by Tony Visconti.

Tuesday 23rd January

Air Studios, 214 Oxford Street, London, England

A studio session which produced a T. Rex jam which was committed to tape.

Friday 26th January

Air Studios, 214 Oxford Street, London, England

Further studio work on '20th Century Boy' and 'Free Angel', though it's possible that just a single tape copy was made.

BBC Television Centre, Wood Lane, Shepherd's Bush, London, England

Marc and T. Rex were present at the above studios for rehearsals for the following day's programme.

Saturday 27th January

BBC Television Centre, Wood Lane, Shepherd's Bush, London, England

T. Rex made a surprise appearance on BBC Television's 'The Cilla Black Show', transmitted on BBC1. The performance was recorded earlier in the day and broadcast later that evening. Two songs were performed on the show; a mimed version of 'Mad Donna' from the forthcoming album and a live duet with Cilla Black on 'Life's A Gas'. The performance was firmly in the realms of kitsch with Marc's voice noticeably croaky at times on the latter song. The band were paid £500 for the performance.

Sunday 28th January

Marc and June go on a second trip to Barbados.

'BOLAN BOOGIE' WEST GERMAN TOUR

Sadly Marc seemed tired and a little worse for wear for the majority of these concerts. Consequently the band turned in some poor performances. Most of the songs performed were extended versions, sometimes to quite ridiculous lengths. For example, the version of 'Telegram Sam' performed in Vienna clocked in at some 12 minutes. Despite the shoddy quality of the concerts, the band turned in a killer performance for German television on Radio Bremen's 'Musikladen'. For each concert the band received a guarantee of £1,000 against 60% of the receipts.

Tuesday 13th February

The band departed Heathrow for Berlin at just after at 10.30 in the morning, arriving at 2.15 in the afternoon.

Sportpalast, Berlin, West Germany

The band's after-concert hotel is the Bristol Hotel Kempinski.

Wednesday 14th February

The band flew from Berlin to Bremen in the late afternoon.

Radio Bremen Studios, Bremen, West Germany

T. Rex appeared on the German programme 'Musikladen', the successor to 'Beat Club'. Two songs

MAMA CONCERTS PRESENTS

T.REX

BOLAN BOOGIE

Grugahalle
Essen
16. Februar
Freitag
20⁰⁰Uhr

Vorverkauf
Höing im Handelshof
Verkehrsverein im Hauptbahnhof
Buchhandlung Baedeker
Zigarrenhaus Kaiser, Schwarzlei Kela
Kaufhof-Reisen, Innenstadt Essen
Büchermarkt, Innenstadt Essen
An den Kassen und den bekannten
Vorverkaufsstellen der Grugahalle
Co-Produktion: Mama Concerts
R. Schulte-Behrendorf

flyer

were filmed, '20th Century Boy' and 'Buick Mackane'.

As with previous editions of 'Beat Club', two takes of '20th Century Boy' were recorded and then mixed together. The first take featured the whole band, while the second take featured just Bolan on guitar and vocals. The audio and visual recordings were then mixed together. The performance was broadcast on 21st February. 'Buick Mackane' was left incomplete, only a first take being filmed. At the time it was left unbroadcast, but was shown by accident at the end of an Osmonds' special on 17th March 1974!

Originally it was thought that the performance took place on 19th February. It now transpires that this was the mastering date.

The band spent the night at the Park Hotel.

Thursday 15th February
The entourage was driven from Bremen to Düsseldorf and had a day off. For this night and the following the band stayed at the Hilton Hotel in Düsseldorf.

Friday 16th February
Grugahalle, Essen, West Germany
Set list: 'Chariot Choogle', 'Baby Strange', 'Metal Guru', 'Telegram Sam', 'Buick Mackane', 'Jeepster', 'Hot Love', 'Get It On', '20th Century Boy', 'Instrumental Jam'
This gig most likely featured the debut concert performance of '20th Century Boy'.

Saturday 17th February
The band flew from Düsseldorf to Hamburg in the early afternoon.
Fontenay Lounge, Intercontinental Hotel, Hamburg
Prior to that evening's concert at 4 p.m., there was a photo session which featured the whole band plus an Angie Bowie look-a-like modelling. The lounge had been especially decorated for the session. After this, Bolan and Mickey Finn gave press interviews.
Planten un Blomen Halle 7, Hamburg, West Germany

Sunday 18th February

The band flew from Hamburg to Nuremburg via Frankfurt, departing in the late morning and arriving at just after 2 p.m.

Neue Messehalle, Nuremburg, West Germany

Following the concert the band spent the night at the Grand Hotel.

Monday 19th February

The band flew from Nuremburg to Vienna via Frankfurt, again leaving in the late morning and arriving just around two in the afternoon.

Halle D, Stadthalle, Vienna, Austria

Set list: 'Chariot Choogle', 'Baby Strange', 'Metal Guru', 'Telegram Sam', 'Spaceball Ricochet', 'Buick Mackane', 'Jeepster', 'Hot Love', 'Get It On'

By this stage Bolan had dropped the acoustic set from the live repertoire, which makes the performance of 'Spaceball Ricochet' something of an oddity.

The band's hotel for the evening was the Bristol Hotel.

Tuesday 20th February

T. Rex travelled by plane from Vienna to Frankfurt, leaving in the mid-afternoon. The band were based at the Intercontinental hotel in Frankfurt for this and the following two nights.

Stadthalle, Offenbach, West Germany

Set list: 'Telegram Sam', 'Baby Strange', 'Metal Guru', 'Buick Mackane', 'Jeepster', 'Get It On'

The concert was shorter than usual and featured a truncated set list. After 10 minutes Bolan left the stage due to his anger with a defective microphone. After a delay, he and the band returned to the stage to finish the performance.

Originally the Deutsches Museum, Munich concert was scheduled for this date.

Wednesday 21st February

Originally a concert at the Stadthalle in Frankfurt was planned for this date.

Broadcast on the ARD network of 'Musikladen' including '20th Century Boy'. See entry for 15th February.

The band have a day off in Frankfurt.

Thursday 22nd February

The band were driven from Frankfurt to Saarbrücken for that night's show.

ATSV-Halle, Saarbrücken, West Germany

Overnight accommodation was at the Hotel Christine.

Friday 23rd February

The band return to Frankfurt by road, before catching the 14.10 flight to Munich, arriving in the city at just after three.

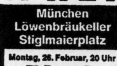

Sonntag, 25. Februar 1973
18,00 Uhr

Mannheim · Große VFR Sporthalle
am Maimarkt

MAMA CONCERTS PRESENTS

T.REX

BOLAN BOOGIE

12,00 DM
incl. .MWSt. zuzüglich Vorverkaufsgebühr

Keine Haftung für Sach- und Körperschäden.
In keinem Falle Rückerstattungsanspruch
auf den Kaufpreis. · Vor Mißbrauch wird gewarnt.

Kongressaal, Deutsches Museum, Munich, West Germany
For this night and the following two, the band were based at the Sheraton Hotel in Munich.

Saturday 24th February

Sporthalle, Cologne, West Germany
It appears that this concert was cancelled. The band were booked into the Sheraton Hotel in Munich and this is mentioned in two itineraries as a day off.
The Stadthalle, Offenbach concert was originally planned for this date.

Sunday 25th February

The band returned to Frankfurt from Munich by plane before travelling to Mannheim by road.

Grosse VFR Sporthalle, Mannheim, West Germany
The overnight hotel was the Steigenberger Hotel.

Originally a concert at the Frederich Eberthalle in Ludwigshafen was planned for this date.

Monday 26th February

The band returned to London, departing Frankfurt in the late afternoon and arriving in London just before five.

Tuesday 27th February

Air Studios, 214 Oxford Street, London, England
A mix of '20th Century Boy' was produced for use on 'Top Of The Pops'.

Wednesday 28th February

BBC Television Centre, Wood Lane, Shepherd's Bush, London, England
Only one performance of '20th Century Boy' was recorded for BBC Television's 'Top Of The Pops'. This was transmitted on the 1st March, 8th March and 15th March editions of the show.

Thursday 1st March

Initial broadcast on BBC 1's 'Top Of The Pops' of '20th Century Boy'. See entry for 28th February.

Friday 2nd March

20th Century Boy / Free Angel (EMI T. Rex MARC 4)
Though still successful, '20th Century Boy' stalled at number 3 in the UK singles chart.

"Guitars tremble, Marc howls, and it's gang awa' with another in his series of rhythmic entertainments. There are overtones of 'I Wanna Be Your Man' ... It's full of nervous energy (and) the beat is more danceable than 'Easy Action'...".

Melody Maker

"It's been said that this is a pretty crucial time for Bolan. Certainly I would have thought now was the time to release something quite unexpected on to the market ... this is a very solid driving bass start, (which) opens up to reveal another variation on 'Telegram Sam' ... I just think it's a bit sad that he hasn't extended his musical capabilities as far as he might have done...".

Penny Valentine, Sounds

"After 'Metal Guru', 'Solid Gold Easy Action', and 'Children Of The Revolution', I thought they'd lost their touch. But lo and behold, there's Marc's thunder guitar majestically assaulting you. The lyrics and melody are better than of late ... The weakest part of the entire disc is the chorus ... Still it's his best since 'Telegram Sam' and that can't be bad."

NME

Thursday 8th March
Second transmission of the '20th Century Boy' appearance on 'Top Of The Pops' (BBC 1). See entry for 28th February.

'BOLAN BOOGIE' EUROPEAN TOUR
Following the series of German dates and a short break, T. Rex played further dates in other European countries. During a break in the tour schedule, the band entered Rosenberg Studios in Copenhagen to lay down a number of tracks. As with the German dates, the band were to be paid £1,000 per show against 60% of the door. The Brussels concert was an exception to this.

It is particularly difficult to establish the exact sequence of events of this tour due to the amount of rescheduling and the number of conflicting tour itineraries.

Saturday 10th March
T. Rex flew on a chartered flight to Le Bourget Airport, Paris, departing Heathrow at nine in the morning and arriving in Paris at eleven.

"Variete En Studio", Studio 17, Les Buthe Chaumant, Paris, France
Television recording for French television's 'Devine Qui Est Derrier La Porte', a Saturday night variety show similar to 'The Cilla Black Show', only worse. Two songs were performed, 'Children Of The Revolution' and '20th Century Boy', both of them being mimed to the original discs. A rehearsal was held at 12.30 p.m., followed by a dress rehearsal at 5 p.m. The show was broadcast live from 8.30 p.m. The band were paid 1,250 French Francs each for the performance.
After the concert they stayed at the Hilton in Paris.

Sunday 11th March
The band have a day off, spending a second night at the Paris Hilton.

Monday 12th March
Olympia, Paris, France
Set list: 'Telegram Sam', 'Metal Guru', 'Jeepster', 'Get It On' (incomplete)
A soundcheck was set for 3 p.m. with the show scheduled for 9 p.m. The band received £1,000 for the performance.

Tuesday 13th March
The band flew back from Le Bourget airport to Heathrow in the early afternoon. Originally it appears they were due to travel on to Gothenburg, staying at the Hotel Rusinen.

Thursday 15th March
Final broadcast of '20th Century Boy' on 'Top Of The Pops' (BBC 1). See entry for 28th February. T. Rex flew from London to Gothenburg, arriving at just after half past one in the afternoon.

Scandanavium, Gothenburg, Sweden

Originally this night's concert was scheduled for the Konserthus in Stockholm.

Friday 16th March

Tanx (EMI T. Rex BLN 5002)

'Tenement Lady', 'Rapids', 'Mister Mister', 'Broken Hearted Blues', 'Shock Rock', 'Country Honey', 'Electric Slim And The Factory Hen', 'Mad Donna', 'Born To Boogie', 'Life Is Strange', 'The Street And Babe Shadow', 'Highway Knees', 'Left Hand Luke'

Marc Bolan – guitar, vocals; Mickey Finn – percussion; Steve Currie – bass; Bill Legend – drums; Tony Visconti – backing vocals, mellotron; Howard Casey – saxophone; Bernard (?) or Andre Herve – piano; Sue And Sunny, Barry St. John, Vicky Brown – backing vocals.

Recorded at Strawberry Studios, Paris; EMI Toshiba Studios, Tokyo; Air Studios, London.

Like 'The Slider', 'Tanx' peaked at number 4 in the UK album chart. In the USA the album failed to emulate or build on the success of 'The Slider' reaching a lowly 102 in the album charts.

"I like 'The Slider' ... it captured all that simplicity and choogling panting (the fans) had paid their money to see ...

'Tanx' moves T. Rex some steps on from that album, yet in a funny way, some steps back too, to the lyrical feel of yesterday. 'Electric Slim And The Factory Hen', for instance, comes over strong. 'Tanx' is in its own way a strong album. It will be interesting to see how it does ... his teeny audience ... have grown a lot over two years ...".

Penny Valentine, Sounds

"(Bolan) understands rock 'n' roll and he's been nearly as good at it as he says he is – but lately he seems to have lost the crucial knack of writing good hooks ... To his credit he's been trying to vary the pace ... 'Tanx' is a nice album ... but, even so it's not as good as 'The Slider' ... He's relaxed on it, indulging himself and losing tension in whole swathes of forgettable mediocrity ... the second side just passes me by ... excepting 'The Street And Babe Shadow', whose swirling organ and ripsnorting tenor sax offset the tune's proper monotony ... Side one has some goodies: 'Shock Rock' and 'Country Honey' display the kind of energy that's been missing lately, 'Broken Hearted Blues' is pretty and 'Electric Slim And The Factory Hen' is the pick of the album – deceptively soft and swaying ...".

Richard Williams, Melody Maker

"Overall the 13 tracks tend to vary enormously in merit, with a substantial amount of the standard T. Rex thump 'n' grind coming somewhere in between. I guess it's all down to how you like your T. Rex served.

For me it's the calmer, more relaxed tracks that are the most palatable ... "Electric Slim And The Factory Hen" is an example of this, with an easy flowing melody line, backed up by strings...

On the other hand, "Shock Rock" is an abomination made utterly banal by two lines of lyrics ... which are just repeated a few times.

Over on side two though, interest begins to wane ... as it gets back to the standard T. Rex we all know, if not exactly love...

Finally the album ends on an odd note with "Left Hand Luke", one of those long ... slowly-building efforts ... with everything included that you can think of. Maybe this is the direction Bolan intends to take in the future."

James Johnson, NME

The entourage travel from flew from Gothenburg to Malmö in the early afternoon. They were booked into Sct. Jorgens Hotel. Apparently Marc threatened to pull the night's concert due to his dissatisfaction with the car that EMI Sweden had sent to collect the band from the airport.
Olympen, Lund, Sweden

"T Rex are big off stage but oh, so small on it.

... T. Rex is nothing but a big fraud. In the focus stands guitarist/singer, Marc Bolan, classi-fied by many as the sex symbol of the 70s.

Marc does gimmicks that were already old four years ago. As a guitar player he is boring and even mediocre and tries to compensate by shaking his hips and so on. A weak and pale super-star!

By his side: Mickey Finn. He was already present when the T was written Tyrannosaurus. Back then he filled some purpose with his bongos. He supported Marc in a sufficient way, but today he is a pure luxury. His drumming cannot be heard in the electronic noise; ungrateful, unnecessary.

Add to this Steve Currie on bass, who was not able to keep in time on the faster numbers. Nothing but a scandal!

Behind the drums: Bill Legend, who really was the best in the band. It was said after last year's T. Rex concert in Copenhagen, but it deserves to be repeated: see through the bubble! It's time to puncture it. It contains very little music, but a lot of gimmicks.

Many in the audience were cold to what was presented on stage and they should be praised. Swedish audiences won't accept any tricks.

Bosse Hansson, Sydsvenska Dagbladet

Saturday 17th March
The tour party travelled from Malmö to Århus via Copenhagen, arriving in Århus at five in the afternoon. They were booked into the Hotel Atlantic.
Velby Risskoven Hallen, Århus, Denmark

Sunday 18th March
The entourage travel from Århus, via Copenhagen, to Oslo, arriving in the mid-afternoon. They were booked into the Grand Hotel for that night and the following one. The rest of the day was a free one.

Monday 19th March

Chateau Neuf, Oslo, Norway
Set list: 'Chariot Choogle', 'Baby Strange', 'Metal Guru', 'Telegram Sam', 'Buick Mackane', 'Jeepster', 'Hot Love', 'Get It On'
Originally the concert at the Scandanavium in Gothenburg was planned for this date. The Oslo concert was originally planned to have been held at the Eckebergshallen.

Tuesday 20th March

The band flew from Oslo to Copenhagen in the early afternoon, arriving just before half past two.
Rosenberg Studios, Vanloese, Copenhagen, Denmark
A tape dated this day was prepared containing 'All My Love', 'Liquid Gang', 'The Groover', 'Down Home Lady', 'Midnight' and 'Superbad'. This was something of a mega-session as a total of six tracks appear to have been recorded during the day's proceedings. The session was booked to begin at 7 p.m.

A concert at the Konserthuset, in Gothenburg was originally scheduled for this evening. In the event, the concert was brought forward a few days and the venue changed.

The band were booked into the Hotel 3 Falke in Copenhagen for this night and the following two.

Information gleamed from Bolan's passport seems to indicates that he flew into Utrecht in Holland on this date. However, this is extremely unlikely. Either the place is wrong or the date is (perhaps 1975). Utrecht is a minor airport.

Wednesday 21st March

Falkoner Teatret, Frederiksberg, Copenhagen, Denmark
Tony Visconti came on at this concert to play extra bass guitar for the encore of 'Get It On'. Earlier in the day Marc gave press interviews at the Palace Hotel in Copenhagen.

Thursday 22nd March

Rosenberg Studios, Vanloese, Copenhagen, Denmark
Recording session which produced 'Saturation Syncopation' and 'Delanie' and probably some additional work on the songs recorded two days earlier. The session began at noon.
Fyns Konserthuset, Odense, Denmark
This concert, though scheduled, was cancelled in favour of the above recording session.

Friday 23rd March

The band flew from Copenhagen to Brussels in the mid-afternoon. They were booked into the Westbury Hotel.

Saturday 24th March

Westbury Hotel, Brussels, Belgium
Marc was filmed prior to the evening's concert for the Belgian music programme 'Veronica's'. Besides giving an (arrogant) interview, he also performed a unique acoustic version of '20th Century Boy'.
National Voorst, Brussels, Belgium
As an exception to the rule, the band were guaranteed £2,000 against 70% of the door for this particular concert.

Marc's passport again seems to indicate that he used the airport at Utrecht in The Netherlands, but this is almost certainly the wrong year.

Sunday 25th March

The tour party flew back from Brussels to London in the late afternoon.

Tuesday 27th March

Air Studios, 214 Oxford Street, London, England

Rough mixes of 'All Of My Love', 'The Groover' and 'Delanie' were produced. Another tape box from the same date lists a total of nine rough mixes, 'All My Love', 'Liquid Gang', 'The Groover', 'Down Home Lady', 'Super Bad', 'Saturation Syncopation' (with a note from Marc titling the song 'All Alone'), two takes of 'Delanie' (one of which with a duff ending) and 'Midnight'.

Wednesday 4th April

Air Studios, 214 Oxford Street, London, England

A master mix of 'Midnight' was completed.

Saturday 7th April

Air Studios, 214 Oxford Street, London, England

Studio session which produced a song titled on the tape box 'Demo for Ringo'.

Tuesday 10th April

Town Hall, Watford, Hertfordshire, England

Marc joined Electric Light Orchestra on stage for their encore.

April

Air Studios, 214 Oxford Street, London, England

Around the time of the Watford concert Bolan joined the Electric Light Orchestra at Air Studios, playing guitar on 'Ma-Ma-Ma-Belle', 'Dreaming Of 4,000' and the outtake 'Everyone's Born To Die'. The first two tracks appeared on the album 'On The Third Day', with 'Ma-Ma-Ma-Belle' also being released as a single. Jeff Lynne also used Bolan's Gibson Flying V guitar for the solo on 'Showdown'.

Saturday 14th April

Marc and June flew to Los Angeles on business and to prepare for the forthcoming US tour.

April

A & M Studios, Los Angeles, California, USA

Ringo Starr studio session during which Marc overdubbed his guitar part on 'Have You Seen My Baby' for the 'Ringo' album.

Saturday 28th April

The other members of T. Rex flew out from London to Los Angeles.

Sunday 29th April

Unknown venue, Los Angeles, California, USA

The band rehearse at an unidentified studio, possibly Wally Heider Studios, for the forthcoming performance at Santa Monica Civic. The rehearsal was scheduled to last from 10 a.m. to 12 midnight.

Monday 30th April
Wally Heider Studios, Los Angeles, California, USA
Recording session which produced a version of 'Carsmile Smith And The Old One', 'Satisfaction Pony', 'Pink', 'Blackjack' and an untitled demo. It's possible that this tape contains material recorded the preceding day.

Tuesday 1st May
Civic Auditorium, Santa Monica, California, USA
While Marc was on his business trip to the States Warner Brothers hastily organised a special concert appearance on ABC television's 'In Concert' programme. The rest of the band were quickly flown over to the USA. Also appearing on the bill were Dr. John, Johnny Nash, Jeff Beck and Slade.

At least two songs were included in the final broadcast, 'Jeepster' (which was edited to remove the line "I'm gonna suck ya") and 'The Groover'. A third song, an instrumental, which survives on audiotape, was probably also shown, though film of this performance has yet to be located. This instrumental has sometimes been wrongly described as a version of 'Squint Eye Mangle'; it isn't. The show was networked in the USA on 8th June. T. Rex were augmented by Gloria Jones and Stephanie Spruill on backing vocals.

Each member of the band was paid $1,425.96 for the performance. A further $3,500 was paid for synchronisation and performance rights.

Wednesday 2nd May
Bolan and the band return to London from Los Angeles.

Thursday 3rd May
Unconfirmed film studio, London, England
Following a 12.30 lunch date, the promo film for 'The Groover' was shot at an unknown film studio. The shoot had a budget of £750. Following this there was a Warrior Music presentation of gold albums "for sales of more than 100,000." For which title(s) is not known, though 'Tanx' is the likely candidate.

Friday 4th May
Air Studios, 214 Oxford Street, London, England
Mixes of BBC versions of 'The Groover' and 'Midnight' were produced. A second tape from that day lists the song 'Pink' on the tape box. In different handwriting 'Mister Motion' and 'Squint Eye Mangle' and '7" Fan Club Flexi' are listed. These additions may have been made many years after the recording session, particularly in view of the fact that 'Mister Motion' and 'Squint Eye Mangle' appear to have been recorded some days later.

Sunday 6th May
Air Studios, 214 Oxford Street, London, England
Mixes were produced of 'Satisfaction Pony', 'Carsmile Smith And The Old One', 'Blackjack' and 'Saturday Night'. 'Saturday Night' is listed as a demo.

Monday 7th May

Air Studios, 214 Oxford Street, London, England

A shorter alternate mix of 'The Groover' was produced. A second tape includes a different rough mix of the song.

Friday 11th May

Apple Studios, London, England

Date for a studio session which produced 'Squint Eye Mangle' and 'Mister Motion'.

Thursday 24th May

Air Studios, 214 Oxford Street, London, England

Rough mixes of 'Squint Eye Mangle' (titled 'Squint Eyes' on the tape box) and 'Blackjack' were completed.

Wednesday 30th May

BBC Television Centre, Wood Lane, Shepherd's Bush, London, England

One performance of 'The Groover' was filmed for BBC Television's 'Top Of The Pops'. The segment was used on the 1st June and 15th June editions.

Friday 1st June (?)

Initial broadcast of 'The Groover' on 'Top Of The Pops' (BBC 1). See entry for 30th May. There is a question over the broadcast date. It may have been transmitted the day before.

The Groover / Midnight (EMI T. Rex MARC 5)

The single reached number 4 in the UK singles chart.

"Instantly recognisable as a T. Rex single – steady beat, full sound, Marc's voice chanting the lyric in a severely limited number of notes, screaming back up vocals, prominent bass thud, heavy guitar fills ... The thing I find a bit un-nerving is that it needn't have been T. Rex playing on the record at all – any competent producer could have fed in the relevant information from their past singles and made this one just as well."

Steve Peacock, Sounds

"So that same old beat starts chugging, grunting voices intone "T ... R ... E ... X" and Marc's voice slithers in indistinguishable lyrics. In short, very much the mixture as before ... Discerning listeners would do well to check out the B-side, an infinitely superior track called 'Midnight', which features some very presentable guitar ... At least there's some constructive thought in there somewhere."

Charles Shaar Murray, NME

Thursday 7th June

Marc gives press interviews in the back garden at Newton's restaurant in the King's Road in Chelsea, London to selected journalists including Roy Carr, amongst others. Pictures were taken by Mike Putland and Pennie Smith.

Friday 8th June

Broadcast on ABC TV in the USA of the 'In Concert' performance recorded in April. See earlier entry.

JOHN SCHER PRESENTS

GARDEN STATE SUMMER MUSIC FAIR

JULY 26TH AT 7:30 P.M.
THREE DOG NIGHT
T-REX
TICKETS $5.50

JULY 30TH, 31ST, AUGUST 1ST
GRATEFUL DEAD
THE BAND
TICKETS $6.00

AUGUST 12TH AT 7:30 P.M.
SANTANA
TICKETS $5.50

AUGUST 18TH AT 7:30 P.M.
GRAND FUNK
RAILROAD
TICKETS $5.50

AUGUST 25TH AT 7:30 P.M.
BEACH BOYS
POCO
TICKETS $5.50

AUGUST 31ST AT 7:30 P.M.
ALLMAN BROS.
BAND TICKETS $5.50

ROOSEVELT STADIUM
ROUTE 440,
JERSEY CITY, N.J.
Tickets available at all Tick-
etron outlets. Call for Info.
(212) 644-4400 also at Capi-
tol Theatre box office in
Passaic, N.J. (201) 778-2888

Friday 15th June
Repeat broadcast of 'The Groover' on 'Top Of The Pops' (BBC 1). See entry for 30th May.

Sunday 17th June–Monday 25th June
Musicland Studios, Munich, West Germany
Studio sessions for the 'Zinc Alloy And The Hidden Riders Of Tomorrow' project. Contemporary reports in the German magazine 'Bravo' indicate that some twenty tracks were taped. Bolan's notebook from the time suggests that the following were recorded: 'Galaxy', 'Painless Persuasion Vs. The Meathawk Immaculate', 'Change', 'Sitting Here', 'Dance In The Midnight', 'Nameless Wildness', 'Saturday Night', 'Carsmile Smith And The Old One' (album version), 'Liquid Gang' (album version), 'Truck On (Tyke)', 'Interstellar Soul', 'You've Got To Jive To Stay Alive', 'Hope You Enjoy The Show', 'Spanish Midnight', 'The Avengers (Superbad)' (album version) and 'Plateau Skull'. Gloria Jones and Pat Hall were present at the sessions. Jack Green also attended, though his contribution to the sessions was minimal. The band stayed at the Sheraton Hotel for the duration of their stay.

Monday 18th June
Musicland Studios, Munich, West Germany
On this particular day versions of 'Carsmile Smith And The Old One', 'Liquid Gang' and 'Interstellar Soul' were recorded.

Wednesday 20th June
Marquee Studios, London, England
A tape from this studio appears to have been produced on this date. The tracks listed on the track sheet are 'Look To Your Soul', 'Down Home Lady' and 'All My Love'. The producer is listed as Tony Visconti. However, the band were recording in Munich on this date. The tape is possibly a Munich tape put into an empty Marquee Studios box.

Saturday 23rd June
Sheraton Hotel, Munich, West Germany
T. Rex, minus Marc, but plus Tony Visconti on guitar and vocals play an impromptu set of cover versions in the hotel bar.

July

Press announcements were made that Jack Green had been added to the T. Rex line up as second guitar player, mainly for live performances.

NORTH AMERICAN TOUR

For the summer tour of America, some bright spark in the A & R department at Warner Brothers came up with the idea of T. Rex going out as support act to AOR behemoths Three Dog Night. In theory the idea was good. Where T. Rex had some kind of following (California for example) they would headline at smaller concert halls. In large arenas, which they couldn't hope to fill, they would play as support act to Three Dog Night. The actual results were something of a disaster. It might as well have been a pairing of Iggy And The Stooges with The Carpenters, such was the musical and audience expectation mismatch.

What was unfortunate was that though they were frequently messy, T. Rex were also often excellent. Gloria Jones and Sister Pat Hall provided extra strength in the vocal department. Bill Legend and Steve Currie had become a solid, pounding rhythm section and Jack Green and Marc complimented each other, with Green giving Marc the freedom to put on a show without having to worry so much about carrying the group's sound.

However, little thought had been given to the live repertoire. Though the tour was supposed to be promoting the 'Tanx' album, only one song, 'Born To Boogie', was featured in the live set. Songs from 'The Slider' still made up most of the performance material. To make matters even stranger, Marc was opening concerts with the unreleased 'Hope You Enjoy The Show' and at some shows was also performing a second unreleased song, 'Plateau Skull'.

Thursday 19th July

Marc flies into Chicago O'Hare airport before moving on to Milwaukee. For this and the following night the overnight hotel is the Holiday Inn in Milwaukee.

Friday 20th July

Milwaukee Arena, Milwaukee, Wisconsin, USA

Saturday 21st July

Chicago Stadium, Chicago, Illinois, USA
Support to Three Dog Night.
Overnight accommodation was arranged for the Playboy Towers hotel.

Sunday 22nd July

Cobo Hall, Detroit, Michigan, USA
Support to Three Dog Night.
For this night and the next the tour party stayed at the Statler Hilton in Detroit.

Monday 23rd July

The band have a day off in Detroit.

Tuesday 24th July

The entourage fly from Detroit to Memphis. The tour party spends the next two nights at the Holiday Inn-Rivermont in Memphis.

T. Rex are doing it across America

Are you ready?

DATE	LOCATION
7/20	Milwaukee Arena, Milwaukee, Wisconsin
7/21	Chicago Stadium, Chicago, Illinois
7/22	Cobo Hall, Detroit, Michigan
7/25	Mid South Coliseum, Memphis, Tennessee
7/27	Miami Sports Auditorium, Miami, Florida
7/28	Curtis Hixon Hall, Tampa, Florida
7/29	Omni, Atlanta, Georgia
7/31	Hirsch Auditorium, Shreveport, Louisiana
8/1	Mobile Municipal Auditorium, Mobile, Alabama
8/2	Royal Stadium, Kansas City, Missouri
8/3	Civic Auditorium, Baltimore, Maryland
8/4	Nassau Coliseum, New York City, New York
8/5	Dillion Stadium, Hartford, Connecticut
8/10	Civic Theatre, San Diego, California
8/11	Santa Monica Civic Auditorium, Santa Monica, Ca
8/12	Long Beach Auditorium, Long Beach, California
8/14	Paramount Theatre, Portland, Oregon
8/15	Paramount Theatre, Seattle, Washington
8/17	Salt Palace, Salt Lake City, Utah
8/18	Denver Coliseum, Denver, Colorado
8/19	Pershing Auditorium, Lincoln, Nebraska
8/20	Quad City Stadium, Davenport, Iowa
8/21	Kiel Auditorium, St. Louis, Missouri
8/23	City Auditorium, Binghamton, New York
8/24	New Haven Arena, New Haven, Connecticut
8/25	State Farm Arena, Harrisburg, Pennsylvania
8/26	Boston Gardens, Boston, Massachusetts
8/30	Tower Theatre, Upper Darby, Pennsylvania
8/31	Toronto Exposition, Toronto, Ontario, Canada
9/1	Winnipeg Arena, Winnipeg, Manitoba, Canada
9/2	Evansville Rock Festival, Evansville, Indiana

Wednesday 25th July

Mid South Coliseum, Memphis, Tennessee, USA

Support to Humble Pie.

Thursday 26th July

Roosevelt Stadium, Jersey City, New Jersey, USA

Originally a concert with Three Dog Night, as part of the 'Garden State Summer Music Fair II' was scheduled at the venue. The show was cancelled. Instead the band travelled from Memphis to Miami and spent the following two nights at the exotically named Thunderbird Resort Hotel in Miami.

Friday 27th July

Miami Sports Auditorium, Miami, Florida, USA

Though scheduled, this concert was cancelled due to problems with transportation of the group's equipment. Had it taken place, it would have been as support to Three Dog Night.

Saturday 28th July

Curtis Hixon Hall, Tampa, Florida, USA

Overnight accommodation was arranged for the even more exotically named Red Carpet Hawaiian Village hotel for this and the following night.

Sunday 29th July

Omni, Atlanta, Georgia, USA

Support to Three Dog Night.
For this and the following night the tour party stay at the Regency Hyatt House Hotel in Atlanta.

Monday 30th July (?)

Sound Pit Studios, Atlanta, Georgia, USA (?)

Studio session that produced unknown tracks, though 'Sound Pit' is a prime candidate.

Tuesday 31st July

Hirsch Auditorium, Shreveport, Louisiana, USA

Also on the bill were Mountain and Mitch Ryder.
The concert may have taken place at the Fairgrounds. The band stayed at the Sheraton Motor Inn.

Wednesday 1st August

Mobile Municipal Auditorium, Mobile, Alabama, USA

The band were booked into the Admiral Semmes hotel for the night.

Thursday 2nd August

Royal Stadium, Kansas City, Missouri, USA

Support to Three Dog Night. Other bands on the bill were Leslie West's Wild West Show and Ruben And The Jets. It's possible that T. Rex appeared third on the bill. Due to transport problems the group had to use equipment borrowed from Leslie West's band.
The entourage spent the night at the Holiday Inn-Downtown in Kansas.

Friday 3rd August

Civic Auditorium, Baltimore, Pennsylvania, USA

Support to Three Dog Night.

Overnight accommodation was arranged at the Holiday Inn-Downtown.

Saturday 4th August

Nassau Coliseum, Uniondale, Long Island, New York, USA

Support to Three Dog Night.

For the following two days the band used the St. Regis Hotel in New York as its base.

Sunday 5th August

Dillon Stadium, Hartford, Connecticut, USA

Support to Three Dog Night.

Monday 6th August–Monday 13th August

Marc, June and Mick O'Halloran were booked into the Beverley Wilshire in Beverley Hills while the rest of the band were based in Los Angeles. However, given conditions in Marc and June's marriage at the time, it's uncertain who was really located where.

Tuesday 7th August–Thursday 9th August (?)

Elektra Studios, Los Angeles, California, USA

Further studio sessions for the 'Zinc Alloy And The Hidden Riders Of Tomorrow' project. It's likely that 'Teenage Dream', 'Sound Pit' and 'Explosive Mouth' were the songs recorded here.

Friday 10th August

Blackjack / Squint Eye Mangle (EMI 2047)

Released under the name Big Carrot, in reality this single was a T. Rex jam featuring Gloria Jones, Sister Pat Hall and Stephanie Spruill on vocals. The disc failed to reach the charts.

A hand-written note from Marc reveals that the disc was originally scheduled to appear on the T. Rex label.

"Keen to buy a coupla T. Rex backing track are you? Well here's your chance ... You'll thrill to that gasping T. Rex guitar sound, snap blood vessels straining to hear The Master singing in the middle distance ... If I was a harsher man, I'd say "egocentric drivel" and leave it at that."

John Peel, Sounds

Civic Theatre, San Diego, California, USA

Set list: 'Hope You Enjoy The Show', 'Chariot Choogle', 'Born To Boogie', 'The Groover', 'Buick Mackane', 'Jeepster', 'Plateau Skull', 'Get It On'

Saturday 11th August

Civic Auditorium, Santa Monica, California, USA

Set list: 'Telegram Sam', 'Jeepster', 'Hot Love', 'The Groover', 'Get It On' (incomplete)

'Like his two previous attempts to knock America on its glitter ass, he still misses the punch and falls flat on his little pug nose. This time he's playing louder and strutting more confidently, and his band has improved enormously ... (which) means they now keep time and play most of the right notes.

T. Rex played for almost two hours, with a cumulative effect of massive Novocain injections. Bolan's songs tend to sound alike anyway, each one based on a catchy repetitive theme – but catchy for three or four minutes on record. Extended to ten, twenty or thirty minutes in concert, those same songs go way past boredom.

Mercifully, there was no encore – the audience was either too bored or too stunned to demand one; the house lights came up quickly, so apparently Bolan had no intention of anticlimaxing."

Judith Sims, Rolling Stone

"For Marc Bolan, a crowded American auditorium is a rare and welcome sight, yet it is not enough to help a flawed concert in a floundering career. T. Rex peaked before they reached America and the band has nose-dived here ever since.

(Bolan) displays no grace and he knows neither style nor subtlety. Instead, he parades aimlessly across the stage, drowning in his own feedback, catching a fresh breath only by rendering a song from 'Electric Warrior' ...

It is hard for an American concert-goer to understand how T. Rex climbed so high in the English rock scene."

Peter Jay Philbin, Melody Maker

"For an act that was all but written off after its last extremely disappointing album and its modest 1972 tours, T. Rex ... put on a vigorous, fast paced Saturday night at the Santa Monica Civic Auditorium for a generally enthusiastic, but, I'm afraid, ultimately unconvinced glitter and rouge audience.

The problem with T. Rex and its leader Marc Bolan at this point appears more mental than musical. I think the difficulty Bolan ... is having in this country has gotten to him and, rather than making him rise to the challenge, is turning him into a desperate performer. He used every imaginable rock cliché Saturday...

On the group's first major US tour in February of 1972, it was clear that Bolan had both the potential personality ... and musical instincts ... to become a huge success here. His 'Bang A Gong' single became a Top Ten hit.

But it was also clear that Bolan did not have enough exciting concert numbers to cause anywhere near the frenzy that the group generates in England ... If he could come up with a few more tunes with the infectious, driving rock and roll spirit of 'Jeepster' or 'Bang A Gong', T. Rex might become a huge hit.

Unfortunately, 'The Slider' his next album, failed to provide that material, so Bolan's second tour

... failed to enhance the group's standing. In fact it detracted. The band seemed sloppy ... As he returned to England, Bolan said he felt things were going as well as could be expected, but he must have been worried privately. The next album ('Tanx') was a stiff, making things even more critical.

Except for the large decorative patches of grey in his otherwise black curly hair, Bolan looked pretty much the same as he did last August ... But his music was different – both in arrangement and execution. Instead of the short, three minute recreations of his hit singles (the style of the first tour), Bolan extended the songs into longer pieces.

It's a move that can be taken either as a sign of increased heaviness or that he hasn't got any good new material. While I suspect it's largely the latter, I'd rather hear more of a good song than lots of weak ones. So, that's an improvement. The band (drums, guitar, bass, percussion and two fine female back-up singers) were more taut and effective than last year. So, musically, T. Rex was much improved.

But Bolan himself was a disturbing disappointment. For most of the evening, he seemed little more than a computerised kewpie doll ... his expressions alternating from intense and brooding to sudden smiles ... For his best number, 'Jeepster', he threw in every cliché imaginable ... He went from a Chuck Berry duckwalk to a leap in the air to falling on his knees to prowling the stage ... Later, he even shoved the neck of the guitar through the legs of one of the back-up singers, an elementary bit of symbolism indeed.

After 'Jeepster', Bolan took time out to tell the audience ... that if the audience (didn't) applaud a lot during the next number, it would be his last of the evening. The applause was apparently satisfactory, however, and he did an extra song.

As a special reward, he told the audience he was going to smash his favourite, ten year old guitar on stage. He then hurled it to the floor, took a whip from a nearby amplifier and lashed at the guitar. My my, I expected to see someone rush from the wings with a gasoline can any second.

If Bolan doesn't have anymore artistic self respect than to engage in such antics, he isn't really worth our attention. He may make it with a young audience that hasn't seen it all before, but that's a rather empty victory. It's too bad because Bolan really knows how to produce some good rock and roll."

Robert Hillburn, Los Angeles Times

Sunday 12th August
Long Beach Auditorium, Long Beach, California, USA

Tuesday 14th August
Paramount Theatre, Portland, Oregon, USA
The tour party stayed at the Portland Hilton.

Wednesday 15th August
Paramount Northwest, Seattle, Washington, USA
Overnight accommodation was arranged for the Edgewater Inn in Seattle.
Following an argument and issuing an ultimatum, June Bolan left the tour in Seattle and effectively ended her relationship with Bolan.

Thursday 16th August
Pacific Exhibition Gardens, Vancouver, British Columbia, Canada
The group stayed at the Bayshore Inn in Vancouver.

Friday 17th August
Salt Palace, Salt Lake City, Utah, USA
Support to Three Dog Night.
Overnight accommodation was set for a hotel named Howard Johnson's.

Saturday 18th August
Denver Coliseum, Denver, Colorado, USA
Support to Three Dog Night.
The concert may have taken place at the Fey Colisseum.
The hotel for this night was called Radisson.

Sunday 19th August
Pershing Auditorium, Lincoln, Nebraska, USA
Support to Three Dog Night.
This night's hotel was the Radisson Cornhuster.

Monday 20th August
'Mississippi State Fair', Quad City Stadium, Davenport, Ohio, USA
Support to Three Dog Night.
The band stay at the Sheraton at Rock Island in Illinois.

Tuesday 21st August
The band flew from Davenport to St. Louis
Kiel Auditorium, St. Louis, Missouri, USA
For this night and the following the band are housed at Stouffer's Riverfront Inn.

Thursday 23rd August
City Auditorium, Binghamton, New York, USA
Support to Three Dog Night.
The band stay overnight at the Treadway Inn in Binghamton.

Friday 24th August–29th August
For this period the band are based at the St. Regis Hotel in New York.

Friday 24th August
New Haven Arena, New Haven, Connecticut, USA
Support to Three Dog Night.

Saturday 25th August
State Farm Arena, Harrisburg, Pennsylvania, USA
Support to Three Dog Night.

Sunday 26th August
Boston Gardens, Boston, Massachusetts, USA
Support to Three Dog Night.

Set list: 'Hope You Enjoy The Show', 'Chariot Choogle', 'Born To Boogie', 'Buick Mackane', 'Jeepster', 'Hot Love', 'Get It On'

Tuesday 28th August

Electric Lady Studios, New York, New York, USA

Recording session which saw 'Till Dawn' and 'Venus Loon' put down on tape.

Wednesday 29th August

Electric Lady Studios, New York, New York, USA

Further work was done on 'Till Dawn' and 'Venus Loon' at this session. It's also possible that one or two other titles were recorded at these sessions.

Thursday 30th August

Tower Theatre, Upper Darby, Pennsylvania, USA

The band stay at the Sheraton Hotel in Philadelphia.

Friday 31st August

T. Rex enter Canada at Malton, Ontario.

Canadian National Exhibition Grandstand, Toronto, Ontario, Canada

Support to Three Dog Night.

"After a leisurely 20-minute pause the English group, T. Rex, appeared. The group couldn't do much to enliven the crowd even when its conga player descended from the stage to toss tambourines into the audience.

T. Rex's set ended in an orgy of smoke and feedback during which lead guitarist Marc Bolan threw his guitar about the stage and then whipped it with a microphone cord."

Robert Martin, The Globe And Mail, Toronto

"A three-hour plus concert featuring Montreal's April Wine, England's T. Rex and Los Angeles' Three Dog Night attracted 21,000 people and a lot of problems not only for the groups and their fans, but for ushers and police at the CNE Grandstand Friday night.

... the problems started with T. Rex. After an hour trying to stir up the crowd with its music, the group's lead singer, Marc Bolan, started to beg people in the crowd to respond.

Unfortunately, some did. Hundreds poured out of the stands to crowd near the restraining fence, and immediately the police hustled everybody back to their seats.

A 45-minute delay followed before Three Dog Night came on."

Peter Goddard, The Toronto Star

The tour party spent the night at the Holiday Inn-City Centre.

Saturday 1st September
Winnipeg Arena, Winnipeg, Manitoba, Canada
Support to Three Dog Night

"It didn't matter whether you went to see and hear Three Dog Night or to learn a little more about the amazingly good group T. Rex, everyone should have received their money's worth Saturday in the Winnipeg Arena.

It was billed as Three Dog Night's night in Winnipeg, but for "glam-rock" fans it was the discovery of T. Rex, a group that has before received little recognition in Winnipeg.

Three Dog Night was good ... but T. Rex, an English group that is growing in popularity no matter where it goes, stole the show.

T. Rex, as lead singer Marc Bolan said, is not as popular here as in England. It took awhile for Winnipeggers to get used to the group's type of music, but once fans warmed up, the wilder T. Rex got.

Without doubt it had to be the best show to hit Winnipeg since Alice Cooper was in town.

From their latest release 'Born To Boogie' (it was written for a movie) to their final number 'Bang A Gong', which ended with Bolan's amplifier blowing up after a sound and realistic bullwhipping, fans were treated to some of the best rock entertainment ever seen in Winnipeg.

Three Dog Night lived up to expectations – good. But it was T. Rex that won more new fans in Winnipeg with an unexpected, sterling performance."

Brian Cole, Winnipeg Free Press

The North Star Inn was used for this night's stay.

Sunday 2nd September
T. Rex exit Canada at Winnipeg.
Evansville Rock Festival, Roberts Municipal Stadium, Evansville, Indiana, USA
T. Rex support The Edgar Winter Group. Also on the bill were Dr. John and Buddy Miles.
Overnight accommodation is set for the Galt House hotel in Louisville, Kentucky.

TONIGHT!
EATON'S and **Levi's** present
THREE DOG NIGHT with **T-REX**
WINNIPEG ARENA/8:00 P.M.
Arena Box Office opens 7:00 p.m.

Monday 3rd September
NBC Television Studios, Los Angeles, California, USA
T. Rex record a slot for NBC's 'Midnight Special'. Two songs, recorded live in the studio, were

broadcast: 'Hot Love' and 'Get It On'. However, it's possible that other titles may have been committed to tape. This performance featured Jack Green, Gloria Jones and Sister Pat Hall. The show was networked in the USA on 28th September.

Tuesday 4th September
Marc flew back to the UK.

Saturday 8th September
Air Studios, 214 Oxford Street, London, England
Further work was done on 'Till Dawn' and 'Venus Loon' at this session. This probably included string overdubs.

Wednesday 12th September
Bolan goes on holiday to Nassau, Bahamas.

Monday 24th September
Air Studios, 214 Oxford Street, London, England
A master mix of 'Bolan's Blues', otherwise known as 'Plateau Skull' was completed at this session.

Friday 28th September
Transmission date in the USA of the performance recorded for NBC's 'Midnight Special'. See entry for 3rd September.

September / October
At some point around this time, Marc and June Bolan vacated the flat in Bilton Towers. Marc moved into a flat with Gloria Jones, located in the Polygon, The Avenue, St. John's Wood, London.

Sunday 7th October
Advision Studios, 23 Gosfield Street, London, England
A studio session which saw two instrumental jams, imaginatively titled 'Jam #1' and 'Jam #2' recorded on tape.

October
Air Studios, 214 Oxford Street, London, England
Overdub session for the 'Zinc Alloy And The Hidden Riders Of Tomorrow' album involving Paul Fenton on drums.

Saturday 13th October
Air Studios, 214 Oxford Street, London, England
Overdub session for the 'Zinc Alloy And The Hidden Riders Of Tomorrow' album, involving Paul Fenton on drums and Danny Thompson on double bass. In addition to recording overdubs, another jam involving Bolan, Thompson, Fenton, Tony Visconti and possibly Jack Green was also recorded at this session. The tape box contains the instructions "Condense into 3 mins" written in Marc's hand.

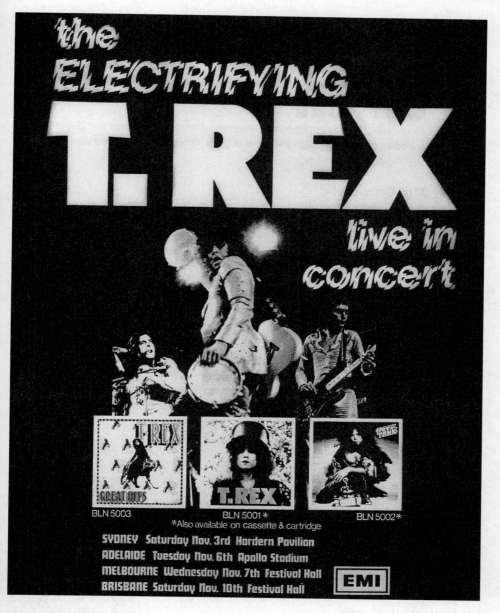

Friday 19th October

Great Hits (EMI T. Rex BLN 5003)

'Telegram Sam', 'Jitterbug Love', 'Lady', 'Metal Guru', 'Thunderwing', 'Sunken Rags', 'Solid Gold Easy Action', '20th Century Boy', 'Midnight', 'The Slider', 'Born To Boogie', 'Children Of The Revolution', 'Shock Rock', 'The Groover'

Surprisingly, the album only reached 32 in the charts, the clearest sign yet that T. Rex's reign at the top was coming to a close.

October 1973 (?)

Air Studios, 214 Oxford Street, London, England
An undated EMI tape box, probably from October, was produced, containing rough mixes of 'The Avengers (Superbad)', 'Saturday Night', 'Change', 'Galaxy', 'Sitting Here', 'The Leopards (Featuring Gardenia And The Mighty Slug') and 'Carsmile Smith And The Old One'.

FAR EAST TOUR

For this series of dates, T. Rex performed as a five piece band. Gloria Jones and Sister Pat Hall were not included as part of the stage line-up due to visa problems. The band were paid a fee of £20,000 for the Australian dates.

Tuesday 23rd October

T. Rex depart from Heathrow Airport for Tokyo at one o'clock in the afternoon.

Wednesday 24th October

T. Rex arrive at Haneda Airport, late the following morning. They were taken to their hotel, the Hilton in Tokyo.

Hilton Hotel, Tokyo Japan
Press interviews were given at the above hotel.

Thursday 25th October

Budokan Hall, Tokyo, Japan
Set list: '20th Century Boy', 'Chariot Choogle', 'Telegram Sam', 'Buick Mackane', 'Jeepster', 'Tokyo Blues', 'Get It On'
'Tokyo Blues' was an ad-libbed piece built around the same song structure as 'Plateau Skull'. Marc was at his arrogant worse here at this show, mistaking Japanese reticence for a lack of appreciation and berating the audience for this.

Friday 26th October

The band have a day off in Tokyo.

Saturday 27th October

Ichirithu Taiikukan, Nagoya, Japan
Set list: '20th Century Boy', 'Chariot Choogle', 'Telegram Sam', 'Buick Mackane', 'Jeepster', 'Get It On'
The band's overnight hotel was the Kanko Hotel.

Sunday 28th October

Koseinenkin Hall, Osaka, Japan
The Royal Hotel was used for overnight accommodation.

Monday 29th October

Yubin Chokin Hall, Hiroshima, Japan
Set list: '20th Century Boy', 'Chariot Choogle', 'Telegram Sam', 'Buick Mackane', 'Jeepster', 'Get It On'
The band stay at the Grand Hotel for this night and the following.

T.REX

T. レックス 公演

10月27日⊕ P.M. 6:30
名市大体育館 (裏面地図参照)

主催■名古屋市立大学大学祭実行委員会
後援■東芝レコード
提供■ユニバーサルナゴヤ

前売券 2,800円

Tuesday 30th October
The band have a day off in Hiroshima.

Wednesday 31st October
The band flew from Hiroshima to Fukuoka.
Shin-Nittetu-Taiikukan, Yahata, Japan
The overnight hotel is the Kokura Nikkatso Hotel.

Thursday 1st November
The tour party leave Fukuoka for Tokyo where a suite is arranged for day use at the Hilton Hotel. Bolan and entourage depart Haneda Airport for Sydney, leaving at 8 in the evening.

Friday 2nd November
T. Rex fly into Sydney Airport, arriving just before 8 a.m. local time. A press conference was given at the airport. Following this, they were then taken to the hotel, the Hyatt Kingsgate in Sydney, where they stayed for the next three days.

Saturday 3rd November
Hordern Pavilion, Sydney, New South Wales, Australia
Set list: '20th Century Boy', 'Chariot Choogle', 'Telegram Sam', 'Buick Mackane', 'Jeepster', 'Get It On'

Sunday 4th November
Unconfirmed television studio, Sydney, New South Wales, Australia (?)
Marc is interviewed on the ten minute music show 'G.T.K.', broadcast at 6.30 p.m. The show was networked on ABS 2. This is unconfirmed. The interview may have been on another programme.
Hordern Pavilion, Sydney, New South Wales, Australia

Monday 5th November (?)
The band were scheduled to fly from Sydney to Melbourne and then to Adelaide, arriving in the early afternoon.

Tuesday 6th November
Apollo Stadium, Adelaide, South Australia, Australia

Wednesday 7th November
The band left Adelaide in the late morning and flew Melbourne, arriving at just after midday. Accommodation for this night and the following is set at the Old Melbourne Motor Inn.
Festival Hall, Melbourne, Victoria, Australia
Set list: '20th Century Boy', 'Chariot Choogle', 'Telegram Sam', 'Buick Mackane', 'Jeepster', 'Hot Love', 'Get It On'

Thursday 8th November
A provisional second date at the Festival Hall in Melbourne was pencilled in for this day.

Friday 9th November

The band fly from Melbourne to Brisbane, arriving just before 1 p.m. On arriving in Brisbane they are taken to their hotel, Lennons Plaza Hotel, and have a day off.

Saturday 10th November

Festival Hall, Brisbane, Queensland, Australia

Set list: '20th Century Boy', 'Chariot Choogle', 'Telegram Sam', 'Buick Mackane', 'Jeepster', 'Hot Love', 'Get It On'

Sunday 11th November

Bolan flies on to Los Angeles for various sessions and to meet up with Gloria Jones.

Monday 12th November

MRI Studios, 1680 North Sycamore Avenue, Hollywood, California, USA

A tape containing 'Get 'Em Up', 'Power Of Love' and 'No No No' was produced on this day. These are Richard Jones tracks. Marc is listed as producer on the tape box.

Friday 16th November

Truck On (Tyke) / Sitting Here (EMI T. Rex MARC 6)

Breaking a long sequence of Top Ten hits, the single only reached 12 in the charts.

"Marc could and should do better than this ... it is disappointing to find him with much the same formula as before. The production is clean and powerful, with a distinctive descending guitar riff and solid drums. But (with) heavy emphasis on a rather worn out hook phrase ... it all becomes an empty exercise. 'Sitting Here', on the B side ... is much better and shows more imagination."

Melody Maker

"Four injunctions to Tyke to truck on, a shriek, four more injunctions, a second shriek and we're off on another Bolan chartbound sound ... 'Truck On (Tyke)' is a curiously lifeless and colourless offering and one wonders whether this particular space age cowboy is last year's space age cowboy ... I heard the word cosmic in there ... I also found myself wondering what gangster's legs look like ... For the last seventy seconds (there's) little but the title oft repeated to a listless guitar riff ...".

John Peel, Sounds

MRI Studios, 1680 North Sycamore Avenue, Hollywood, California, USA

'Sailors Of The Highway' and 'Ghetto Baby' were recorded at these sessions for the Sister Pat Hall album. The tape box contains the note "For Warners". This version of 'Sailors Of The Highway' features Marc on lead vocals.

Saturday 17th November

MRI Studios, 1680 North Sycamore Avenue, Hollywood, California, USA

A session which saw basic tracks for 'Tell Me Now', 'Jitterbug Love' and 'Black Cat (12 Bar Blues)' put down on tape. All tracks were recordings with Sister Pat Hall on lead vocals. A note saying "For Warner Brothers" is also on the tape box.

Another tape, probably a composite, containing 'Power' (probably 'Power Of Love'), 'No No No', 'Tell Me Now', 'Jitterbug Love' and 'Black Cat' was also produced on this date.

There are suggestions that Scott Edwards played bass and jazz drummer Paul Humphreys were the rhythm section for these sessions. It is more likely that Wayne Douglas was the bass player and the drummer was someone else – possibly Ed Green.

November

Following the initial sessions for the Sister Pat Hall album, Bill Legend is fired from T. Rex, allegedly due to hearing problems which were adversely affecting his performance.

November (?)

Air Studios, 214 Oxford Street, London, England

An undated Air Studios tape, probably from either late November or early December, was compiled featuring a number of Sister Pat Hall and T. Rex tracks. These were: 'Sailors Of The Highway' (Sister Pat Hall version with Marc on vocals), 'Change', 'Gardenia' (probably 'The Leopards'), 'Galaxy', 'Nameless Wildness', 'Sugar Plum Fairy' and 'Ghetto Baby'. 'Sugar Plum Fairy' is completely unknown elsewhere. It may be a familiar song under a different title.

Tuesday 27th November

Air Studios, 214 Oxford Street, London, England

Master mixes of 'Hope You Enjoy The Show', 'You Got To Jive To Stay Alive' and 'Nameless Wildness' were achieved. See entry for 15th February 1974.

Thursday 29th November

Air Studios, 214 Oxford Street, London, England

Mixes of 'Interstellar Soul', 'Change' and 'The Avengers (Superbad)' were completed at this session.

Monday 3rd December

Air Studios, 214 Oxford Street, London, England

Mixes for 'Satisfaction Pony', 'Saturday Night' and 'Look To Your Soul' were completed. The tape box contains a note to not include the songs on the album.

Thursday 13th December

Air Studios, 214 Oxford Street, London, England

Mixes of 'Liquid Gang', 'Carsmile Smith And The Old One' and 'Nameless Wildness' were completed. The word "copy" is written on the tape box. 'Nameless Wildness' is a rough mix. The other two songs are master mixes.

Friday 14th December (?)

Granada Television Studios, Manchester, Lancashire, England

The only television appearance to promote 'Truck On (Tyke)' took place on Granada Television's 'Lift Off With Ayshea', a children's pop programme which went out in the late afternoon at early tea-time. Bill Legend had left the band by now so Mickey Finn was back to his favourite role of miming the drum part. Also Marc sang without guitar leaving Jack Green, in his only British TV appearance with the band, to mime the guitar part. The show was broadcast on 19th December.

Monday 17th December
Air Studios, 214 Oxford Street, London, England
Two mixes of 'Galaxy' were completed on this day, with the second one providing the master. The first mix, though listed on the session sheet, is missing from the tape. Also mixed were 'The Leopards (Featuring Gardenia And The Mighty Slug)', 'Nameless Wildness' with two edit sections and three takes of 'Till Dawn'. However, once again the session sheet and the tape contents differ from each other. Only one version of 'Till Dawn' is on the tape'. This is a four-minute rough mix.

Wednesday 19th December
Broadcast on ITV networks in the UK of 'Lift Off With Ayshea' featuring 'Truck On (Tyke)'. See earlier entry.

Wednesday 26th December
Marc flies to Nassau for a holiday with Gloria Jones.

1974

1974 commenced with the ill-thought out 'Zinc Alloy And The Hidden Riders Of Tomorrow' tour. The album didn't reach the shops until more than a month after the tour had ended. The set list consisted of hit singles and songs from 'The Slider', with only 'Teenage Dream' from the new album being performed live. Also, little thought appeared to have been given as to what the expanded line-up was supposed to achieve. Instead of a powerful wall of sound, the band frequently sounded bloated.

Surprisingly/stupidly no London date was included in the tour. In fact it was to be a further two years before T. Rex were to perform again in London, making a gap totalling more than three years between London shows. Further concert dates were planned for the months of April and May. These were to commence around the 16th or 17th of April. One of these was planned to have been a major London gig. In the final event, nothing happened. Instead, Bolan, accompanied by Gloria Jones, went on holiday to Malaga before electing to retreat to America, revamp the band and spend time recording in Los Angeles. Davey Lutton took over the drummer's stool and Gloria Jones was fully integrated into the line-up, playing clavinet and providing backing vocals. By the spring Jack Green and Sister Pat Hall were out of the line-up, with the latter's solo album also being shelved. In July or August Bolan further bolstered the line-up by adding former Keef Hartley keyboard player Peter 'Dino' Dines.

Following the failure of 'Tanx' in the US market, Warner Brothers dropped T. Rex from the label. For a short period of time Atlantic were interested in signing the group and releasing the 'Zinc Alloy And The Hidden Riders Of Tomorrow' album. In the end, Bolan signed a one-off deal with the recently established Casablanca label. Label boss Neil Bogart requested a new album as he was not keen on most of 'Zinc Alloy'. The resulting album, 'Light Of Love', featured eight new songs, plus three from 'Zinc Alloy'. The album was not released in Britain until the following year, under a different title and featuring an amended track listing.

The final T. Rex tour of North America, supporting 'Light Of Love', took place in the autumn of 1974. Most of the dates were support slots, though there were a few dates as headliners, mainly at clubs or in Canada. Performances were erratic, but frequently messy and tired, featuring a bloated and lethargic Bolan and a sluggish band. Though the group had its supporters, the tour disappointed more than it delivered and the accompanying album failed to break the top 200 album chart. T. Rex were never to perform in either the USA or Canada again. Neither were any further records released in those territories during Bolan's lifetime.

Friday 4th January
Marc flies out of Nassau.

'TRUCK OFF' BRITISH TOUR

Pink Floyd's sound and lighting men, Arthur Max and Graham Flemming were employed for the tour. In addition, the line-up of T. Rex was expanded to include Howie Casey on tenor sax, Dick Parry on baritone sax, Davey Lutton on drums and Paul Fenton on second drum kit. Gloria Jones and Sister Pat Hall also rejoined the line-up after missing out on the Australian and Japanese shows. After the tour and some recording, only Davey Lutton and Jack Green were retained, though Jack Green was to leave the band in the spring, following recording sessions in Munich.

Monday 21st January

Marc and the band took a mid-morning flight to Newcastle, arriving at 10 in the morning.

City Hall, Newcastle, Northumberland, England

Set list: '20th Century Boy', 'Chariot Choogle', 'Telegram Sam', 'Jeepster', 'Teenage Dream', 'The Groover', 'Born To Boogie', 'Metal Guru', 'Hot Love', 'Get It On'

"Marc smiled, strutted and attacked his guitar with perhaps more enthusiasm than expertise ... his playing consists of little more than a series of cadenzas over one chord, which tends to make extended jams a trifle monotonous.

The band were at their best on mid-tempo tunes with a funky backbeat ... but on the faster numbers, matters got out of hand. 'Jeepster' gave up rather than finished after a series of solos by Marc in which the exhausted drummers missed the beat and Steve Currie frantically signalled a now-or-never decision, "Stop it!"

Chris Welch, Melody Maker

Overnight accommodation was arranged at the Five Bridges Hotel.

Tuesday 22nd January

Apollo Theatre, Glasgow, Lanarkshire, Scotland

Set list: '20th Century Boy', 'Chariot Choogle', 'Telegram Sam', 'Jeepster', 'Teenage Dream', 'The Groover', 'Born To Boogie', 'Metal Guru', 'Hot Love', 'Get It On'

Press interviews and an interview for local radio were done after the show.

Overnight accommodation was arranged at the Albany Hotel.

Wednesday 23rd January

For this night and the following three, the Portland Hotel in Manchester became the base of operations.

Thursday 24th January

City Hall, Sheffield, Yorkshire, England

Set list: '20th Century Boy', 'Chariot Choogle', 'Telegram Sam', 'Jeepster', 'Teenage Dream', 'The Groover', 'Born To Boogie', 'Metal Guru', 'Hot Love', 'Get It On'

Friday 25th January

Teenage Dream / Satisfaction Pony (EMI T. Rex MARC 7)

The first and only single to feature a Visconti / Bolan production credit. The song peaked at 13 in the charts.

"Surprise, surprise! Marc sings out – and at last, it really is the new T. Rex sound ... A sweep-

John Smith Productions present
MARC BOLAN & T-REX ON TOUR
AS ZINC ALLOY & THE HIDDEN RIDERS OF TOMORROW

TRUCK OFF

January 21 City Hall Newcastle
22 Apollo Centre Glasgow
24 City Hall Sheffield
26 Free Trade Hall Manchester
27 De Montfort Hall Leicester
28 Odeon New Street Birmingham
TICKETS ON SALE FROM USUAL BOX OFFICES FROM JAN 2ND (EXCEPT BIRMINGHAM FROM JAN 6TH)

CITY HALL NEWCASTLE	CITY HALL NEWCASTLE		CITY HALL

CITY HALL
NEWCASTLE

Monday,
21st January,
1974

T. REX
IN
CONCERT

Area
£1·50

E 19

Box Office
Duplicate

CITY HALL
NEWCASTLE

Monday,
21st January,
1974

T. REX
IN
CONCERT

Area
£1·50

E 19

This Portion
to be given up

Phillips Printers Ltd., Newcastle upon Tyne

CITY HALL
Northumberland Road, Newcastle upon Tyne 1

Monday, 21st January, 1974, at 7.30 p.m.

TONY SMITH FOR JOHN SMITH ENTERTAINMENTS
present

T . REX

IN CONCERT

plus Supporting Act

AREA £1·50   SEAT   E 19

Booking Agents: City Hall Box Office
Northumberland Road, Newcastle upon Tyne (Tel. 20007)
This Portion to be retained.

ing orchestra, with blues impregnated piano and gospel soaked back-up vocals, on a beautifully produced Wagnerian rock ballad. Even as 'Truck On (Tyke)' fades from the chart, so will the 'Dream" of old Bolan soar higher."

Chris Welch, Melody Maker

"... The new single is pretty different for T. Rex and yet at the same time, remains pretty much the same. Piano and strings embellish a medium tempo and Marc returns to (the) Larry The Lamb vocal quality that made Tyrannosaurus Rex such an intriguing group.

... Lyrically he swings from his own wordy surrealism to a parody of mid-period Dylan and it's not an entirely happy mixture ... The girl (singers) sound good and there's a fierce little guitar break ... At 4.55 it does go on a bit and I have an uneasy feeling that 'Teenage Dream' won't go very far in the charts."

John Peel, Sounds

"While the shimmering strings shimmy out the nostalgic intro to Paul Anka's 'Diana', the ladies of the choir drop their knitting to enquire jadedly: "Whatever happened to the Teenage Dream?" I don't know, but I think someone just smoked it! ... Zinc Zimmerman and The Hidden Riders Of Mars (?) step clumsily on some cold congealed turkeyburgers while cranking out this amazingly inarticulate mean teen lament. A very strange brew which ... (contains) a guitar solo which sounds like a ferret – or maybe Mickey Finn – being suffocated ... lets return to THAT guitar solo. Heaven knows, that should never have been accepted as a final take for at certain junctures it veers so far off it shatters windows. Bolan and his producer Tony Visconti have been around long enough to recognise a good solo from a dud one."

Roy Carr, NME

Saturday 26th January
Free Trade Hall, Manchester, Lancashire, England
Set list: '20th Century Boy', 'Chariot Choogle', 'Telegram Sam', 'Jeepster', 'Teenage Dream',
'The Groover', 'Born To Boogie', 'Metal Guru', 'Hot Love', 'Get It On'
During the concert Mickey Marmalade was knocked out on stage after he hit his head on a
Genie tower while dodging a rotten egg thrown at Marc.

Sunday 27th January
De Montfort Hall, Leicester, Leicestershire, England
Set list: '20th Century Boy', 'Chariot Choogle', 'Telegram Sam', 'Jeepster', 'Teenage Dream',
'The Groover', 'Born To Boogie', 'Metal Guru', 'Hot Love', 'Get It On'
Overnight accomodation was set for the Magnum Hotel.

Monday 28th January
Odeon, Birmingham, Warwickshire, England
Set list: '20th Century Boy', 'Chariot Choogle', 'Telegram Sam', 'Jeepster', 'Teenage Dream',
'The Groover', 'Born To Boogie', 'Metal Guru', 'Hot Love', 'Get It On'
Marc's chauffeur Alphi O'Leary was critically injured by whiplash in a car accident when a bus
ran into his Range Rover while carrying the band's bags. He was diagnosed with a broken neck
and given the Last Rites. He survived but he never returned to work for Marc. Following his
recovery he went on to work for Eric Clapton.

Saturday 2nd February
BBC Television Centre, Wood Lane, Shepherd's Bush, London, England
The only 'Top Of The Pops' performance of 'Teenage Dream' was recorded on this date and featured Marc appearing solo on the show, minus the rest of the band. The appearance was transmitted on 7th February.
   The version of the song performed was markedly different to that released as a single with
extensive lead guitar fills from Marc and saxophones replacing the orchestral parts.

Sunday 3rd February
Marquee Studios, London, England
Rough mixes of 'Nameless Wildness', 'Till Dawn' without lead guitar and 'Till Dawn' with lead
guitar were prepared on this date.
   A second tape box suggests that a Sister Pat Hall session, featuring a version of 'Sunken
Rags', was held at MRI on this date. This is almost certainly wrong. Either the session was held
at MRI in November, or alternately the session date is correct and Bolan just used an old MRI
tape box that he had with him at the time.

Thursday 7th February
Broadcast date for the only transmission 'Teenage Dream' on 'Top Of The Pops' (BBC 1). See
entry for 2nd February.

February
Unconfirmed BBC Radio Studio, London, England
At some point early in the month Marc went into a BBC radio studio to record an edition of 'My

Top Twelve', a show in which he chose twelve songs to make up an imaginary album. His choices were: 'Back Off Boogaloo' – Ringo Starr, 'I'll Never Need More Than This' – Ike And Tina Turner, 'Eleanore' – The Turtles, 'Clean Up Woman' – Betty Wright, 'Brown Sugar' – The Rolling Stones, 'She's A Woman' – The Beatles, 'The Wind Cries Mary' – Jimi Hendrix Experience, 'What Did I Do To Lose You' – Gloria Jones, 'Marjorie' – Joe Cocker, 'Yes, We Can Can' – The Pointer Sisters, 'My Generation' – The Who.

Wednesday 13th February

Air Studios, 214 Oxford Street, London, England

Recording session which saw the Sister Pat Hall versions of 'City Port' and 'Do Your Thing' recorded.

Friday 15th February

Air Studios, 214 Oxford Street, London, England

A tape containing rough mixes of 'You Got To Jive To Say Alive', 'Hope You Enjoy The Show' and 'Nameless Wildness' was produced on this date. However, another source dates this as being from 27th November 1973, which is more likely.

Sunday 17th February

Broadcast date for the 'My Top Twelve' programme on BBC Radio One. See earlier entry.

Wednesday 20th February

Scorpio Sound, Euston, London, England

Recording session for the Sister Pat Hall project which produced a rough mix of 'When I Was A Boy' (title on the tape box). The song is actually 'When I Was A Child'.

Friday 22nd February

Scorpio Sound, Euston, London, England

A session which produce versions of 'Think Zinc' and a lengthy version of 'Solid Baby'.

Saturday 23rd February

Scorpio Sound, Euston, London, England

Studio session which produced 'Space Boss', another take of 'Solid Baby' (a.k.a 'Solid Baby – Funky Baby') and an edit for Sister Pat Hall's 'Do Your Thing'.

Wednesday 27th February

Scorpio Sound, Euston, London, England

Mixes of 'Solid Baby' and 'Think Zinc' were completed on this date.

Thursday 28th February

Scorpio Sound, Euston, London, England

Studio session which produced 'Sky Church Music'.

Friday 1st March

A Creamed Cage In August / Zinc Alloy And The Hidden Riders Of Tomorrow (EMI T. Rex BLNA 7751)

'Venus Loon', 'Sound Pit', 'Explosive Mouth', 'Galaxy', 'Change', 'Nameless Wildness', 'Teenage

Dream', 'Liquid Gang', 'Carsmile Smith And The Old One', 'You've Got To Jive To Stay Alive–Spanish Midnight', 'Interstellar Soul', 'Painless Persuasion Vs The Meathawk Immaculate', 'The Avengers (Superbad)', 'The Leopards (Featuring Gardenia And The Mighty Slug)'

Marc Bolan – vocals, guitar; Mickey Finn – percussion; Steve Currie – bass; Bill Legend – drums; Jack Green – guitar; Tony Visconti – mellotron, guitar; Lonnie Jordan – piano; Danny Thompson – double bass; Paul Fenton – drums; B. J. Cole – pedal steel guitar; Gloria Jones, Sister Pat Hall, Richard Jones – backing vocals.

Recorded at Musicland Studios, Munich; Elektra Studios, Los Angeles; Electric Lady Studios, New York; Sound Pit Studios, Atlanta; Air Studios, London.

Produced by Tony Visconti and Marc Bolan.

The album peaked at 12 in the UK album charts. It was not released in the USA.

"... with the help of Tony Visconti, the Bolan sound has become even more vibrant, slightly dotty and sharply professional ... It's a futile exercise to probe too deeply into T. Rex music. What matters is the overall combination of the Bolan charisma, the pulse of rock and the inspiration by which the components are married. And there's a lot more life, guts and twists of the unexpected here than on many a more serious work ... 'Venus Loon', the opener, is one of Marc's funkiest compositions, with some original changes ... 'Sound Pit' is exciting, almost frenzied ... 'Explosive Mouth' is tortured ... 'The Leopards' has the ring of true greatness ... The slow tempo and beautiful choral backing help make this one of T. Rex's most thoughtful performances. If the fantasy was replaced by substance and the words took on true meaning, then Marc could achieve his dream – to gain real respect as an artist".

Chris Welch, Melody Maker

"A thousand curses on his baco–foil jackets and may his mascara run all over his lip gloss in the heat of the spotlights ... my idea of purgatory would be to be marooned on a desert island with a gramophone and a copy of this album ... OK, so he's hired a bunch of musicians who'd need to be trussed and gagged before they did a duff gig ... but the effect is the same old Trexery dressed up a bit with the odd neat solo ... it's unlikely to win any new converts."

Steve Peacock, Sounds

"I was hoping the spangled dwarf was going to pull of something approaching musical competence just so I could do my small bit to redress the balance in the war of tin nerves.

With the opening reverberation of 'Venus Loon' I was ready to believe Bolan had finally pulled himself and his music together. It's a tight, jerking number substantially different from the Truck On Tykishness of most of his recent singles ... and it has little of the predictability of previous works.

But the Loon toon, along with 'Teenage Dream' and a few guitar passages on 'Explosive Mouth' and 'Liquid Gang' are the album's only plausible moments.

For the remainder, Bolan has conjured up a series of ponderous titles that he uses as a vehicle to project his inane curly-haired stud image. Either that, or he's lamenting the demise of past edifices like 'Telegram Sam' and ye 'Metal Guru'.

The whole thing puts you in mind of a half-cocked production-line band content at one stab of glory."

Andrew Tyler, NME

"Yes, the bad moon bopster returns, so watch out! ... and then there's Marc guitar playing. Apart from the appallingly bad solo on 'Teenage Dream', it's not bad at all. 'Venus Loon', the opener, has a compelling, if familiar feel, as do the next two … Then just when you think it's going to be samey he throws in 'Galaxy' with its catchy hook and strings, and 'Change' … If the second side is a little tedious, it begins and ends well. 'Liquid Gang' is the enigmatic opener … Then there's more of this well-produced but mostly repetitive stuff before 'The Leopards (Featuring Gardenia & The Might Slug)' ends it in truly slimy symbolism and slinky style. No-one can say that Marc Bolan is out of the game yet … but if he ain't still got those teenage ears, there's not enough here to recruit a new army of fans."

PH, Record & Radio Mirror

Wednesday 6th March
Scorpio Sound, Euston, London, England
Two takes of the song 'Hi' (as written on the tape box) were recorded on this day. These are the acoustic versions of 'High' recorded with Sister Pat Hall.

Thursday 7th March
Scorpio Sound, Euston, London, England
Two rough mixes of 'Think Zinc' were completed on this date.

Friday 8th March
Scorpio Sound, Euston, London, England
Studio session which produced work on the Sister Pat Hall versions of 'Sunken Rags', 'City Port' and 'Ghetto Baby'.

Wednesday 13th March
Scorpio Sound, Euston, London, England
A tape containing mixes of 'Tell Me' and 'Jitterbug Love' was produced on this day. A second tape containing 'City Port', 'High' and edit sections for 'Do Your Thing' was also produced. A third tape containing the master of 'City Port' also dates from this session.

Saturday 16th March
Air Studios, 214 Oxford Street, London, England
Rough mixes were produced of 'Jitterbug Love' (the Sister Pat Hall take which includes vocals by Marc) and 'Think Zinc'.

Thursday 21st March
Scorpio Sound, Euston, London, England
Studio session that produced four takes of 'Metropolis Incarnate'.

Monday 25th March
Scorpio Sound, Euston, London, England
A studio session which produced 'Light Of Love', 'Metropolis Incarnate' and 'Why Stay'.

Thursday 28th March–Sunday 31st March
Musicland Studios, Munich, West Germany
Four days of recording sessions at the above studio, though it's possible the sessions began on 23rd March and the session tape for the 25th March has been placed in the wrong studio box.

Further work was done on the above songs. These sessions involved Jack Green, Steve Currie, Davey Lutton and Mickey Finn. It's possible that some involvement in an album for Canadian DJ Dougie Pringle may have taken place at this time, though it's more likely this took place a year later at the Chateau d'Herouville.

A "country" song called 'Preacher' was also put down on tape at this group of sessions as was a short instrumental version of 'Saturation Syncopation'. Additional songs which were probably recorded at these sessions include a version of Rick Nelson's 'I'm In Love Again', 'Na Na Na' and an instrumental jam.

Tuesday 2nd April

Studio Wandsbeck, Hamburg, West Germany

To promote 'Teenage Dream' in Germany, Marc appeared on the ZDF programme 'Disco 74'. Like with his earlier 'Top Of The Pops' performance he appeared solo, miming to the song. The show was broadcast on 13th April. At some point in the proceedings Bolan also performed an acoustic medley of songs. This was not broadcast and which songs made up the medley is not known.

Friday 5th April

Scorpio Sound, Euston, London, England

A tape with the word "outtakes" written on the session sheet was produced. This contained various mixes and fragments of 'Ghetto Baby', 'When I Was A Child' and 'Sailors Of The Highway'.

Saturday 6th April

Scorpio Sound, Euston, London, England

A tape containing the master mix of Sister Pat Hall's version of 'Jitterbug Love' and a nearly complete rough mix of 'Sunken Rags' was made.

Tuesday 9th April

Scorpio Sound, Euston, London, England

Studio session which produced versions of 'Get It On', 'It's A Shame' (a.k.a. 'Jitterbug Love') and 'Sunken Rags' for the Sister Pat Hall album. It's not sure whether this session involved recording, overdubbing or mixing. Certainly the latter two songs had all but been completed prior to this date. It is however possible that she was now off the scene and the project was beginning to change into an album for Gloria Jones. Film of Bolan and Jones rehearsing 'Get It On' was almost certainly shot around this time.

A hand written note from Marc reveals that planned running order for the Sister Pat Hall album was as follows: 1. 'Jitterbug Love' 2. 'Tell Me Now' 3. 'Ghetto Baby' 4. 'Sailors Of The Highway' 5. No song listed 6. 'Do Your Thing' 7. 'Sunken Rags' 8. 'City Port' 9. 'Neighbourhood'. The final song appears to have been the original title for 'When I Was A Child'. Among the musicians on the album were Gloria Jones on piano and Danny Thompson on bass guitar.

Saturday 13th April

Broadcast of 'Teenage Dream' on 'Disco 74' on the ZDF network in West Germany. See entry for 3rd April.

Monday 15th April
Scorpio Sound, Euston, London, England
A tape containing the master mix of 'Do Your Thing' along with the master mix of the middle edit section of the song was produced on this date.

Wednesday 17th April
Marc and Gloria fly to Malaga for a holiday, staying at the San Pedro Hotel in Marbella.

Monday 22nd April
EMI, Abbey Road, London NW10, England
A tape containing 'Think Zinc' was produced at the above studio on this date. This was probably done for purposes of the single that was released on Ariola in Germany and other European territories. Why the track wasn't released in the United Kingdom is not clear.

Tuesday 23rd April
EMI, Abbey Road, London NW10, England
Another tape containing a version of 'Think Zinc' was produced on this date.

Wednesday 24th April
Scorpio Sound, Euston, London, England
While Marc was on holiday, a master tape of Sister Pat Hall material was compiled. This contained 'Sailors Of The Highway', 'When I Was A Child', 'Ghetto Baby', 'Jitterbug Love', 'City Port', 'High' and 'Do Your Thing'. A tape containing 'Tell Me' also exists for this date.

Friday 26th April
Bolan and Gloria Jones leave Spain from Madrid and fly on to Los Angeles.

Monday 29th April
MRI Studios, 1680 North Sycamore Avenue, Hollywood, California, USA
A tape containing a Sister Pat Hall version of 'Get It On' was produced on this date. This is probably the version which was recorded on 9th April.

Friday 3rd May
MRI Studios, 1680 North Sycamore Avenue, Hollywood, California, USA
A session which saw versions of 'Do I Love Thee', 'Dishing Fish Wop' (a.k.a. 'Golden Belt'), 'Girl In The Thunderbolt Suit' and 'Token Of My Love' recorded.

Friday 10th May
MRI Studios, 1680 North Sycamore Avenue, Hollywood, California, USA
A tape containing 'Sunken Rags' and 'Tell Me' was produced on this date. It's possible that these are the versions from the Sister Pat Hall sessions, but now with Gloria Jones' vocals overdubbed.

Tuesday 14th May
MRI Studios, 1680 North Sycamore Avenue, Hollywood, California, USA
Recording session which produced two versions of 'Light Of Love' and additional work on 'Token Of My Love'.

Friday 17th May

MRI Studios, 1680 North Sycamore Avenue, Hollywood, California, USA

Studio session which produced work on a new version of 'The Children Of Rarn' and 'Teenage Angel'. The latter being another version of 'Metropolis Incarnate'. Additionally a tape containing 'Light Of My Love' (as written on the tape box) and 'Token Of My Love' was also produced on this day. It's possible that some further work was done on these songs or the tape was produced purely for reference purposes.

Monday 20th May

MRI Studios, 1680 North Sycamore Avenue, Hollywood, California, USA

Studio session which produced further work on 'The Children Of Rarn' project and an early run through of 'Video Drama'. Additionally, a tape was made containing 'City Port' and 'When I Was A Child' from the Sister Pat Hall album sessions. This tape has the word "copy" written on the track sheet.

Tuesday 21st May

MRI Studios, 1680 North Sycamore Avenue, Hollywood, California, USA

Studio session which produced further work on and/or different versions 'Do I Love Thee', 'Henry's Fish Wop' and 'One From Column 13'. The latter track is possibly a version of 'I Really Love You Babe'. A second tape from the same day contains rough mixes of 'Solid Baby', 'Space Boss' and ''Till Dawn'.

Thursday 23rd May

MRI Studios, 1680 North Sycamore Avenue, Hollywood, California, USA

Recording session which produced 'Precious Star', 'Girl In The Thunderbolt Suit', 'Baby Boomerang' and more work on 'Golden Belt', listed under the title 'Dishing Fish Wop'. For what reason 'Baby Boomerang' was recorded remains unknown. Handwritten notes by Gloria Jones seem to indicate that there may well have been plans to record a version with her singing with Junior Walker providing saxophone, for release in Japan. The note is, however, undated.

Tuesday 28th May

MRI Studios, 1680 North Sycamore Avenue, Hollywood, California, USA

Studio session which saw 'Burrito Blue Jean Wop' (a.k.a. 'Girl In The Thunderbolt Suit'), 'Video Drama' and 'Every Lady' committed to tape. It's possible that more than one take of 'Video Drama' was recorded.

Friday 31st May

MRI Studios, 1680 North Sycamore Avenue, Hollywood, California, USA

A tape containing a nearly complete version of 'Video Drama', a version of 'Token Of My Love' with a guide vocal, instrumental and vocal versions of 'Every Lady', further takes of 'Video Drama', a rough mix of 'Precious Star' and an instrumental version of 'Stand By Me' was compiled on this date. A studio jam is also mentioned on the track sheet, but does not appear on the tape.

In addition a mono seven inch reel was also produced containing 'Girl In The Thunderbolt Suit', 'Precious Star', 'Golden Belt', 'Do I Love Thee' and 'I Really Love You Babe'.

Tuesday 4th June

MRI Studios, 1680 North Sycamore Avenue, Hollywood, California, USA

A tape containing three versions of 'Token Of My Love' and 'Girl In The Thunderbolt Suit' was produced on this date. This session was probably dedicated to mixing.

Saturday 8th June

MRI Studios, 1680 North Sycamore Avenue, Hollywood, California, USA

A tape containing 'Token Of My Love' and 'Precious Star' exists for this date. This was probably a mixing / overdubbing. The tape contains the master versions.

Monday 10th June

MRI Studios, 1680 North Sycamore Avenue, Hollywood, California, USA

A tape containing a slightly longer master mix of 'Space Boss' and a slightly shorter master mix of 'Till Dawn' was produced on this date.

June

Bolic Sound Studios, Inglewood, California, USA

Marc guests on an Ike and Tina Turner recording session, recording guitar parts for 'Sexy Ida (Part Two)' and possibly other, as yet, unreleased songs.

Friday 21st June

Jasper C. Debussy / Hippy Gumbo / The Perfumed Garden Of Gulliver Smith (Track 2094 013)

Almost two years after it had originally been planned, the 'Jasper C. Debussy' was finally given a full release. Needless to say, it didn't make the charts.

The Beginning Of Doves (Track Select 2410 201)

'Jasper C. Debussy', 'Lunacy's Back', 'Beyond The Rising Sun', 'Black And White Incident', 'Observations', 'Eastern Spell', 'You Got The Power', 'Hippy Gumbo', 'Sara Crazy Child', 'Rings Of Fortune', 'Hot Rod Mama', 'The Beginning Of Doves', 'Mustang Ford', 'Pictures Of Purple People', 'One Inch Rock', 'Jasmine 49', 'Charlie', 'Misty Mist', 'Cat Black', 'Sally Was An Angel'

A cash-in album put out by Track featuring a collection of Marc Bolan solo demos and early Tyrannosaurus Rex recordings made in between November 1966 and December 1967. Originally Track planned to release the album in the summer of 1972 under the title 'Hard On Love'. Bolan was able to prevent this via court action.

The record failed to chart.

'Jasper C. Debussy', 'Hippy Gumbo', 'Charlie', 'Jasmine 49', 'Eastern Spell', 'Mustang Ford', 'Cat Black', 'Hot Rod Mama', 'Black And White Incident', 'Observations', 'You Got The Power', and 'Pictures Of Purple People' were Marc Bolan solo demos from 1966.

'Lunacy's Back', 'Beyond The Rising Sun', 'Sara Crazy Child', 'Rings Of Fortune', 'The Beginning Of Doves', 'One Inch Rock', 'Misty Mist' were Tyrannosaurus Rex demos.

'Sally Was An Angel' is part of a Tyrannosaurus Rex demo spliced with part of the John's Children version.

Friday 5th July

Light Of Love / Explosive Mouth (EMI T. Rex MARC 8)

The single peaked at 22 in the charts.

"A rather tedious single from Marc "Suddenly so fat" Bolan ... "La la la la la la the light of love," warbles Marc in his usual irritating manner ... England's best selling poet bites the dust. A nation mourns. So long Marc, it's been good knowing you."

Melody Maker

"Better tuck this one under my straining belt as it already displays symptoms of bursting burst-like into the charts ... The single moves off from the jetty with la la la la's which Marc warbles in trad Tyrannosaurus Rex manner while ladies la along with him. The track is simple percussive mulch ... and the whole is danceable, simplistic and much more engaging than 'Whatever Happened To The Teenage Dream' ... There are suggestions of a quite pretty tune in there somewhere and it's better Bolan than we've had in a while."

John Peel, Sounds

"The new improved T. Rex? Well almost. After a faceless flirtation with the great image shuffle, the metal midget is back to doing what he knows best: pounding a time-eroded cliché into senseless 70's enjoyment... there's enough here to keep fans of the 'Electric Warrior' period hopeful."

NME

Unconfirmed film studio, Paris, France
Filming of the promotional film for the 'Light Of Love' single.

Saturday 6th July
Marc returns to Los Angeles for further recording sessions.

Wednesday 10th July
MRI Studios, 1680 North Sycamore Avenue, Hollywood, California, USA
Recording session which saw further work on 'Golden Belt'. It's possible that Dino Dines was a member of the band by the time of this session.

July
Victorine Film Studios, Nice, France
In the later part of the month the band flew out to Nice with their partners for several weeks of rehearsals for the forthcoming tour of North America. The group stayed at the Negresco Hotel in Nice and rehearsed on a sound stage at the above film studios.

While helping to unload equipment into the studio Mickey Marmalade broke two fingers when a Hammond organ fell onto his hand.

It's more likely that Dino Dines joined the band at this stage.

August
At the end of the month Marc and Gloria flew back to the USA while the rest of the band returned to Britain. Bolan was certainly in New York on the 26th August as a visa for Monte Carlo was issued on this date.

September (?)
MRI Studios, 1680 North Sycamore Avenue, Hollywood, California, USA
Studio session which produced 'Zip Gun Boogie'.

Thursday 5th September
MRI Studios, 1680 North Sycamore Avenue, Hollywood, California, USA
A studio session which produced versions of 'Cry Baby' and 'High'. It's likely that these are Gloria Jones tracks.

September (?)
Scorpio Sound, Euston, London, England
An undated tape box exists from Scorpio Sound containing 'Zip Gun Boogie' and a demo entitled 'Love To Your Mama'.

Sunday 22nd September
Mickey Finn, Steve Curry, Davey Lutton and Dino Dines fly out to Los Angeles to be met by Mickey Marmalade and taken on to the Beverley Rodeo Hotel.

Monday 23rd September
S.I.R. Studios, 6251 Santa Monica Boulevard, Hollywood, California, USA
Rehearsal for the forthcoming tour.

Tuesday 24th September
S.I.R. Studios, 6251 Santa Monica Boulevard, Hollywood, California, USA
Rehearsal for the forthcoming tour.
MRI Studios, 1680 North Sycamore Avenue, Hollywood, California, USA
The master tape for 'Zip Gun Boogie' was produced on this date.

NORTH AMERICAN TOUR
What was to be the final T. Rex tour of North America was a somewhat messy affair. Dates were scheduled, re-scheduled and then cancelled. The original schedule (see appendix) contained a number of shows at venues that were not part of the normal North American tour circuit.

The band mainly played support slots in bigger halls and headlined at clubs. For support slots, T. Rex usually played a six-song set. Headline performances saw the set expanded to nine songs. Unusually, Marc seemed to realise that he had an album to promote and many of the songs which had been part of the live set for two or more years were dropped in favour of new material. These songs included 'Light Of Love', 'Solid Baby', 'Token Of My Love' and 'Precious Star' which were never performed in front of British audiences. Strangely, Bolan chose to also include his latest single 'Zip Gun Boogie' in the set. The record was never issued in North America.

Wednesday 25th September
Marc and T. Rex, plus Tony Howard and Mickey Marmalade fly from Los Angeles to Philadelphia. Mick O'Halloran plus his road crew of Chris David and Nodge Davies also fly out from London to Philadelphia.

Thursday 26th September
Tower Theatre, Upper Darby, Pennsylvania, USA
Set list: 'Jeepster', 'Light Of Love', 'Solid Baby', 'Token Of My Love', 'Telegram Sam', 'Teenage Dream', 'Zip Gun Boogie', 'Precious Star', 'Get It On'

Support to Blue Oyster Cult.

"... with Bolan's second statement, "This is the first time we've played on a stage in nine months," smacking of something like an apology, the situation seemed mighty bleak ...

But the chaos that ravaged T. Rex's shows here last year seemed a thing of the past as drummer Davey Lutton first, and then Bolan pounded out the introduction to 'Jeepster'. His rhythm guitar work has tightened up beyond belief – whereas last year his riffs seemed sloppy and overbearing, he now plays with the punch and self-assuredness most complementing the straightforward approach he gives his songwriting.

Bolan followed with 'Light Of Love' from his new album of the same title, injecting a boyish vocal enthusiasm which practically carried the song alone. His class composition ... 'Telegram Sam' ... showed off the rest of his new band ... all playing as a highly cohesive unit – one thing Bolan has never previously benefited from.

His recently improved guitar expertise, stretching over to his lead playing as well, held together the slow drawn-out verses of 'Teenage Dream' in the familiar tradition of Hendrix, utilizing fuzz and sustain with flawless control.

The only disappointment of the show followed immediately with Bolan introducing 'Zip Gun Boogie' as his "next single". Lame lyrics and unimaginative and repetitive guitar progressions make it obvious that Bolan should stop thinking single and just let the material write itself ...

After 'Precious Star' he closed with 'Bang A Gong' and all hell broke loose. Bolan opened up on guitar, keyed on Currie's pulsating bass, and roared to the finish... He switched from his Les Paul to a Fender Stratocaster... tambourined his fretboard to death, laid his instrument down, whipped it repeatedly, picked it up and hurled it an amp which had been electronically rigged to explode upon impact amidst a cloud of smoke. The kids were wide-eyed."

Steve Weitzman, Zoo World

Friday 27th September
Memorial Auditorium, Worcester, Massachusetts, USA

Saturday 28th September
Ideal Park, Johnstown, Pennsylvania, USA
An outdoors show which featured Rush as support band.

Sunday 29th September
Veterans Memorial Auditorium, Columbus, Ohio, USA
Support to Lynyrd Skynyrd.

Monday 30th September
Marc spends his birthday in New York.

Wednesday 2nd October
Joint In The Woods, Parsippany, New Jersey, USA
Set list: 'Jeepster', 'Telegram Sam', 'Light Of Love', 'Solid Baby', 'Precious Star', 'Zip Gun Boogie', 'Token Of My Love', 'Teenage Dream', 'Get It On' (May be incorrect)
After the gig Marc was interviewed by Lisa Robinson for 'Rock Scene' magazine.

Saturday 5th October

WNEW–FM Studios, New York, New York, USA

Marc was interviewed on the above station to explain the cancellation of that night's gig. Originally T. Rex were scheduled to support Blue Oyster Cult at the Academy Of Music. Though Blue Oyster Cult went ahead with their performance, T. Rex did not play. Instead it appears the group gave the following performance.

Clemson University, Clemson, North Carolina, USA

Support to American Breed.

Sunday 6th October

Cumberland County College, Fayetteville, North Carolina, USA

Tuesday 8th October

Long Beach Auditorium, Long Beach, California, USA

Television recordings for 'Don Kirshner's Rock Concert'. Though a complete T. Rex set was filmed, only four songs were included in the final broadcast: 'Jeepster', 'Zip Gun Boogie', 'Token Of My Love' and 'Get It On'. All versions of the songs were extended lengthy versions.

Though the broadcast programme featured performances from Ross and Isis, the actual concert actually featured Eric Carmen/The Raspberries and Roger McGuinn.

Friday 11th October

Warner Theatre, Fresno, California, USA

Saturday 12th October

Long Beach Auditorium, Long Beach, California, USA

This appearance, a support slot to Blue Oyster Cult, was cancelled due to Bolan having throat problems. He was treated by a Dr. Newman, father of singer Randy Newman.

Sunday 13th October

Golden Hall, San Diego, California, USA

Originally the concert was scheduled for the following night at the Civic Theatre. The concert was cancelled due to Marc's continuing throat problems.

Monday 14th October

Show Palace, Phoenix, Arizona, USA

Support to Blue Oyster Cult. Golden Earring were also on the bill.

Wednesday 16th October

Arena, Medford, Oregon, USA

Friday 18th October

Paramount Theatre, Portland, Oregon, USA

Support to Blue Oyster Cult.

Saturday 19th October

Paramount Northwest, Seattle, Washington, USA

Support to Blue Oyster Cult.

Sunday 20th October

T. Rex enter Canada at Victoria

Memorial Arena, Victoria, British Columbia, Canada

Monday 21st October

Pacific Coliseum, Vancouver, British Columbia, Canada

Blue Oyster Cult play as support act.

"One of several North American tours brought (Bolan) to the Pacific Coliseum Monday night, where he faced a rough audience ... Bolan is short, imagine a five-foot Faust ... He sneers, pouts, slinks to the mike, and at times blesses the front rows with a sudden bright smile. Oh, he's got it, all right.

The audience didn't think so. They were fatigued from a long, slow warm-up; hockey acoustics that shattered the perfect wailing highs of a skinny, black, back-up girl and muffled Bolan's adenoidal drone; the excellent record tracks degenerated into thick-textured boogie, rock sludge.

A few nubile boppers in the front ... were reaching for his sweaty towel and screaming on cue. But, for the rest, a few were hostile and many were leaving. The white neon star that lit up on stage seemed to mock him."

Don Stanley, Vancouver Sun

Wednesday 23rd October

Stampede Corral, Calgary, Alberta, Canada

Blue Oyster Cult play as support act.

"T. Rex fans were nervous at half-time Wednesday night ... Like, they just weren't a little bit nervous, they were real nervous ... Their hero was in trouble.

Their hero is Marc Bolan ... who is the leader and founder of T. Rex, a group rumoured to have been the hottest band in England for a couple of months two years ago.

So how was Bolan going to follow that absolutely brilliant, artistically sensational, astonishing, vividly symbolic performance by the other band on the bill Blue Oyster Cult?

What could Bolan possibly do? Blue Oyster Cult ended their set with the stage completely submerged in smoke bombs, the three electric guitarists playing three notes in unison while slowly leaning back into the smoke until they too were completely covered up ...

Intermission. Then the lights went off and the T. Rex fans were simply tense as the emcee shouted for Calgary to welcome England's number one group, T. REX! And the light went back on and there was Bolan crucified on a big neon star mounted on a platform rising from the stage. Whew! He was going to do it! He was going to out-flash Blue Oyster Cult.

Yeah, sure, but once Bolan jumped off the star platform and started playing his guitar everything pooped out. He had basically mediocre musicians like a conga player and an organist trying to follow him, but they all ended up out of tune and bumping into each other because Bolan wasn't going anywhere, he was standing completely still. It sounded like a guy who used to know how to play guitar and forgot, and is now working from the last lingering memories.

There was this back-up singer hidden behind a speaker column that was great though. She had a strong, powerful voice, and she was really in tune. When she joined in on the choruses it made the slick little melodies that Bolan writes come to life.

I left right after Bolan introduced a song called 'Teenage Queen' (sic). When nobody in the crowd acknowledged the tune, he shouted "What's the matter with you? That's only the number one song in England!" There was this steady stream of people leaving and I followed them.

But hang on there. Just because Blue Oyster Cult stole the show from T. Rex doesn't mean it's any good, either.

In fact, Blue Oyster Cult is terrible ...".

Eugene Chadbourne, Calgary Herald

Thursday 24th October
Kinsmen Fieldhouse, Edmonton, Alberta, Canada
Blue Oyster Cult play as support act.

"Marc Bolan, star of the English rock group T. Rex, stared out at the full house crowd of 7,000 at the Kinsmen Fieldhouse last night and made a frank confession.

"Us superstars are human sometimes. Only sometimes."

Bolan, by the way, is a superstar. At least in England anyway. And for the second time he and his band are trying to crack the lucrative North American market and spread that superstardom a bit further. The first effort, a few years ago, failed dismally.

But they aren't going to do it with shows like last night's. The only thing that saved T. Rex's act from being totally boring was the offensive loudness.

And Bolan handled things in his own particular superstar fashion. He was rude.

For instance, when someone in the crowd yelled something to Bolan, the short, pudgy star called back: "If you shout at me mister, I'll come down there and break your nose."

T. Rex's act is a degenerate form of rock music, with more emphasis placed on the show than the music.

Bolan, dressed up like a supersonic Robin Hood, made his entrance propped atop a huge, flashing star.

During the show he used the star as a platform.

To close he turned his guitar up to full, laid it down in front of him, then crawled on top of it. He also whipped it with a leather chord, bounced it off the stage floor and threw it into an amplifier.

The whole time the guitar was making the sound of a sick cow.

Indicative of the show's quality, people were leaving in droves long before Bolan made his superstar finish.

Much more enjoyable was the music of Blue Oyster Cult ...".

Joe Somberger, Edmonton Journal

Saturday 26th October
The Gymnasium, University Of Manitoba, Winnipeg, Manitoba, Canada
Blue Oyster Cult play as support act.

Sunday 27th October
T. Rex exit Canada from Winnipeg.
The band arrived in Chicago and stayed at the Playboy Towers hotel which became their base until the morning of 9th November.

Monday 28th October–Saturday 2nd November
Paragon Studios, Chicago, Illinois, USA
In total T. Rex spent a total of nine days recording at Paragon Studios. Details of the exact material recorded at the sessions are not known, as all the session tapes appear to be missing. However, it is highly likely that the following songs were recorded at the sessions: 'Sanctified' (two takes), 'I Never Told Me', 'Chrome Sitar', 'Casual Agent', 'By The Light Of A Magical Moon' (two takes), 'Love For Me', 'New York City', 'Sparrow', 'Dawn Storm', 'Saturday Night' and a take of 'Sensation Boulevard'.

Wednesday 30th October

Salt Palace, Salt Lake City, Utah, USA

This concert was cancelled.

Friday 1st November

Zip Gun Boogie / Space Boss (EMI T. Rex MARC 9)

While Bolan is out of the UK, this single is released with little in the way of promotion. It reaches 41 in the charts.

"Fantastic start with really vicious guitars and what sounds faintly like a fairground organ ... Then in comes Marc whining and groaning his way through something about a zip gun boogie coming on strong, whatever that may be. There's an initial catchiness about it ... but by the time we've heard about the zip gun boogie for the three hundredth time, it's just another boring Bolan record ... this record will do little to challenge his rapidly diminishing status in pop. "

Colin Irwin, Melody Maker

"Well, whatever happened to Marc's imagination? Here he seems totally at a loss for a good idea and sticks once more to a basic blues / rock and roll chord structure, which isn't a bad thing in itself other than the fact he's been doing it for a long time now and doing it badly at that. The instrumentation ... is ugly and the lyrical content is banal even by Bolan's standards. It isn't even played particularly well and the addition of a heavy riff... has all the panache of Uriah Heep. Hasn't he cottoned on to the fact that his records aren't selling anymore?"

Steve Clarke, NME

Sunday 3rd November

Day off.

Monday 4th November–Tuesday 5th November

Paragon Studios, Chicago, Illinois, USA

Wednesday 6th November

Day off.

Thursday 7th November

The band took a short flight from Chicago to St. Louis in the late afternoon.

Kiel Opera House, St. Louis, Missouri, USA

Support to Kiss.

Following the concert the band return to Chicago, arriving just before 1 a.m.

Friday 8th November

Aragon Ballroom, Chicago, Illinois, USA

It's unclear whether this concert was as headline act or as support to Kiss. The venue's website suggests the former.

Saturday 9th November

For that night's concert the group flew from Chicago to Evansville in the early afternoon.

Roberts Municipal Stadium, Evansville, Indiana, USA
Set list: 'Jeepster', 'Telegram Sam', 'Light Of Love', 'Teenage Dream', 'Zip Gun Boogie', 'Get It On'
Support to Guess Who.
The band's accommodation was arranged for the Jackson House Hotel.

Sunday 10th November
The group travelled from Evansville to Cleveland via Indianapolis, beginning their four-hour journey in the mid-afternoon. They were booked into the Keg And Quarter hotel for this night and the following.

Monday 11th November
Agora Ballroom, Cleveland, Ohio, USA
Set list: 'Jeepster', 'Telegram Sam', 'Token Of My Love', 'Teenage Dream', 'Zip Gun Boogie', 'Get It On'
Support from Carmen.
The show was recorded and broadcast by WMMS–FM, Cleveland. It's probable that the set list is incomplete. These were the songs which were broadcast.

Tuesday 12th November
The group flies from Cleveland to New York in the early afternoon. They stayed at the St. Moritz hotel, which was to become their base until the 19th November. Marc bought a Gibson Les Paul, serial number 01945 for $450 from a Jerry A Blaha.

Wednesday 13th November
The band travelled by road to that night's concert.
Mr. D's, Elmwood Park, New Jersey, USA

Thursday 14th November
The band took the short flight to Allentown in the late afternoon, arriving around 6 p.m.
Rockne Hall, Allentown, Pennsylvania, USA
Following the concert, the band return to New York by road.

Friday 15th November
The band travel by road to the
Trenton concert.
War Memorial Theatre, Trenton, New

Jersey, USA
Set list: 'Jeepster', 'Telegram Sam', 'Light Of Love', 'Zip Gun Boogie', 'Token Of My Love', 'Teenage Dream', 'Get It On'
Support came from The Sensational Alex Harvey Band.
Following the concert, the band returned to New York by road. En route the band's vehicles were pulled over by the New Jersey Highway Patrol for speeding, with the members of the entourage being given "a hard time" by the police.

Saturday 16th November
The band travel by road to Portchester.

Capitol Theatre, Portchester, New York, USA
Support to ZZ Top

Sunday 17th November
The band have a day off in New York while the road crew drive from New York to Detroit.

Monday 18th November
Day off in New York.

Tuesday 19th November
The band flew to Detroit just after midday. They were booked into the St. Regis Hotel. This became their base until 23rd November. In the early part of the evening they flew to Grand Rapids for that evening's show.

Thunder Chicken, Comstock Park, Grand Rapids, Michigan, USA

Wednesday 20th November
The band took a late afternoon flight to Lansing for the evening's gig.

Brewery, Lansing, Michigan, USA
Following the show the group returned to Detroit, arriving shortly before midnight.

Thursday 21st November
Michigan Palace, Detroit, Michigan, USA
Support to ZZ Top

Friday 22nd November
Michigan Palace, Detroit, Michigan, USA
Support to ZZ Top.
This was to be the last ever T. Rex concert appearance in North America and the last with Mickey Finn.

Saturday 23rd November
While the members of T. Rex flew back to the U.K., Marc, Gloria and Mickey Marmalade flew on to Los Angeles to stay at the Beverley Wilshire Hotel, before moving into 1250 Del Resto Drive, Beverley Hills, a house rented from antique dealer John Good.

Tuesday 26th November

Stage West, Hartford, Connecticut, USA

A concert was scheduled at the above venue, but it was cancelled.

Wednesday 27th November (?)

MRI Studios, 1680 North Sycamore Avenue, Hollywood, California, USA (?)

Recording session which produced the basic tracks for 'Casual Agent', 'Sanctified', 'Chrome Sitar', 'My Little Baby' and 'Sparrow'. It's also possible that some overdubs were recorded for 'New York City' and 'All Alone' at this session. Finally there is a question mark hanging over the actual venue for this session. It may have taken place at Paragon Studios in Chicago (a month earlier).

Friday 29th November

State Fairgrounds, Tampa, Florida, USA

Though the concert was scheduled, the appearance never took place.

Thursday 5th December

MRI Studios, 1680 North Sycamore Avenue, Hollywood, California, USA

A studio session that produced work on 'My Little Baby', 'New York City', 'Cry Baby', 'All Alone'. It's probable that the version of 'Cry Baby' recorded here is a different version from that recorded in September and is the version which appears on the Gloria Jones album 'Vixen'. The T. Rex band members were not present for these sessions. Instead session musicians were used. These were likely to include drummer Ed Green on drums, Scott Edwards on bass, Sylvester Rivers on keyboards, and guitarists Ray Parker and Sugar Bear.

Wednesday 11th December

MRI Studios, 1680 North Sycamore Avenue, Hollywood, California, USA

Recording session produced the basic tracks for 'Dawn Storm' and 'Jupiter Liar'. A second tape containing 'Teenage Dream' was also made. This tape has the words "Copy tape for Casablanca" written on it. This version featured a shortened introduction and the Silver Surfer verse edited out. For what purpose the tape was made remains unknown, though it is likely that it was being considered for single release.

Friday 13th December

MRI Studios, 1680 North Sycamore Avenue, Hollywood, California, USA

A recording session which saw work on 'Calling All Destroyers' (plus horns), 'Chrome Sitar' and 'All Alone' was held on this day.

1975

1975 was the year that Marc moved back to Britain. The move seems to have been prompted largely by the failure of the 'Light Of Love' album in the USA and increasing recognition that T. Rex was not going to be able to repeat its international success in that country. As a result of paying so much attention to "conquering" America, the core T. Rex audience in Europe had been neglected and had resultantly dwindled in numbers.

Even though Bolan returned to the United Kingdom, there was still little activity on the live front. 1975 saw a handful of summer dates at British seaside resorts. These featured extremely short 45–50 minute sets and were played mainly to test the waters and to see what kind of audience the group still had. Bolan stayed clear of risking major appearances in larger metropolitan areas.

Originally a tour was scheduled for November 1975. However this was postponed until the following year. Though no tour schedule was officially announced, tickets for a concert at the Mayfair Ballroom in Newcastle were erroneously put on sale, before being withdrawn. The decision to postpone the tour probably had two reasons. Firstly, the release date for 'Futuristic Dragon' was postponed until the following year. Secondly, the birth Rolan Bolan in September put all tour plans on hold for a while.

On the record release front, British audiences had to be content with the 'Bolan's Zip Gun' album. Most of the album had been available as the US release 'Light Of Love' since September the previous year and import copies were not too hard to come by. As a result, sales of 'Bolan's Zip Gun' were poor. The release of the follow-up album, 'Futuristic Dragon', most of which had been completed by the end of February, was held up. It was originally slated for summer release, then postponed to the autumn. Eventually the disc appeared in January 1976. As a result, many of the projects that Marc began recording that year never saw the light of day during his lifetime.

January
Bolan and Gloria Jones moved into an apartment in the Estoril B building, Avenue Princess Grace, Monaco. Prior to flying on to Los Angeles from Monte Carlo, Marc made a stopover in London where he gave several press interviews, including an infamous one to Roy Carr of NME.

Wednesday 29th January
Bolan and Gloria Jones, accompanied by Mickey Marmalade, return to Los Angeles. While they are on the plane, back in London, Tony Howard sacks Mickey Finn from T. Rex.

Friday 31st January
MRI Studios, 1680 North Sycamore Avenue, Hollywood, California, USA
Recording session which probably produced further work on 'Calling All Destroyers'.

Wednesday 12th February

MRI Studios, 1680 North Sycamore Avenue, Hollywood, California, USA

Date which saw a tape containing 'Sensation Boulevard', 'By The Light Of A Magical Moon', 'Get It On' ('Bang A Gong' on the tape box) and 'Sensation Boulevard' (with vocals) produced. The version of 'Get It On' is the slow version which later appeared as 'Get It On (Part 2)' on Gloria Jones's 'Vixen' album.

Friday 14th February

Bolan's Zip Gun (EMI T. Rex BLNA 7752)

'Light Of Love', 'Solid Baby', 'Precious Star', 'Token Of My Love', 'Space Boss', 'Think Zinc', 'Till Dawn', 'Girl In The Thunderbolt Suit', 'I Really Love You Babe', 'Golden Belt', 'Zip Gun Boogie'
Recorded at MRI Studios, Hollywood; Scorpio Sound, London; Electric Lady Studios, New York.
Produced by Marc Bolan. Engineered by Gary Ulmer, Mike Stavrou and unknown.
Marc Bolan – vocals, guitar; Steve Currie – bass; Davey Lutton – drums; Gloria Jones – clavinet and backing vocals; Mickey Finn –percussion; Bobbye Hall Porter – percussion; Dino Dines – keyboards; Paul Fenton – drums on 'Solid Baby' and 'Think Zinc'; Sister Pat Hall – backing vocals on 'Solid Baby', 'Space Boss', 'Think Zinc', 'Till Dawn'; Uncredited – keyboards; Howard Casey (?) – saxophones.
The album fails to make the charts.

"... In case you don't recall the Bolan Sound circa '73, here's a quick rundown: Open with stomping hands and handclaps, solo. Continue drums, noisily, without one variation, running throughout like a demented running stitch.

Zigzag on top of that with fuzzy guitar, its executions obviously subordinate to the swaying of Marc's lithe young form ... Add, for the purposes of '75, perhaps a shade more dehumanised ooh-ooh chorus in the far distance.

And to complete, the (some say) hypnotic, (others say) mastubatory intimacy of that breathy voicebox, repeat the same catchphrase approximately 153 times per track ... And that in a nutshell is 'Bolan's Zip Gun'.

A far cry from the pure voices and guitars of the old Rex days. And yes, it might drive you mad, except that after six or seven minutes you don't really notice whether it's playing or not.

Any spare accolades floating about would have to go to keyboardist Dino Dines who manages some sneaky dilution of the monotony with a touch of Kung Fu temple bells here ('Golden Belt'), a bar or two of honky-tonk there ('Token Of My Love').

Meanwhile sidekick Mickey Finn has finally split ... So this looks like the end of T. Rex As We Knew Them ... Farewell, Mugger Pixie."

Kate Phillips, NME

"The tragedy of being super successful and drastically over exposed is that a natural rejection sets in from those who reject or become tired of the ingredients that invite success in the first place. The younger fans who gave Marc his freedom from the underground scene of the sixties ... have grown up and moved on ... Meanwhile the jackals of the industry swoop in for the kill, pleased to sink claws into a sitting target ... Yet the music here is not so bad. 'Light Of Love' is a good riff and Bolan can still boogie on tunes like 'Precious Star'... Dino Dines plays raunchy piano and Davey Lutton gets a smart, cracking sound. If this had been some pub rock band from Southend, there would be rave reviews and centre spread analysis, but this is Marc Bolan, and he can't do anything right ... 'Space Boss' ... rocks with uncredited tenor sax honking over a stomping rhythm section ... Suitably banal lyrics from Marc too ... Wasn't early pop supposed to be silly, but rocking? And on a tune like 'Think Zinc' you have bizarre stomping lunacy with production ... There are a lot worse musicians and certainly a lot worse bands making it and 'Girl In The Thunderbolt Suit' and the howling harmonicas of 'I Really Love You Babe' ... have more spirit than some of the newer pop packages."

Chris Welch, Melody Maker

"... What sounded like good, simple fun two years ago comes off sounding like inferior exercises in self-indulgence today. There's nothing on this album that's nearly as infectious or as instantaneous as the days he used to 'Get It On'. But then again, perhaps it isn't Marc, perhaps we just don't care like we used to ... As far as the vinyl goes, it's mild unassuming rock and roll with Bolan pouting and mincing through the lyrics. 'Girl In The Thunderbolt Suit' is directly related to a couple of rockers on Lou Reed's 'Transformer'. There's handclaps a plenty and lots of crass sounds. In the final analysis, all you're left with is a headache."

Barbara Charone, Sounds

Monday 24th February
Bolan accompanied by Gloria Jones arrived in London early in the morning. They stayed at the Carlton Tower Hotel for the length of their stay. They also travelled to various radio stations in Glasgow, Edinburgh, Liverpool, Manchester and Sheffield promoting 'Bolan's Zip Gun'.

Wednesday 26th February
Studio 3, London Weekend Television Studios, Kent House, London Bridge, London, England
Recording of an interview segment for 'Saturday Scene'. Marc was interviewed by Michael Wale.

Friday 28th February
Air Studios, 214 Oxford Street, London, England
A tape was produced on this date containing mixes of 'Sensation Boulevard', 'Casual Agent', 'Jupiter Liar', 'Chrome Sitar', 'All Alone', 'New York City' and 'Calling All Destroyers'.

Saturday 1st March
Broadcast at 10.20 of Marc's interview with Michael Wale on the Saturday morning show 'Saturday Scene'.

Monday 17th March
Strawberry Studios, Chateau d'Herouville, Pontoise, Paris, France (?)

Tuesday 18th March
Strawberry Studios, Chateau d'Herouville, Pontoise, Paris, France (?)

Wednesday 19th March
Strawberry Studios, Chateau d'Herouville, Pontoise, Paris, France
T. Rex recorded basic tracks for 'Billy Super Duper' and 'Depth Charge' on this date. In total

there were three days of sessions which were, in Marc's words, a "waste of time". Clive Franks, Elton John's engineer was employed to man the mixing desk, before walking out. His name is not mentioned on the tape box for these particular tracks. No further details of what material was attempted are available, though it's possible that material recorded with Canadian DJ Dougie Pringle may have been put on tape at these sessions.

April

Marc's Home, Estoril B building, Avenue Princess Grace, Monaco, France
Following the Chateau sessions, Bolan returns to Monaco. While there he spends time rehearsing the script for the planned film 'Obsession' with tour manager Mickey Marmalade. The film was due to star David Niven and Cappucine and to be filmed in Monaco. In the final event, the film was not made.

Wednesday 9th April

Unconfirmed studio, Monaco, France (?)
Studio rehearsal including work on 'Swahili Boogie Woogie'.

Sunday 13th April

Marc's Home, Estoril B building, Avenue Princess Grace, Monaco, France
A home recording of 'Dynamo' was made on this date.

April

Prior to flying to Munich for recording sessions, Bolan flies into London to meet up with Gloria Jones who has been staying in London for medical reasons prior to the birth of their child. They stay at Brown's Hotel.

Saturday 19th April

T. Rex fly into Munich from London for recording sessions at Musicland Studios. Marc is delayed while he experiences a "heart attack" i.e. high blood pressure and palpitations caused by excessive drinking the night before departure.

Tuesday 22nd April

Musicland Studios, Munich, West Germany
A studio session which saw rough versions of 'You're Gonna Move', 'Saturday Night', an instrumental version of Jimi Hendrix's 'Purple Haze' and a studio jam entitled 'Daze' committed to tape.

Friday 25th April

Musicland Studios, Munich, West Germany
Studio session which saw a song entitled 'Suit' recorded. This was an early version of 'Soul Of My Suit'. Also recorded were several rough takes of 'Teen Riot Structure'.

Saturday 26th April

Musicland Studios, Munich, West Germany
Recording session which included the song 'Slave Police' being put down on tape. Also further takes of 'Teen Riot Structure' were recorded.

Sunday 27th April

Musicland Studios, Munich, West Germany

Recording session which saw a version of 'Lalena' recorded with Donovan singing put down on tape. The recording appears to be lost.

Wednesday 30th April

Musicland Studios, Munich, West Germany

Possible date for a recording session which saw further work on 'Slave Police' and 'Lalena' taking place.

Following the sessions, where Bolan had "enjoyed" a stormy relationship with engineer Mack (now well-known for his work with Queen), he and T. Rex are "banned" from future use of the studio. Following the sessions Bolan and Jones returned to Monaco, while the rest of the band returned to London.

Sunday 11th May

After a quick visit to the UK Marc flies into New York, before moving on to Los Angeles.

May

Marc and David Bowie attend a reception for Gary Glitter in New York. By the time they arrived Glitter had already left.

May / June

Marc, returns to live in England, hiring a house at 25 Holmead Road, Fulham, London. Gloria Jones joined him later.

Wednesday 10th June

Pied Bull, Angel, Islington, London, England

T. Rex conducted at least one rehearsal at the above pub venue prior to their concerts. Gloria Jones did not attend as she was still in Los Angeles at the time.

Gooseberry Studios, 19 Gerrard Street, London, England

Following the rehearsal, Bolan, plus the band, went on to the above studio and committed versions of 'Jeepster', '20th Century Boy' and 'Teenage Dream' to tape. Why they should have done this remains unknown. A possible reason is that they were demos for radio sessions.

Friday 20th June

New York City / Chrome Sitar (EMI T. Rex MARC 10)

The first T. Rex single release in eight months returns the band to the single's chart. It reached a high point of 15.

"'New York City' starts with electronics and sighing over a crisp stroll, and then the chorus is poured on, and finally Marc raises his fuzzy head and breaks into song. To be honest, I get the impression that Marc the producer is trying to hide Marc the singer. The record is so cluttered and fussy, and it is most annoying to catch glimpses of ... some rather dandy guitar work buried beneath all the nonsense. Reckon Marc needs to get back to the essentials ...".

John Peel, Sounds

"The grave is dug, the coffin buried and earth poured on top, but still comes the cries from within, "I'm not dead, I'm still the King of Pop." The voice is faint now ... But he's gonna need something really exceptional to lift him from that coffin now and this trivia, though better than of late, is scarcely enough. Miss."

Colin Irwin, Melody Maker

University Of Exeter, Exeter, Devon, England

A secret concert intended to promote the forthcoming single and to warm up for the tour. Marc appeared on a bill which also featured Caravan and Ronnie Lane's Slim Chance. Caravan headlined with T. Rex coming on stage between them and Ronnie Lane's group.

June

Scorpio Sound, Euston, London, England

'Live' alternate versions of 'New York City' and '20th Century Boy' were recorded at this session, along with jingles for 'Capital Radio' in London and 'Piccadilly Radio' in Manchester. A demo with Gloria Jones entitled 'You're So Handy' was also recorded.

Tuesday 1st July

Trident Studios, St. Anne's Court, Soho, London, England

A version of 'New York City' was prepared for 'Top Of The Pops' on this date. This programme marked the debut of Eric Hall dressed as Eric The Frog. What a prat.

Wednesday 2nd July

BBC Television Centre, Wood Lane, Shepherd's Bush, London, England

The first appearance on BBC 1's 'Top Of The Pops' in nearly eighteen months saw T. Rex miming to 'New York City'. The performance was used on 3rd July and 31st July editions of the programme.

Thursday 3rd July

Transmission date of the 'New York City' slot on 'Top Of The Pops' (BBC 1). See entry for 2nd July.

Sunday 6th July

Capital Radio Studios, Euston, London, England

Marc appeared on the afternoon youth magazine programme 'Hullabaloo'. In addition to being interviewed by Maggie Norden, T. Rex also performed a studio session. However, it's more likely that this session had been recorded some days earlier at Scorpio Sound which was situated in the same tower block as the Capital Radio studios.

The session was made up of four songs: '20th Century Boy', 'New York City', 'Soul Of My Suit' and 'Get It On'. At the time 'Soul Of My Suit' was unreleased and featured a totally different arrangement to that which was used on the final released version over eighteen months later.

Tuesday 8th July

Piccadilly Radio Studios, Manchester, Lancashire, England

Marc was interviewed by Andy Peebles on his afternoon radio show.

Capital Radio Studio, Euston, London, England

Transmission date for Marc presenting Capital Radio's evening "progressive" show 'Your Mother Wouldn't Like It'. The show had propably been recorded on tape some days prior to broadcast.

BRITISH TOUR
Sunday 13th July

Manx Radio Studios, Douglas, Isle Of Man

Prior to the evening's concert, Marc was interviewed on Manx Radio.

Palace Lido, Douglas, Isle Of Man

Set list: 'Jeepster', '20th Century Boy', 'Teenage Dream', 'Zip Gun Boogie', 'New York City', 'Soul Of My Suit', 'Hot Love', 'Get It On'

Tuesday 15th July

Thames Television Studios, Euston, London, England

Marc was interviewed on the 'Today' show. He appeared alongside Telly Savalas and began to usurp Alan Hargreaves' role as interlocutor. This eventually led to a short series of slots with Marc as interviewer later that year.

MRI Studios, 1680 North Sycamore Avenue, Hollywood, California, USA

A tape was produced containing the following Richard Jones tracks: 'Love Is Here To Stay' (2 takes), 'Pure Magic' (2 takes) and 'Loving You'. The tape box contains the instruction "To remix by Marc' and 'Loving You' is noted as "B–Side".

Wednesday 16th July

BBC Television Centre, Wood Lane, Shepherd's Bush, London, England

A second performance of 'New York City' for BBC 1's 'Top Of The Pops' saw T. Rex running through a live take of the song. This take featured the song taken at a much quicker pace than on the record. The slot was broadcast on 17th July.

Thursday 17th July

Transmission date on BBC 1 for the second performance of 'New York City' filmed for 'Top Of The Pops'. See entry for 16th July.

Friday 18th July (?)

Granada Television Studios, Manchester, Lancashire, England

T. Rex performed 'New York City' on Granada Television's children's pop show 'Rock On With 45'. This take also featured the band playing live in the studio. The show was networked at different times on the various ITV networks.

Wednesday 23rd July

Tiffany's, Great Yarmouth, Norfolk, England

Set list: 'Jeepster', '20th Century Boy', 'Teenage Dream', 'Zip Gun Boogie', 'New York City', 'Soul Of My Suit', 'Hot Love', 'Get It On'

Thursday 24th July

Broadcast date in the London area for the edition of 'Rock On With 45' featuring the 'New York City' performance.

Friday 25th July
Pier Pavilion, Hastings, Sussex, England
Set list: 'Jeepster', '20th Century Boy', 'Teenage Dream', 'Zip Gun Boogie', 'New York City', 'Soul Of My Suit', 'Hot Love', 'Get It On'

Saturday 26th July
Transmission date (in London) for 'Rock On With 45' (ITV) which featured the performance of 'New York City' recorded on 18th July.
Leas Cliffe Hall, Folkestone, Kent, England
Set list: 'Jeepster', '20th Century Boy', 'Teenage Dream', 'Zip Gun Boogie', 'New York City', 'Hot Love', 'Get It On'

Thursday 31st July
Broadcast date for a repeat of the first 'Top Of The Pops' performance of 'New York City'. See entry for 2nd July.

July (?)
MRI Studios, 1680 North Sycamore Avenue, Hollywood, California, USA
An undated tape box containing a vocal-less version of the Richard Jones track 'Pure Magic' possibly dates from this time.

July (?)
MRI Studios, 1680 North Sycamore Avenue, Hollywood, California, USA
A second undated tape box, but again certainly dating from this period, was produced. This contains the Richard Jones tracks 'Pure Magic' and 'Loving You' was produced around this time.

July / August (?)
Unidentified Studio
A third undated tape, containing the Richard Jones tracks 'Pure Magic' and 'Love Is Here To Stay' was produced around the summer of 1975. This also contains T. Rex's 'Depth Charge'. The studio is also unknown. The most likely candidate is MRI.

Friday 1st August
Scorpio Sound, Euston, London, England
A studio session which saw a different/early take of 'Dreamy Lady' recorded.

Monday 4th August
Yorkshire Television Studios, Leeds, Yorkshire, England
Marc guested on the Yorkshire Television produced programme 'Pop Quest' handing out prizes and being interviewed. The show was transmitted on 12th September. (Changed from September).

Friday 8th August
Thames Television Studios, Euston, London, England
Marc made his second appearance on Thames Television's 'Today', this time being interviewed alongside Nigel Dempster, Patrick Cosgrave and Vicki Hodges. The show was broadcast live.

Tuesday 12th August

Transmission date on ITV networks for 'Shang-A-Lang', the Bay City Rollers hosted pop show, which featured the promo film of 'New York City'.

Sunday 17th August

T. Rex were offered a concert performance at a gala performance at the European Cup Final Of Athletecism in France.

Thursday 28th August

Scorpio Sound, Euston, London, England

A total of three tape boxes seem to exist for this date. One tapebox indicates that 'Dreamy Lady' was recorded on this date. A second tapebox suggests a recording session which produced some work on 'Dock Of The Bay', 'Christmas Bop' and 'Do You Wanna Dance'. A blues/jazz jam was also recorded on this date. A third tapebox indicates that there was also a mixdown session for 'Silver Lady' (a working title for 'Dreamy Lady'), 'Do You Wanna Dance', 'Get It On' (presumably one of the Gloria Jones versions) and 'Dock Of The Bay. It's possible that the final two tapes are composites of material which had been recorded earlier in the month.

Summer

Marc's House, 25 Holmead Road, Fulham, London, England

Sometime in the late summer Marc had a jam session with The Walker Brothers at his home.

Friday 5th September

Trident Studios, St. Anne's Court, Soho, London, England

Studio session which included further work on 'Do You Wanna Dance', 'Dock Of The Bay' plus two versions of 'Ain't That A Shame' – a long and a short version.

Friday 12th September

Transmission date on ITV networks for 'Pop Quest'. See earlier entry.

Friday 19th September

Scorpio Sound, Euston, London, England

Studio session which saw a version of 'London Boys' put down on tape.

Thursday 25th September

Thames Television Studios, Euston, London, England

Marc interviews John Mayall for 'Today'. The interview is broadcast live.

Friday 26th September

Dreamy Lady / Do You Wanna Dance / Dock Of The Bay (EMI T. Rex MARC 11)

The single fails to emulate the success of its predecessor, peaking at 30 in the charts.

"Good value from Marc on this maxi-single ... and could provide him with a welcome return to the charts. The one new song is a typical Bolan boogie over a shuffle backing with some excellent echoey vocal reminiscent of the past decade during the verses ...".

Chris Charlesworth, Melody Maker

"Marc's latest is a rhythmic little item which ought to merit some marginal disco action ..."Oh Dreamy Lady, won't you come to my bed?" Poor kid, though he does have a way with words ... Wait a second. Listen to that vocal. This is Bryan Ferry at 78. Flip 'Do You Wanna Dance' and 'Dock Of The Bay'. Still trying to compete with / make Bowie jealous. "He could have been Donny Osmond, but he wanted to be Mick Jagger. Schmuck. Print it." Dick Clarke 1973."

Lester Bangs, NME

"I like T. Rex, I think that this is good, very good ... This reminds me of the old T. Rex with Steve Took ... I used to be really into Tyrannosaurus Rex. I've got all their albums, and this sounds like the old Marc coming out again ...".

Gary Holton of the Heavy Metal Kids, Sounds

Birth of Bolan and Gloria Jones's son Rolan Seymour Feld.

Tuesday 30th September
London Weekend Television Studios, Kent House, Southbank, London, England
Marc makes his first performance on Mike Mansfield's show 'Supersonic'. The show was broadcast on 4th October and featured a performance of 'Dreamy Lady' which had a marginally different mix and vocal line from that on the disc. The song was not broadcast in its complete form, instead coming in just before the second verse, thus suggesting that Marc had sung the verses the wrong way round. The whole band plus Paul Fenton on congas were shown playing in the background. Marc also introduced The Hollies.

Thursday 2nd October
Thames Television Studios, Euston, London, England
Marc interviewed Keith Moon for the 'Today' show. Moon was on his worst/funniest behaviour and sent Marc up terribly during the interview.

Saturday 4th October
London Weekend Television Studios, Kent House, Southbank, London, England
Bolan was interviewed by presenter Sally James on the early morning children's show 'Saturday Scene'.

Later that day, there was the initial broadcast of 'Supersonic' featuring the first performance of 'Dreamy Lady'. The transmission took place in the London Weekend Television area. Other ITV channels broadcast the show one week later, on the 11th October. See entry for 23rd September.

Friday 10th October
Air Studios, 214 Oxford Street, London, England
Studio session which produced further work on 'Futuristic Dragon' and 'Christmas Bop'. In addition a tape was made of 'Dreamy Lady' with the words "LWT" written on the box. This was the mix which was used for the forthcoming appearance on 'Supersonic'.

Saturday 11th October
Scorpio Sound, Euston, London, England
Recording session which saw versions of 'Funky London Childhood', 'London Boys', 'Dreamy

Lady' and 'Do You Wanna Dance' produced. Two mixes of each track were produced, one with vocals and one an instrumental. The first two songs were recorded for Thames Television's 'Today' programme. The latter two were recorded for use by the BBC.

Tuesday 14th October

London Weekend Television Studios, Kent House, Southbank, London, England

Marc made a second solo appearance on 'Supersonic' performing a different version of 'Dreamy Lady', the version which had been prepared some days earlier, on the 10th October at Air Studios. The show was transmitted in the London area on 18th October.

Wednesday 15th October

Thames Television Studios, Euston, London, England

T. Rex recorded performances of two songs, 'Funky London Childhood' and 'London Boys', for Thames Television's 'Today' show. Both songs used the tapes recorded a few days earlier, but Bolan sang a live vocal. The band appeared as a quartet of Bolan, Currie, Dines and Lutton; Gloria Jones was not present at the recordings. 'Funky London Childhood' was broadcast on 16th October and 'London Boys' was broadcast on 3rd November.

Thursday 16th October

Transmission on Thames Television's 'Today' programme of 'Funky London Childhood' which had been recorded the day before. See entry for 15th October.

Friday 17th October

Air Studios, 214 Oxford Street, London, England

Date for a session which saw work on both 'Futuristic Dragon' and 'Christmas Bop'.

Saturday 18th October

Transmission date for the second performance of 'Dreamy Lady' recorded for Supersonic. This transmission date was (again) for the London area only. Other areas broadcast the programme anything up to a week later. See entry for 14th October.

Monday 20th October

Thames Television Studios, Euston, London, England

The final two interviews Marc conducted for 'Today', with Stan Lee, creator and publisher of the American Marvel Comics group, and Roy Wood, were recorded on this date and broadcast on separate programmes later that month.

Tuesday 21st October

Basing Street Studios, Basing Street, London, England

A studio session which saw further work on 'Ain't That A Shame' as well as the recording of the 'Top Of The Pops' version of 'Dreamy Lady'.

Wednesday 22nd October

BBC Television Centre, Wood Lane, Shepherd's Bush, London, England

The only 'Top Of The Pops' performance of 'Dreamy Lady' was recorded on this date and broadcast the following night, 23rd October.

Thursday 23rd October

Transmission date for the version of 'Dreamy Lady' recorded for 'Top Of The Pops' (BBC 1). See entry for 22nd October.

Monday 28th October

Air Studios, 214 Oxford Street, London, England

Date for a session which saw additional overdubs recorded for 'Christmas Bop'.

Tuesday 29th October

Air Studios, 214 Oxford Street, London, England

Date for another session which saw further work on 'Christmas Bop'.

Friday 31st October

Air Studios, 214 Oxford Street, London, England

Additional dubbing / production work on 'Futuristic Dragon (Introduction)' took place at this session.

October (?)

Unknown Radio Studio, London, England (?)

Marc was interviewed by Alan Thompson, supposedly for radio syndication in North America. It's not known if the interview was ever actually broadcast.

Monday 3rd November

The live version of 'London Boys' recorded for 'Today' was broadcast on this date. The programme was only shown in the London area. See entry for 15th October.

Thursday 6th November

Air Studios, 214 Oxford Street, London, England

A tape containing the crossfade between 'Futuristic Dragon (Introduction)' and 'Jupiter Liar' was compiled. In addition a tape was also produced which contained guitar tracks on one channel and a version of 'Depth Charge' (with piano) on the other.

Saturday 8th November

Air Studios, 214 Oxford Street, London, England

The master tape of the 'Futuristic Dragon' album was compiled on this date.

Thursday 13th November

MRI Studios, 1680 North Sycamore Avenue, Hollywood, California, USA

A tape containing 'Casual Agent' was produced on this date. Which version and for what purpose remains unknown.

November (?)

MRI Studios, 1680 North Sycamore Avenue, Hollywood, California, USA

An undated tape from this period contains an acoustic demo of 'Universe' (on the tape box Bolan has written the title 'Let's Face The Music') and two mixes of 'Futuristic Dragon (Introduction)'.

Tuesday 25th November
Broadcast date for a short interview segment concerning publishing in the music business on BBC Radio One's 'Insight' programme.

Tuesday 11th December
MRI Studios, 1680 North Sycamore Avenue, Hollywood, California, USA
Studio session which produced the versions of 'Funky London Childhood' and 'London Boys'.

Friday 14th December
Christmas Bop / Telegram Sam / Metal Guru (EMI T. Rex MARC 12)
The planned release of this single was cancelled.

1976

1976 began with the biggest T. Rex tour of Britain since Autumn 1971. Though there were some good performances, on the whole the tour was something of a mess, largely through being poorly planned. For example, why play in St. Albans and yet not in Aylesbury? Aylesbury had a long established venue, 'Friars', which probably would have been a better choice. The idea of attempting to return to the roots sadly misfired. Ticket prices were also comparatively high and many of the smaller venues in the smaller towns were only filled to half capacity. In the bigger cities, ticket sales were healthier, but even then many of the shows were far from sold out. The tour could well have done with being half the final size.

After the tour Marc seemed to begin the process of a serious rethink of the T. Rex sound. Gloria Jones left the band to pursue her solo career. Marc seemed to decide that a more back to basics approach was needed, which coincided quite neatly with the nascent punk movement in Britain. The first indication of this was the 'I Love To Boogie' single. In the summer of 1976, Miller Anderson was added to the band, mainly for live work. Anderson was an excellent guitar player, who had worked with Dino Dines in the Keef Hartley band. Live, the band started to become a bit more powerful, though Davey Lutton's lacklustre drumming remained a weakness.

On record the band also still had problems igniting, as the 'Laser Love' single showed. What could have been another '20th Century Boy' was instead a rather tepid release. The record stalled just outside the top 40. Davey Lutton seemed to bear the brunt of this failure and was sacked. As a result Steve Currie, who was Lutton's closest colleague in the band, quit. Their places were quickly filled by bassist Herbie Flowers and drummer Tony Newman, both solid and respected musicians with a huge pedigree. They had been David Bowie's rhythm section on the 'Diamond Dogs' album and subsequent tour. Flowers had also played sessions for nearly every one under the sun. Newman had been drummer with Jeff Beck amongst others. They were a far more muscular rhythm section than Currie and Lutton. Only Dino Dines remained of the musicians who had been members of T. Rex at the beginning of the year. Even then, the new line-up's live debut in December 1976 was something of a disappointment, with what appeared to be an under-rehearsed performance for the Christmas edition of 'Supersonic' at The Royal Theatre in London.

Monday 5th January

MRI Studios, 1680 North Sycamore Avenue, Hollywood, California, USA
Three versions of the Richard Jones track 'Loving You' were made at this particular session.

Tuesday 6th January

MRI Studios, 1680 North Sycamore Avenue, Hollywood, California, USA
A tape containing 'Shadow Of The Night', 'Would You Like To Know', 'Fall For You' (probably 'I'm

A Fool For You Girl'), 'Savage Beethoven' and 'Bust My Balls' was compiled on this date. The first track is a Richard Jones song; the second track is a Gloria Jones one. The latter three have "Demo project' in Marc's handwriting written against them.

A second tape from that day includes another mix of the Richard Jones track 'Love Is Here To Stay'.

Monday 12th January

BBC Television Centre, Shepherd's Bush, London, England

Marc was interviewed on the BBC programme 'Nationwide' as part of a new national anti-smoking campaign. The interview was broadcast live.

Sunday 18th January

Capital Radio, Euston, London, England

Marc was interviewed by Maggie Nordern on the 'Hullabaloo' show. He also answered questions from listeners on a phone-in section. Tracks from the forthcoming 'Futuristic Dragon' album were also played.

Friday 30th January

Futuristic Dragon (EMI T. Rex BLN 5004)

'Futuristic Dragon (Introduction)', 'Jupiter Liar', 'Chrome Sitar', 'All Alone', 'New York City', 'My Little Baby', 'Calling All Destroyers', 'Theme For A Dragon', 'Sensation Boulevard', 'Ride My Wheels', 'Dreamy Lady', 'Dawn Storm', 'Casual Agent'

Marc Bolan – vocals, guitar, synthesiser; Steve Currie – bass; Gloria Jones – clavinet and backing vocals; Dino Dines – keyboards; Davey Lutton – drums; Paul Fenton – percussion; Bobbye Hall Porter – percussion; Tyrone Scott – backing vocals; Uncredited – saxophones; Uncredited session musicians. See entry for 5th December 1974.

Recorded at MRI Studios, Hollywood; Paragon Studios, Chicago; Scorpio Sound, London.

Produced by Marc Bolan; Engineered by Gary Ulmer, Marty Feldman and Mike Stavrou.

Disappointingly, the album only spent one week in the charts reaching 50.

"In the five or six years since the release of 'Electric Warrior', Marc Bolan has moved neither forwards or backwards – just sideways. The only real difference between his recent songs and his past work is the former's mass production quality.

This went out of control for a while ... but things seem to have settled down now. There are still banks of soaring chorals and prolonged synthesiser on 'Futuristic Dragon', but at least it's all rather more sparingly used. In fact ... the album has a positive affinity to the past ... from the George Underwood cover ... through the rear sleeve hand-written fantastical scroll ... to some of the song's lyrics. Can't be a bad thing.

Indeed the album's opener and title track is very much a cross between 'Elemental Child' (guitar frenzy) and 'The Children Of Rarn' (elven charm) and sets the scene for better things. Not that they come on as strongly as you might have hoped.

The aforementioned multi-instrumentation more often than not serves as a disguise for simplistic songs that ... shouldn't really last much over a minute. 'New York City' is, of course, the prime example, with a mere 27 words sustaining Bolan for the best part of four minutes ... 'Jupiter Liar' and 'Dawn Storm' are also culprits.

Bestrax are 'Calling All Destroyers', speedy, with Bolan puffing appropriately ... and 'Casual Agent', notably for its beautifully nonsensical lines ...

'Futuristic Dragon' is, by no stretch of the imagination, a great album and will no doubt be seen by many merely as additional vinyl fuel for Bolan's musical pyre ...

Myself, I can't help but like the LP, can't help but enjoy Bolan's vocal inflections, his alliterative, if puzzling lyrics and, most of all, his gall to keep releasing albums, when it must be admitted, the greater part of his creative urge disappeared a long time ago. And so what if the 'Jeepster' riff crops up all of three times?"

Geoff Barton, Sounds

February (?)
London Weekend Television Studios, Kent House, Southbank, London, England
Marc was interviewed by Sally James on London Weekend Television's 'Saturday Scene', a Saturday morning children's show for kids and teenage degenerates.

Monday 2nd February
Unknown Studio, London, England
Rehearsal for the upcoming tour with the sound crew.

Tuesday 3rd February
Unknown Studio, London, England
Rehearsal for the upcoming tour with the sound crew.

Wednesday 4th February
Air Studios, London, England (?)
Studio time was booked for listening to the unreleased Sister Pat Hall album tapes. This was probably done with the intention of finding material that could be reworked and included on the planned Gloria Jones album.

'FUTURISTIC DRAGON' BRITISH TOUR

For the tour, Gloria Jones rejoined the line-up of T. Rex on keyboards and backing vocals. In addition, a friend of Gloria's from Los Angeles, Tyrone Scott, was also drafted in on keyboards and backing vocals. The band was slick and well rehearsed with the three-keyboard line-up bolstering the live sound. On the other hand, Bolan was frequently drunk. Besides forgetting the lyrics to some songs, he often had vocal problems.

Though the tour was ostensibly to support the new album, very little was actually played from 'Futuristic Dragon'; in fact, only the two singles which appeared on the album, 'New York City' and 'Dreamy Lady' were staples of the live set. The tour programme indicated that 'Futuristic Dragon' and 'Calling All Destroyers' might form part of the set list. They were never performed. Instead, Bolan chose to perform the unreleased 'Funky London Childhood'. The reminder of the set-list was of the 'greatest hits' variety, with 'Children Of The Revolution' and 'Solid Gold Easy Action' surprisingly making their live debuts.

Several concerts were planned which never made it to the final schedule. These are included in the appendix.

Thursday 5th February
Central Hall, Chatham, Kent, England
No professional photographers were allowed at this concert.

Friday 6th February

City Hall, St. Albans, Hertfordshire, England

Set list: '20th Century Boy', 'Jeepster', 'Funky London Childhood', 'New York City', 'Solid Gold Easy Action', 'Children Of The Revolution', 'Telegram Sam', 'Debora', 'One Inch Rock', 'Ride A White Swan', 'Life's A Gas', 'Dreamy Lady', 'Teenage Dream', 'London Boys', 'Hot Love', 'Get It On'

"It was only the second date of Marc Bolan's current tour, but in the words of one pleasantly surprised old T. Rex fan, "He's delivered the goods okay."

Mr. Bolan, however, was not happy. Musically he obviously enjoyed the gig, but having to perform to a less than half filled hall did nothing to boost the ego ... In conversation he never stops boasting in an effort he must know impresses no-one but himself. Not even an enthusiastic audience is going to be impressed by claims to having sold eleven million copies of 'Hot Love', when looking around them they see barely 400 other spectators.

And spectators is probably the best way to describe the audience at St. Albans City Hall last Friday evening. Except for the small crowd of glitter shriekers at the foot of the stage, most of us were there to gawp at the phenomena of Mr. Bolan and T. Rex. All the local press were there to gather pictures for next week's family newspaper and an hour after the concert had ended, tearful fans were still waiting outside to hopefully touch their fading pop idol.

Many of them had probably not been to the concert with tickets priced at £2, a fact Mr. Bolan appeared annoyed about. But with him charging well in excess of a thousand pounds to play a hall only licensed to accommodate 1,000 people, he – or his advisers – were clearly responsible in part for the excessively priced tickets.

Opening with the number '20th Century Boy' Marc and T. Rex who for this tour are his old lady, Gloria Jones, Steve Currie, Davey Lutton, Dino Dines and Tyrone Scott concentrated on playing a tight funky set of mostly old numbers ... There were surprisingly few from his new LP, 'Futuristic Dragon', but he did include the new single 'London Boys'. Everyone in the band played their part, competently and adequately enough to please the handful of fans.

But in making reference to Cliff Richard's previous appearance at the same hall, he on the one hand drew attention to both of them failing to successfully break into the American market and on the other to the comparison that Cliff had sold out two shows in St. Albans in the space of two hours following the box office opening. Marc Bolan won't be boasting to even himself about his St. Albans gig. So ephemeral was Mr. Bolan that a week later it almost seems that the concert never took place."

John Sivyer, Sounds

The band received £360 for the concert.

Saturday 7th February

Leas Cliffe Hall, Folkestone, Kent, England

The band received £350 for the concert.

Sunday 8th February

Cliffes Pavilion, Southend On Sea, Essex, England

Part of the concert was filmed from the audience on cine film complete with original sound. Two songs are known to exist: 'Funky London Childhood' and 'Telegram Sam'.

'Life's A Gas' made its debut in the acoustic section of the show.

The band received £600 for the concert.

FUTURISTIC DRAGON

ALBUM AVAILABLE SOON **ORDER NOW**

T. REX ON TOUR

FEBRUARY 4th
JOHNSON HALL **YEOVIL**
FEBRUARY 5th
CENTRAL HALL **CHATHAM**
FEBRUARY 6th
CITY HALL **ST. ALBANS**
FEBRUARY 7th
LEAS CLIFF HALL **FOLKSTONE**
FEBRUARY 8th
CLIFFS PAVILION **SOUTHEND-ON-SEA**
FEBRUARY 12th
FLORAL HALL **SOUTHPORT**
FEBRUARY 13th
PALACE THEATRE **NEWARK**
FEBRUARY 14th
GRAND PAVILION **WITHERNSEA**
FEBRUARY 15th
EMPIRE THEATRE **SUNDERLAND**

FEBRUARY 18th
LYCEUM **LONDON**
FEBRUARY 19th
QUEENSWAY **DUNSTABLE**
FEBRUARY 23rd
TOWN HALL **BIRMINGHAM**
FEBRUARY 24th
FREE TRADE HALL **MANCHESTER**
FEBRUARY 28th
WINTER GARDENS **NEW BRIGHTON**
MARCH 1st
APOLLO THEATRE **GLASGOW**
MARCH 3rd
LARGE MUNICIPAL HALL **FALKIRK**
MARCH 6th
GRAND HALL **KILMARNOCK**

Wednesday 11th February

EMI Studios, Abbey Road, London, England
A handwritten note for this date suggests that Marc may have done some work at the above studio.

Thursday 12th February

Radio Tees Studios, Stockton On Tees, Teeside, England
An interview was scheduled for 10 a.m. for the above radio station. This was probably rescheduled for Sunday 15th February.

Metro Radio Studios, Newcastle Upon Tyne, Tyne And Wear, England
An interview was set for the above radio station at 1 p.m. This was probably rescheduled for the 15th February.

Unknown venue, Southport, Merseyside, England (?)
Prior to the concert an interview with journalist Spencer Leigh of the Liverpool Illustrated News was scheduled for 7.30p.m.

Floral Hall, Southport, Merseyside, England
Set list: '20th Century Boy', 'Jeepster', 'Funky London Childhood', 'New York City', 'Solid Gold Easy Action', 'Children Of The Revolution', 'Telegram Sam', 'Debora', 'One Inch Rock', 'Life's A Gas', 'Dreamy Lady', 'Teenage Dream', 'London Boys', 'Hot Love', 'Get It On'
After the gig the band stayed at the Clifton Hotel in Southport. The band received £616 for the concert.

Friday 13th February

Unknown venue, Nottingham, Nottinghamshire, England (?)
An interview was scheduled with journalist Brian Hancock at 4 p.m. This may have been rescheduled for 23rd February.

Radio Trent Studios, Nottingham, Nottinghamshire, England
A radio interview was scheduled for 4.30 p.m. at the above radio station.

Palace Theatre, Newark, Nottinghamshire, England
After the show the band stayed at the Robin Hood Hotel in Newark. They received £732 for their performance.

Saturday 14th February

Radio Humberside Studios, Hull, Humberside, England
An interview with Tim Gibson was scheduled for 6.30 at the above radio station.

Grand Pavilion, Withernsea, Humberside, England
The overnight hotel for this date was the Hull Crest Motel in Hull. The band received only £300 for the concert.

Sunday 15th February

Metro Radio Studios, Newcastle Upon Tyne, Tyne And Wear, England
An interview was held at 6 p.m. with Jeff Brown.

BBC Radio Newcastle Studios, Newcastle Upon Tyne, Tyne And Wear, England
An interview with Ian Penman, later of the NME, was conducted for the above radio station at 6.30 p.m.

Unknown venue, Newcastle Upon Tyne, Tyne And Wear, England
Marc was interviewed by Bill Bradshaw of the Halifax Evening Courier at 7 p.m.

Radio Tees Studios, Stockton On Tees, Teeside, England

A final pre-concert interview, with Ian Sandall, took place at 7.30 p.m. at the above radio station.

Empire Theatre, Sunderland, Tyne And Wear, England

The band received £1,065 for the concert. After the show the entourage travelled back to London.

Tuesday 17th February

London Weekend Television Studios, Kent House, Southbank, London, England

During a short break in the tour, T. Rex filmed an appearance on 'Supersonic'. The band were due at the television studios at 10.30 in the morning. Two songs were recorded, 'London Boys' and 'Telegram Sam'. Though the performance was mimed, 'Telegram Sam' featured a newly recorded backing track featuring the then current line up of T. Rex. 'London Boys' also showed some differences to the original single mix. Four takes of 'London Boys' and two takes of 'Telegram Sam' were filmed. The show was broadcast on 21st February. Earlier in the day Marc had been photographed for the Daily Mirror by Ron Burton for a promotion for the Burns Flyte guitar which he then later used for Supersonic. Burns were probably extremely happy when, during the performance of 'London Boys', Marc threw the guitar from the raised platform on which he was performing.

Wednesday 18th February

The Lyceum, Strand, London, England

Set list: '20th Century Boy', 'Jeepster', 'Funky London Childhood', 'New York City', 'Solid Gold Easy Action', 'Children Of The Revolution', 'Teenage Dream', 'Telegram Sam', 'Debora', 'One Inch Rock', 'Life's A Gas', 'Dreamy Lady', 'London Boys', 'Hot Love', 'Get It On'

"New and improved. Born to boogie or born to waltz? The star of an ageing teen dream had the cheek to book himself into London's Lyceum Ballroom without a support band and expect to fill the place ... Marc Bolan had the nerve and pulled it off. Although T. Rex didn't pack out this sleazy old dance hall, should many more people have arrived, things would have grown mighty uncomfortable.

... T. Rex came in for so much stick back in 1971 to 72 and the glitter kid answered it all with such bare faced ludicrous panache that all normal grounds of criticism are invalidated. There is no way you can knock Marc Bolan for what he does. After all T. Rex were a great pop band. 'Telegram Sam' and 'Metal Guru' were derivative perhaps ... (but) every song was Bolan's and no one else's which is more than you can say for (others) ...

... Marc Bolan isn't quite as flash as he used to be, though the red rhinestone suit and the bleached streaked hair were as loud as his five-piece band. His voice is slipping too ... he cracked somewhat embarrassingly during solo acoustic versions of 'Debora', 'One Inch Rock' and 'Ride A White Swan'. The old Bolan magic circle warble's wearing a little thin after all these years ...

Running through the old hits like this, Marc Bolan won't come back. The crown was lost years ago and I don't think he'll get it back."

NME

"I met a true love at a T. Rex concert, so he has a special affection. At that time he was assaulting America, expecting everybody to cream without working for it, and nobody did. Last Wednesday at the Lyceum was our first meeting since then.

The band now comprises Dino Dines, Steve Currie, Davey Lutton, Gloria Jones and Tyrone Scott. The latter two are providing some excellent vocalising. They play well, a pumping rhythm machine, but then T. Rex was the original seventies rhythm machine.

They have a great slapping drum sound and a booming bass, and Marc's amalgamation of Chuck Berry and Bo Diddley and other classic early riffs fits well within it. Unfortunately, this leaves the organ to fill in most of the non-rhythmic textures, and just isn't strong enough to succeed.

It took until 'Jeepster', the second song, for the bopping elf to take over and it was great. T. Rex is now down to the hard-core fans for an audience; if they are to grow again they need to attract 'serious' rock fans, which means playing by the rules of that game.

To a large extent they did this. Bolan has an undeniable charisma, and on stage expends a lot of energy; combined with the strengths of the band it has the makings of quite a show.

But where T. Rex should be playing their current compositions, especially when there are thirteen of them on his latest album, he devoted a large portion of the set to a trip down memory lane. Within that context though, 'Children Of The Revolution' and 'Teenage Dream' (which should have been a huge hit) were excellent, and 'Solid Gold Easy Action' made the single sound like a demo in comparison.

All through those songs, and even today, T. Rex has never lost its innocence. While Lou Reed is busy inspecting the subway of his veins, Marc is singing about girls with frogs in their hands.

And yet the person singing these fairy tales looks ... debauched, perfect fodder for any number of Dorian Gray inspired fantasies. And bopping across the stage the way Marc does ... it looked great, but it didn't feel right.

What it signified, I'm not sure but while most of the business people there looked under sufferance, there were, count 'em, seven photographers ... angling for space at the front of the stage. Marc obliged them wonderfully."

John Ingham, Sounds

"There was a time when Marc Bolan was the absolute darling of an audience entranced completely by the glamour and jive of his music and personality ...

Then he started to take himself seriously and his decline became inevitable.

His arrogance and ambition far outstripped his talent either as a musician or a composer and after the initial flash of success he revealed no great originality or imagination. Nay, as panic superseded confidence, he began to seem a grotesque parody of himself.

Marc Bolan played London's Lyceum Ballroom last Wednesday.

It was the saddest spectacle I've witnessed in years. There were no more than a thousand people there to see him and he paraded himself before them like a faded old tart looking for one final trick before fading into final obscurity.

... It really was all so pathetic. He jerked and grimaced about the stage like an obese puppet, though to be fair, he's lost a little weight recently, posing and poncing through 'Children Of The Revolution and 'Whatever Happened To The Teenage Dream' (sic) and other mediocrities. His band was dismally inept and uninspired and at times he seemed to realise that ... it's virtually all over.

Bolan will never reclaim the audience he's lost to other similarly insignificant talents.

Still, why should he worry? He can still go into cabaret."

Alan Jones, Melody Maker

The band received £3,200 for the concert.

Thursday 19th February

Queensway Hall, Dunstable, Bedfordshire, England

Set list: '20th Century Boy', 'Jeepster', 'Funky London Childhood', 'New York City', 'Solid Gold Easy Action', 'Children Of The Revolution', 'Teenage Dream', 'Telegram Sam', 'Debora', 'One Inch Rock', 'Ride A White Swan', 'Life's A Gas', 'Dreamy Lady', 'London Boys', 'Hot Love', 'Get It On'

The band received £600 for the concert.

Friday 20th February

London Boys / Solid Baby (EMI T. Rex MARC 13)

The single scraped into the charts reaching a high point of 40.

"Mmm, this plastic piece is so grotesque that it's sure to shake up the whole neighbourhood. Slip this horrible record on to your turntable and watch your friends disappear. It's horrible. If you've got the courage, maybe you could have fun with this. Miss-hit."

Caroline Coon, Melody Maker

"Would have been a gas ten years ago, when the lyrics would have struck a chord with any scooter kid bent on mayhem in Margate. Today, it sounds like a lot of energy expended to little effect, although I can never bring myself to dislike anything from Bolan, one of British rock's few true originals."

Alan Lewis, Sounds

Capital Radio Studios, Euston, London, England

Prior to travelling to Bournemouth, Marc went to Capital Radio to be interviewed at 2 p. m.

Winter Gardens, Bournemouth, Hampshire, England

The band received a paltry £250 for the concert.

Saturday 21st February

Broadcast date in the London Weekend Television area of 'Supersonic' featuring the versions of 'London Boys' and 'Telegram Sam' filmed on the 17th February.

Monday 23rd February

Holiday Inn, Birmingham, Warwickshire, England

Marc was interviewed by journalist Brian Hancocks. See entry for 13th February.

At 4 p.m. Marc was interviewed at his hotel for BRMB radio. The interview went out live. While being interviewed on air he invited Roy Wood along to that night's show.

TOWN HALL, BIRMINGHAM

DEREK BLOCK presents

T. REX

IN CONCERT — *Special Guests*

LENNIE MACDONALD BAND

MONDAY, 23rd FEBRUARY, 1976,
at 1930 hours

UPPER GALLERY £2.00

B 30

PLEASE RETAIN

LATECOMERS will not be admitted until a convenient break in the programme. Tickets cannot be exchanged or money refunded.

Town Hall, Birmingham, Warwickshire, England
Set list: '20th Century Boy', 'Jeepster', 'Funky London Childhood', 'New York City', 'Solid Gold Easy Action', 'Children Of The Revolution', 'Teenage Dream', 'Telegram Sam', 'Debora', 'One Inch Rock', 'Ride A White Swan', 'Life's A Gas', 'Dreamy Lady', 'London Boys', 'Hot Love', 'Get It On'
The band received £1,945 for the concert, staying overnight at the Holiday Inn.

Tuesday 24th February

FTH
An appointment was scheduled for 2 p.m. for the above. No further information is available to what this may refer to.

Piccadilly Radio Studios, Manchester, Lancashire, England
An interview was scheduled for 2.30 at the above radio station.

Free Trade Hall, Manchester, Lancashire, England
The band received £1532 for the concert. After the show the tour party returned to London.

Thursday 26th February

Granada Television Studios, Manchester, Lancashire, England
Marc, along with Gloria Jones, was present at Granada Television Studios from 9 a.m. for a performance on the programme 'Granada Reports'. Recording of the programme commenced at 1.45 p.m. and finished at 5.30 p.m. The programme was broadcast at 6 p.m. Marc was scheduled to perform two songs, though no details could be located as to which material he performed.

Saturday 28th February

Floral Hall Pavilion, Winter Gardens, New Brighton, Wirral, England
The band received £904 for the concert. After the show the band stayed at the Liverpool Centre Hotel.

Sunday 29th February

The tour party travelled to Glasgow to stay at the Pond Hotel, which became its base for the remainder of the tour.

Monday 1st March

Clyde Radio Studios, Glasgow, Strathclyde, Scotland
Marc was scheduled to be at the above radio station at 1 p.m. for an interview.

Apollo Theatre, Glasgow, Strathclyde, Scotland
The band received £1657 for the concert.

Tuesday 2nd March

This day was scheduled as a day off from the tour.

Wednesday 3rd March

Radio Forth Studios, Edinburgh, Central Scotland, Scotland
Another radio interview timed for 1 p.m. was scheduled at the above radio station.

Municipal Hall, Falkirk, Central Scotland, Scotland
The band received £300 for the concert.

Thursday 4th March
Concert Hall, Civic Centre, Motherwell, Strathclyde, Scotland
The band received £318 for the performance.

Friday 5th March
Scottish Television Studios, Glasgow, Strathclyde, Scotland
Marc was due to be collected by Ed Cookson and taken to Scottish Television Studios at 11 a.m. for a performance on an unidentified television programme. It's possible that this involved an acoustic performance. No further details.

Saturday 6th March
Grand Hall, Kilmarnock, Ayrshire, Scotland
This concert was cancelled. The official reason given was "illness". However, the fact that a mere £187.60 had been taken in advance ticket sales hints at the true nature of the cancellation.

Wednesday 10th March
BBC Television Centre, Wood Lane, Shepherd's Bush, London, England
Only one performance of 'London Boys' was recorded for 'Top Of The Pops'. This was shown on the 11th March edition of the show.

Thursday 11th March
Transmission of the performance of 'London Boys' recorded for 'Top Of The Pops' (BBC 1). See entry for 10th March.

Saturday 20th March
Butts Shopping Centre, Reading, Berkshire, England
A personal appearance by Marc and Gloria in the afternoon, where they signed copies of the 'Futuristic Dragon' album.
Radio 210 Thames Valley Radio Studios, Calcot, Berkshire, England
Following the appearance at Butts Shopping Centre, Marc and Gloria went on to the above radio studios where they were interviewed by Steve Wright. During the programme Marc recited the lyrics to 'Futuristic Dragon (Introduction)'. In addition to the interview, Marc and Gloria recorded a special acoustic session which featured a total of five songs: 'Teenager In Love', 'Dreamy Lady', 'New York City', 'Hot Love' and 'Get It On'. The last three songs were performed as a medley. The session was aired later that evening on Steve Wright's programme 'Radio 210 Club'. A jingle for the radio station was also recorded.

Saturday 27th March
A T. Rex performance was possibly broadcast on 'Supersonic' on this date. No further information.

Sunday 28th March
Capital Radio, Euston, London, England
T. Rex appeared on the 'Hullabaloo' afternoon show for a second time. The show was broadcast live. Marc was once again interviewed by Maggie Norden and this time T. Rex performed live in a Capital Radio studio. Gloria Jones and Tyrone Scott did not take part in the perform-

ince. Backing vocals were supplied by Miquele Brown. Five songs were performed: 'London Boys', 'Funky London Childhood', 'Dreamy Lady', 'Teenager In Love' and 'New York City'. Dreamy Lady' and 'Teenager In Love' were performed as on the tour – acoustic with light backing from the band.

Friday 2nd April
Granada Television Studios, Manchester, Lancashire, England
Marc appears on 'Granada Report', the 6 p.m. local evening news show.
Get It On (Part One) / Get It On (Part Two) (EMI 2437)
Release date for the long talked about Gloria Jones solo single which Marc produced. Despite getting good reviews, the single failed to sell.

"Gloria Jones' 'Get It On', yes Marc Bolan inspired, penned and produced, is so frenetic and fast, it's frightening. It's exhausting enough to hear, let alone dance to. But youth will of course...".

Caroline Coon, Melody Maker

"Did I say the Tina Charles number was fast? Mrs. Bolan performing a Mr. Bolan hit could catch the Concorde. I can just see her shaking that thing and I'm getting quite excited. Also, I like the record."

Phil Sutcliffe, Sounds

Sunday 4th April
Radio Orwell, Ipswich, Suffolk, England
Bolan and Gloria Jones appeared on the show 'Solid Gold Sunday', being interviewed by presenter Keith Rogers who also played a selection of John's Children, Tyrannosaurus Rex and T. Rex records.

Saturday 10th April
London Weekend Television Studios, Kent House, Southbank, London, England
Marc appeared on LWT's 'Saturday Scene' programme. He was interviewed by Sally James. The show was probably broadcast live.

Tuesday 20th April
A session for London's Capital Radio was scheduled for this date. The booking was cancelled.

Saturday 24th April
Marc flies to Helsinki to attend David Bowie's show and to join the Bowie tour entourage for the subsequent Scandinavian dates.

Thursday 29th April
Marc flies out of Stockholm after attending Bowie's show at the Kungliga Tennishallen and returns to London.

Saturday 1st May
Decibel Studios, Stamford Hill, London, England
Recording session which resulted in versions of 'I Believe' and 'Pain And Love'.

Monday 3rd May
Empire Pool, Wembley, Middlesex, England
Marc and Gloria attend David Bowie's concert at the above venue.

Saturday 8th May
Air Studios, 214 Oxford Street, London, England
A tape containing the Gloria Jones version of 'Sailors Of The Highway' was made on this date. It's probable that this was the result of a mixing session, though there may have been some overdubbing of the song.

Tuesday 18th May
Decibel Studios, Stamford Hill, London, England
Recording session which produced three takes of 'Pain And Love'.

May
Decibel Studios, Stamford Hill, London, England
Recording session which produced 'I Love To Boogie'. Initially this track was intended to be just a demo.

Tuesday 1st June
Air Studios, 214 Oxford Street, London, England
Master mixes of 'Love Is Here To Stay', 'Lovin' You', 'Funky London Childhood' and 'London Boys' were made on this day. The first two songs are Richard Jones tracks, produced by Marc. The final song, 'London Boys' may be an alternate version or a remix.

Thursday 3rd June
Air Studios, 214 Oxford Street, London, England
A tape containing three takes of the Gloria Jones track 'Would You Like To Know' was produced on this date.

Friday 4th June
I Love To Boogie / Baby Boomerang (EMI T. Rex MARC 14)
The most successful of the latter T. Rex singles reached a high point of 13 in the charts.

"So it's we love T. Rex time again. Well, well. "Belinda Mae Fender's got a ...", rasps Marc, done right up, if not totally spangled. Very free key, but 'I Love To Boogie' is a must for all high fliers. A hit. After T. Rex though, playing The Beach Boys' 'Good Vibrations' is like staggering out of a brothel into a gaggle of choirboys on their way to matins. A jolting clash of purity and the profane."

Caroline Coon, Melody Maker

"From the new Valentino Bolan, a kind of restrained cross between hey-day Mungo Jerry and the man's own version of Eddie Cochran's 'Summertime Blues' ... The time is right, I reckon, for a Bolan revival ... 'I Love To Boogie', which also has its 'One Inch Rock' links and could well be the resounding summer hit of 76, is wonderfully basic, revolving as it does around the minimal words "I love to boogie, jitterbug boogie on a Saturday night." Hasn't quite got the cataclysmical lyrical poignancy of the frog in her hand line of the recent 'New York City' single, however, but – the B side of this one is 'Baby Boomerang', a 1972 song, from 'The Slider' no less. Why no new tune, Marc? Huh?"

Geoff Barton, Sounds

"... 'I Love To Boogie' (is) terminally vapid, totally devoid of hooks and cursed with a production as flimsy as a wet Kleenex."

Charles Shaar Murray, NME

Saturday 5th June

Air Studios, 214 Oxford Street, London, England
The Gloria Jones tracks 'Drive You Crazy (Disco Lady)' (the title on the tape box) and 'Would You Like To Know' were (probably) mixed on this date.

Monday 7th June

Air Studios, 214 Oxford Street, London, England
Gloria Jones' version of 'Tell Me' was mixed on this date. Further overdubs were also done to the backing track of 'Universe'.

Tuesday 15th June

Hammersmith Odeon, Hammersmith, London, England
Gloria Jones supports Bob Marley And The Wailers at the above venue. Marc attended the concert.

Wednesday 16th June

BBC Television Centre, Wood Lane, Shepherd's Bush, London, England
The first television recording of 'I Love To Boogie' for BBC Television's 'Top Of The Pops' was a live performance and was broadcast on 17th June. It marked the debut of Miller Anderson as second guitar player. Anderson had been hired because Bolan was supposedly not confident about performing live unaccompanied on the show.
Hammersmith Odeon, Hammersmith, London, England
Gloria Jones supports Bob Marley And The Wailers at the above venue for a second night. Marc attended the show.

Thursday 17th June

Broadcast date for the first version of 'I Love To Boogie' recorded for 'Top Of The Pops' (BBC 1). See entry for 16th June.

Saturday 19th June

Ninian Park, Cardiff, Glamorgan, Wales
Marc attends the Ninian Park rock festival, where Gloria is supporting Bob Marley And The Wailers among others. He is later photographed at the event with Robert Plant.

Sunday 27th June

Belle Vue, Manchester, Lancashire, England
Marc attends the Bob Marley And The Wailers concert. Gloria Jones is support act along with Gonzales.

Monday 28th June
Radio Luxembourg Studios, London, England
An interview to promote 'I Love To Boogie' was broadcast live on this date.

Wednesday 30th June
BBC Television Centre, Wood Lane, Shepherd's Bush, London, England
A second live performance of 'I Love To Boogie' was recorded for 'Top Of The Pops' on this date. It was transmitted on 1st July.

Thursday 1st July
Transmission date for the second version of 'I Love To Boogie' recorded for 'Top Of The Pops' (BBC 1). See entry for 30th June.

Friday 2nd July
BBC Radio Studios, Broadcasting House, London, England
Marc guested on 'Rosko's Roundtable', a show devoted to reviewing the new record releases. The programme was broadcast live. Afterwards he went on to a party at Selfridge's Hotel held in honour of EMI A&R man Roy Featherstone who was moving on to become Managing Director of MCA.

Tuesday 13th July
Wimbledon Theatre, Wimbledon, London, England
Set list: 'I Love To Boogie', 'Funky London Childhood', 'Soul Of My Suit', 'New York City', 'Laser Love'
Support came from AC/DC and Leapy Lee.
In a special concert recorded for television, Marc and T. Rex performed multiple takes of the five-song set. Many of these takes broke down due to instruments going out of tune because of the extra lighting required for the television production, or because of sound problems. The resulting footage was then edited down for a 'Supersonic' special entitled 'Rollin' Bolan'. The programme was transmitted on ITV networks on 28th August.

Friday 16th July
Decibel Studios, Stamford Hill, London, England
Recording session which produced three takes of 'Laser Love' and one of 'Life's An Elevator'.

Sunday 18th July
Ritz Ballroom, Manchester, Lancashire, England
Marc attends the Gloria Jones and Gonzales concert at the above venue.

Monday 19th July
Air Studios, 214 Oxford Street, London, England
A Gloria Jones demo session was recorded on this date. Two solo piano demos, 'Cry Baby' and 'Freedom Is All I Know' were committed to tape.

Saturday 24th July
Air Studios, 214 Oxford Street, London, England
Recording session which produced a retake of 'Laser Love'.

Tuesday 27th July
Air Studios, 214 Oxford Street, London, England
Gloria Jones' version of 'Sailors Of The Highway' had some additional work done to it at this session. The tape box suggests that this involved the overdubbing of the piano track.

July
Radio Luxembourg Studios, London, England
Marc was interviewed by Ken Evans about his star sign for 'The Valderma Stars Horoscope Show'.

Monday 2nd August
Marc flew to Los Angeles for a holiday and then recording sessions.

Tuesday 24th August
MRI Studios, 1680 North Sycamore Avenue, Hollywood, California, USA
Three Richard Jones tracks, 'Straight It Up', 'Oblivion' and 'Love Was Here' were recorded on this day. Marc is credited as producer on the tape box.

Saturday 28th August
Transmission date for the 'Supersonic' special 'Rollin' Bolan' on ITV networks. See entry for 13th July.

Sunday 5th September
Marc returns to London from Los Angeles.

Friday 17th September
Laser Love / Life's An Elevator (EMI T. Rex MARC 15)
Release date for the above single which disappointingly only reached number 41 in the charts.

"Didn't Marc Bolan already make this record? I beg your pardon. This is Marc Bolan Boogie D Variation 312. Boles is a star just like Gloria Swanson is a star, but the recorded evidence is becoming more and more irrelevant to that fact."

Angie Errigo, NME

"Schizophrenic blend of standard Bolan instant smash as in 'Get It On', 'Telegram Sam' and the rest – and mid-Sixties rockola ... should make it sooner or later. Don't knock him, he's an original."

Susanne Garrett, Sounds

Saturday 25th September
London Weekend Television Studios, Kent House, Southbank, London, England
Marc appears on 'Saturday Scene' where he is interviewed by Sally James.

September
It's announced that Steve Currie and Davey Lutton have left T. Rex. Their replacements are top session musicians Herbie Flowers and Tony Newman on bass and drums respectively.

September
Marc and Gloria move to 142 Upper Richmond Road, East Sheen, London.

Tuesday 5th October
London Weekend Television Studios, Kent House, Southbank, London, England
Marc appears solo on 'Supersonic' performing kitsch versions of 'Laser Love' and 'Ride A White Swan'. The programme is transmitted on 16th October. 'Laser Love' showed slight differences from the record while 'Ride A White Swan' was a totally new version of the song.

Wednesday 6th October
BBC Television Centre, Wood Lane, Shepherd's Bush, London, England
The only 'Top Of The Pops' performance of 'Laser Love' was recorded on this date and transmitted on 7th October. The new line up of T. Rex made their public debut. The performance of the song showed some minor differences in the mix from that of the record version.

Thursday 7th October
Transmission date on BBC 1 for the edition of 'Top Of The Pops' featuring T. Rex performing 'Laser Love'. See entry for 6th October.

Thursday 14th October
Air Studios, 214 Oxford Street, London, England
Recording and / or mixing session which produced versions of 'Jason B. Sad', 'Hang-Ups', two takes of 'I'm A Fool For You Girl', 'Universe' and 'Laser Love'. Most likely the tape produced on this date is a composite of earlier recording sessions and was for Marc to review tracks for the forthcoming album. 'Hang -Ups' is the master version and 'Jason B. Sad' is likely to be too.

Saturday 16th October
Transmission date for the versions of 'Laser Love' and 'Ride A White Swan' recorded for 'Supersonic' (ITV). See entry for 5th October.

On the same day Marc conducted a telephone interview with Steve Wright for Radio 210 Thames Valley during which he mentioned writing 'Dandy In The Underworld' that day and performing on 'Supersonic' including an aborted plan for him to perform live with Slik.

Thursday 21st October (?)
Granada Television Studios, Manchester, Lancashire, England
Further promotion for 'Laser Love' included an appearance on the Granada produced programme 'The Arrows', another children's late afternoon pop music programme. The performance featured a slightly different version of the song. The appearance was broadcast on 2nd November.

Wednesday 27th October
Air Studios, 214 Oxford Street, London, England
Date for recording session which propably produced the basic tracks for 'To Know You Is To Love You' and 'Tame My Tiger'.

Tuesday 2nd November

Transmission date on ITV networks of the performance of 'Laser Love' recorded for 'The Arrows'. See entry for 21st October.

Wednesday 3rd November

Air Studios, 214 Oxford Street, London, England

Recording session which produced outtake versions of 'Dandy In The Underworld' and the basic track of 'Crimson Moon'.

Thursday 4th November

Trident Studios, St. Anne's Court, Soho, London, England

"Love And Pain" (the title on the tape box) and 'Teen Riot Structure' recorded. A second tape box indicates that 'Teen Riot Structure', 'Blues', 'Groove A Little' and 'Punk No.2' were recorded. It's possible that 'Blues' or 'Punk No.2' could be 'Pain And Love' under another title. It's also possible that the second tape boxes contains mixes only.

Monday 15th November–Friday 19th November

Air Studios, 214 Oxford Street, London, England

A block of studio sessions which produced material for 'Dandy In The Underworld'. Sessions were held every day of this particular week.

Friday 19th November

Air Studios, 214 Oxford Street, London, England

Date for a session which produced further work on 'To Know You Is To Love You' and 'Tame My Tiger'.

Tuesday 23rd November

Trident Studios, St. Anne's Court, Soho, London, England

Recording session for the album version of 'Groove A Little' (listed as 'Punkoid' on the tape box).

November (?)

Air Studios, 214 Oxford Street, London, England

A session which saw Marc recutting the vocals for 'Dandy In The Underworld', 'Groove A Little' and 'Jason B. Sad'. This could be part of the 15th–19th November block.

Friday 3rd December

Vixen (EMI EMC 3159)

'I Ain't Going Nowhere', 'High', 'Tell Me Now', 'Tainted Love', 'Cry Baby', 'Get It On (Part One)', 'Go Now', 'Would You Like To Know', 'Get It On (Part Two)', 'Drive Me Crazy (Disco Lady)', 'Sailors Of The Highway', 'Stagecoach'.

Marc Bolan – guitar; Steve Currie – bass; Bill Legend – drums; Davey Lutton – drums; Dino Dines – keyboards; Wayne Douglas – bass ('Tell Me Now'); Ed Green – drums ('Cry Baby'); Paul Humphrey – drums; Ollie Brown – drums ('Get It On (Part 1)); Scott Edwards – bass; Sylvester Rivers – keyboards; Ray Parker – guitar; Sugar Bear – guitar; Sisters Love – backing vocals; Tyrone Scott – backing vocals; Anwar – backing vocals plus members of Gonzales. Recorded at MRI Studios, Hollywood CA and Scorpio Sound, London ('Tainted Love' and 'Go Now'). Produced by Marc Bolan and Gloria Jones.

"Fine British debut album from Mr. Bolan's old lady – and there's more than a few T. Rex influences. Gloria sounds remarkably like Aretha Franklin on 'I Ain't Going Nowhere'. On 'High' you can tell that Marc was at the controls and there's a weird distorted guitar in the background ... 'Tell Me Now' is a curious mixture of Bolan and soul, but strangely successful. Ms Jones is a talented lady – I bet Marc's proud."

Robin Smith, Record Mirror

"Quite a spirited album from Gloria Jones, co-produced by her paramour Marc Bolan. Good value for the length of twelve tracks, but the material isn't strong enough to sustain interest... there is nothing here as convincing as the songs Gloria co-wrote for Tamla Motown, notably with Pam Sawyer. Vocally, side one captures her nearer her best."

Anonymous, Melody Maker

Tuesday 7th December (?)
Air Studios, 214 Oxford Street, London, England
One session, held on a Tuesday in December saw Marc recording a link for 'I'm A Fool For You Girl'. This is the most likely date.

Friday 10th December
Air Studios, 214 Oxford Street, London, England
A tape containing master mixes of 'Groove A Little', 'Soul Of My Suit' and 'Universe' was produced on this date.

Saturday 18th December
A thirty-second pre-recorded Christmas message was broadcast on London Weekend Television's 'Saturday Scene'.

Sunday 19th December
The Royal Theatre, Drury Lane, London, England
A special live slot was recorded for 'Christmas Supersonic' which was broadcast one week later on 25th December. The concert was for charity and in the presence of Princess Margaret. It also featured the comeback (the first of many) of Gary Glitter who had taken a short retirement.

Three songs were performed at the concert, 'I Love To Boogie', 'Soul Of My Suit' and 'New York City'. Only 'New York City' was included in the final programme, which was just as well as 'Soul Of My Suit' was a bit of a disaster and 'New York City' featured an out of tune guitar – not Miller Anderson's. The show concluded with an all-star finale including Bolan singing "We Wish You A Merry Christmas".

Tuesday 21st December
Olympia, Kensington, London, England
Marc and Gloria attended the opening night of Rod Stewart's stint at Olympia and the after show party.

Thursday 23rd December
Marc and Jeff Dexter arrive in Paris to prepare for an appearance on French television.

Friday 24th December
Unconfirmed Television Studio, Paris, France

Marc appeared live on the French programme 'La Nuit de Noël de Graziella'. This was a programme which was broadcast live from 9.30 p.m. to 1.30 a.m. The programme was divided into several sections. Marc appeared in the section entitled 'Une Viellee de Noël'. This section was transmitted close to the end of the programme, early in the morning of 25th December. The whole show was broadcast on French Television Antenne 2.

Two songs, 'I Love To Boogie' and 'Laser Love' were definitely performed, however it's possible that Marc performed a further two songs. Marc sang live over pre-recorded backing tracks.

Marc had spent the morning rehearsing for the programme. However the live transmission of the show was rather unfortunate for Marc. He was supposed to rise up from under the stage on a platform. The platform got stuck and under the cover of dry ice studio technicians had to help Marc out of his predicament, damaging his shoulder in the process.

Saturday 25th December
Broadcast date for 'Christmas Supersonic' recorded at the Royal Theatre in Drury Lane.

Sunday 26th December
Marc and Jeff Dexter fly back to England.

1977

1977 was the year of the "big comeback". Bolan enjoyed significantly increased media profile. The 'Dandy In The Underworld' album garnered respectable reviews and healthier sales than the preceding two albums. The band completed a successful tour of Britain, which also received favourable reviews. The reverse side to this was that sales of the singles released that year were poor, with only 'Soul Of My Suit' grazing the top 40. And then there was the television series 'Marc'. A camp, kitsch classic or crap? You decide.

In preparation for a major British tour, T. Rex played a short series of club dates in France. For the British tour the band was tight and solid and possibly the best T. Rex line-up. Though it may have lacked the charisma of the classic 1972 line-up, it was a significantly tighter and more professional unit than any that had preceded it.

Sadly, its potential was, to an extent wasted. Following the March dates, T. Rex only performed one further concert date, in Stockholm. Rather than take the band out on the road, to Germany and possibly back to the USA, Bolan decided to concentrate a lot of time appearing on children's television programmes. Great live performances of 'Soul Of My Suit' and 'Dandy In The Underworld' were wasted on shows like 'Supersonic' and 'Get It Together'. These were largely ignored by the very audience Bolan needed to reclaim. The question has to be asked why T. Rex were not appearing on more "serious" music shows such as 'The Old Grey Whistle Test' and 'So It Goes'.

The lack of live work and the decision not to play live on the 'Marc' series caused some tension within the band with Miller Anderson opting to leave, allegedly on a temporary basis. Anderson was a working musician, who preferred to be out on the road playing live. He wasn't interested in miming on a children's television show and, to an extent, he was right.

A second British tour was planned for the autumn of 1977, along with dates in Germany in the spring of 1978. Sadly, these plans were never to be realised. Had they happened there would have been at least another change to the T. Rex line-up. Due to other commitments, Herbie Flowers would have been absent from the band because of previous commitments. In his place, Marc had offered the bass spot to Adrian Shaw of Hawkwind.

Wednesday 12th January
Marc and party travel to Stuttgart.

Thursday 13th January
Suddeutscher Rundfunk, Stuttgart, West Germany
Rehearsal for the SF Stuttgart/WDR Köln co-produced television programme 'Hit Kwiss'.

Friday 14th January
To Know You Is To Love You / City Port (EMI 2572)

Issued as a Marc Bolan and Gloria Jones single and not a T. Rex one. The single didn't appear on the EMI T. Rex label but on the standard EMI label. It also failed to make the charts.

"Marc and Gloria duet on the old Teddy Bears hit ... and fairly innocuous it is too ... things are kept very straight production / arrangement wise. Marc's vocals sound so nasal it could be someone sending him up. Otherwise it's entirely unoffensive ...".

Steve Clarke, NME

"A good idea which doesn't make it because the production is such a mess. Somebody's singing in the wrong key ... This is less a duet than Marc sounding as if he's singing to himself, about himself, naturally, with an ordinary back-up vocalist."

Caroline Coon, Melody Maker

Suddeutscher Rundfunk, Stuttgart, West Germany
Two songs were "performed" for the 'Hit Kwiss' programme: 'Laser Love' and 'Get It On'. The T. Rex line-up consisted of Marc on guitar and vocals, Miller Anderson on bass, Dino Dines on keyboards and an unknown idiot on drums. Both songs were mimed performances. The band was paid a total of DM 3,000 for the performance, plus a further DM 1,000 for hotel expenses. The programme was shown on the ARD network in West Germany on 20th January.

Thursday 20th January
German transmission on the ARD networked SDR of 'Hit Kwiss' featuring 'Laser Love' and 'Get It On'. See earlier entry.

Sunday 23rd January
Air Studios, 214 Oxford Street, London, England
Recording session. Details of what work was done remains unconfirmed.

Tuesday 1st February
London Weekend Television Studios, Kent House, Southbank, London, England
To promote 'To Know You Is To Love You', Marc and Gloria appeared on 'Supersonic'. Though their performance was mimed, the backing track was a different version of the song. In addition Marc recorded a lip-synch mimed version of 'Crimson Moon' which featured a different mix of the song to that included on 'Dandy In The Underworld. Both songs were broadcast on 12th February.

FRENCH TOUR
Originally the tour was planned to consist of eight dates. Some of these were cancelled and replaced by others. Other venues were switched at the last minute.

Wednesday 2nd February
Marc and Tony Howard flew from London to Paris.
Unknown television studio, Paris, France
Marc appeared live on 'Un sur Cinq' on French Antenne 2. The show was broadcast live from

— 231 —

3.50 p.m. with Marc probably appearing around about 6 p.m. in the evening. He appeared, without the band, miming solo to 'Telegram Sam' and 'I Love To Boogie'.

It's likely that the crew arrived in Bordeaux on this day.

Thursday 3rd February

Le Macumba, Vigneux de Bretagne, Nantes, France

Set list: 'Jeepster', 'Visions Of Domino', 'New York City', 'Soul Of My Suit', 'Groove A Little', 'Telegram Sam', 'Hang-Ups', 'I Love To Boogie', 'Dandy In The Underworld', 'Hot Love', 'Get It On'

After the concert the band stayed at the Sofitel hotel in Nantes.

Friday 4th February

Le Macumba, Merignac, Bordeaux, France

After the concert the band stayed at the Novotel Merignac.

Saturday 5th February

Palais des Sports, La Halle Aux Grains, Toulouse, France

The band stayed at the Mercure-Toulouse hotel.

Sunday 6th February

The band and road crew drive from Toulouse to Pau, stating at the Novotel in Lescar.

Monday 7th February

Parc Beaumont, Casino Municipal, Pau, France

Tuesday 8th February

A concert was originally scheduled for an unconfirmed venue in Besançon. In the event Marc flew first to Paris before travelling on to Frankfurt. He was met at Frankfurt airport by Evelyn Hinkel, and from there he continued his journey, by train, to Baden-Baden to meet up with Gloria Jones for a performance on German television.

The band drove from Paris to Nimes.

Wednesday 9th February

Palais d'Hiver, Villeursanne, Lyon, France

The band drove from Nimes to Lyon. However, this concert was cancelled. The official reason was that Marc was "ill". In fact he was still in Baden-Baden.

Thursday 10th February

Hall 19, Palais des Congres, Dijon, France

This concert was cancelled. The band stayed overnight in Paris at the Hotel Nord et l'Est.

Friday 11th February

Marc, possibly accompanied by Gloria Jones, flew from Stuttgart to Paris to meet up with the other members of T. Rex for that night's concert.

Le Nashville, Paris, France

Set list: 'Jeepster', 'Visions Of Domino', 'New York City', 'Groove A Little', 'Soul Of My Suit', 'I Love To Boogie', 'Hang-Ups', 'Hot Love', 'Get It On'

The concert was originally scheduled for Le Bataclan, but due to a problem with ticket prices, it was switched to Le Nashville.

That afternoon, Marc and Jeff Dexter visited the Paris Olympia theatre to watch a Johnny Halliday rehearsal.

Marc stayed at the Hotel d'Isley.

Saturday 12th February

Broadcast date for 'Supersonic' on ITV networks for the edition of 'Supersonic' featuring 'To Know You Is To Love You' and 'Crimson Moon'. See entry for 1st February.

The Empire, Paris, France

A rehearsal for a forthcoming television appearance was scheduled for 1.30 in the afternoon at the above venue.

Salles Omnisport, La Salle Des Fetes, Troarn, Caen, France

Set list: 'Jeepster', 'Visions Of Domino', 'New York City', 'Groove A Little', 'Soul Of My Suit', 'I Love To Boogie', 'Hang-Ups', 'Hot Love', 'Dandy In The Underworld', 'Get It On'

After the concert the tour party stayed at the Novotel in Caen.

Sunday 13th February

Marc and Jeff Dexter travelled by car from Caen to Paris. The band travelled from Caen to Dieppe and then caught the ferry to Newhaven in England.

The Empire, Paris, France

At 3 p.m. Marc was due to be at the above venue. Whether this was for another rehearsal or recording is not known. However, see the next entry. Marc again stayed at the Hotel d'Isley.

Monday 14th February

Unconfirmed Television Studio, Paris, France

Marc and Gloria Jones recorded a performance of 'To Know Him Is To Love Him' for a French television show. No further details as to the name of the show. The programme was broadcast on 24th February and repeated on 2nd March.

Monday 24th February

Broadcast on French television of a performance of 'To Know Him Is To Love Him'. See previous entry.

Wednesday 2nd March,

The Roxy, Neal Street, Covent Garden, London, England

The release party for 'Dandy In The Underworld' was held at the above club, largely known as London's premier punk club. Among the guests were Paul and Linda McCartney, Alvin Stardust, Donovan, Sex Pistols, Billy Idol and The Damned.

In France there was a repeat broadcast of the version of 'To Know Him Is To Love Him' that had been recorded on 14th February.

'DANDY IN THE UNDERWORLD' BRITISH TOUR

The 'Dandy In The Underworld' tour was a more concise affair than the previous year's

shop poster

'Futuristic Dragon' series of dates. Marc had made much of being the 'Godfather Of Punk' and to highlight these credentials he chose The Damned, then one of the hottest bands on the punk scene, to be support act.

For the first time since 1974's North American tour Bolan actively promoted the new album, playing several songs from 'Dandy In The Underworld'. A selection of the older hits still provided a large chunk of the setlist, but many old favourites were dropped from the repertoire.

Unlike many previous T. Rex line-ups, this particular one was a solid, punchy, disciplined outfit. In the past, songs would often wander off into extended jams, with Marc soloing away, and everybody else seemingly unsure of what they were supposed to be doing. For these dates everything was kept tight. Marc only took extended guitar breaks on two songs, 'Hang-Ups' and 'Get It On'. On other songs, such as 'Soul Of My Suit', Marc and Miller Anderson played some neat dual guitar work, often with Anderson taking the more dominant role. The songs were also kept to relatively brief lengths, except for the traditional 'Get It On' workout.

Thursday 10th March

City Hall, Newcastle, England

Set list: 'Jeepster', 'Visions Of Domino', 'New York City', 'Soul Of My Suit', 'Groove A Little', 'Telegram Sam', 'Hang-Ups', 'Debora', 'I Love To Boogie', 'Teen Riot Structure', 'Dandy In The Underworld', 'Hot Love', 'Get It On'

"I had just seen Marc Bolan at the Lyceum in London almost a year ago ... It really was a sad and desperate performance ... He was a mere counterfeit of his old flamboyant image ... He even forgot the lyric of 'Debora'.

Bolan, however, is nothing if not resilient, and a year later, his ego still monstrously intact, he's laying it all down at Newcastle City Hall ... much of the old zip and rush has been restored and is further encouraged by the enthusiastic support of the faithful ...

... off they get to the opening strains of 'Jeepster'. Hell, it still sounds great, even to these jaded ears.

Bolan's entire attitude is more decisive than it was at that last Lyceum catastrophe ... Even if he cannot fully persuade his critics of his regeneration as an artist, he has at least convinced himself. Let's hear it for the band too ... These musicians may not be challenged by the simplistic imperatives of Bolan's compositions, but they are committed professionals, ruthless and exact. There's no lack of conviction in their playing nor excitement in their performance ...

Bolan, it transpires, has not been unaware of recent developments in rock and roll ... He'd probably argue he was a direct predecessor of the current punk stance of cheek and arrogance ... and he may have a point. But what's this? I swear Marc's been delving into The Stooges' repertoire for some of his current licks and that voice, that phrasing ... he's midway through something called 'Visions Of Domino' and he's beginning to sound like, er, Patti Smith ...

Anyway, this is a minor digression. The majority of the show is pure Bolan hyperbole. A smattering of golden groovers ... interspersed with a couple of new ditties from the forthcoming album 'Dandy In The Underworld', the title track of said platter is a real winner. The set concludes with a euphoric rendition of the vintage 'Hot Love' ... and is crowned by a beezer 'Get It On', which features a fierce instrumental coda. Yeah, I enjoyed it, though I had anticipated disaster ... one has to congratulate the old campaigner for coming through. By the tour's end, he may even have revived popular interest in his music. He even remembered the words to 'Debora'. Things must be looking up."

Allan Jones, Melody Maker

"As these performances by Marc Bolan and The Damned ... proved, it's all... a matter of mind and not age whether you can rock and roll or not ... Bolan, a product of the late sixties rock revolution is no spring chicken anymore. Moreover, he's received a unanimous critical thumbs down for so long now ... one wondered if it wouldn't be best for all of us if he didn't throw in the towel.

But on Thursday ... he was back on form with a clean well-tailored set of old and new material, looking thinner and fitter than he has for ages and backed by an excellent band of mature and highly skilled rock musicians.

Marc ... doesn't give it to the audience all on a plate right from the start, but gradually builds his set, so that by the closing lengthy 'Get It On', the audience is totally infected.

The place isn't quite full and the front of the hall is taken up with Marc's committed fans ... Bolan treats his audience with affection, sings well and plays fine guitar. His solos are well constructed and relatively cliché free. Behind, Miller Anderson duplicates the chord parts ... Tony Newman plays exemplary muscular drums, Herbie Flowers is as highly dextrous as ever on bass and Dino Dines is tasteful on keyboards.

Bolan plays a lot of material from his new album 'Dandy In The Underworld' and, given its limitations, it sounds like the best stuff he's come up with in a long time and the band always play well so that even the lame 'I Love To Boogie' sounds good because of their performance. A thoroughly enjoyable evening ...".

Steve Clarke, NME

"The new improved slim-line Bolan Marc Two pirouetted around the stage ... With his corkscrew hair grown back it was like watching him in his early days. 'Jeepster' burst from the speakers, the new band tight and anchor firm.

The new (numbers) had a harder feel, particularly 'New York City'. It was powered along by Herbie Flowers looking like an ageing skinhead on bass. On to 'Debora' played faster than a speeding bullet and then 'I Love To Boogie' Marc looked relieved that the reaction was so good, and launched into a great guitar solo as in the days of yore. At the end of the set the band were left to their own devices Tony Newman flogging himself to death on drums before Marc waltzed back on stage."

Robin Smith, Record Mirror

Friday 11th March

Dandy In The Underworld (EMI T. Rex BLN 5005)

'Dandy In The Underworld', 'Crimson Moon', 'Universe', 'I'm A Fool For You Girl', 'I Love To Boogie', 'Visions Of Domino', 'Jason B. Sad', 'Groove A Little', 'Soul Of My Suit', 'Hang-Ups', 'Pain And Love', 'Teen Riot Structure'
Marc Bolan – vocals, guitars, bass, percussion; Dino Dines – keyboards; Steve Currie – bass on 'Universe', 'I Love To Boogie', 'Visions Of Domino'; Davey Lutton – drums on 'Universe', 'I Love To Boogie', 'Visions Of Domino'; Herbie Flowers – bass on 'Dandy In The Underworld', 'Crimson Moon', 'Jason B. Sad', 'Groove A Little', 'Soul Of My Suit', 'Hang-Ups' and 'Teen Riot Structure'; Tony Newman – drums on 'Dandy In The Underworld', 'Crimson Moon', 'Jason B. Sad', 'Groove A Little', 'Soul Of My Suit', 'Hang-Ups', 'Pain And Love' and 'Teen Riot Structure'; Miller Anderson – guitar on 'Jason B. Sad'; Scott Edwards – bass on 'I'm A Fool For You Girl'; Paul Humphrey – drums on 'I'm A Fool For You Girl'; Steve Harley – vocals on 'Dandy In The Underworld'; Paul Fenton – drums on 'Visions Of Domino'; Gloria Jones – backing vocals; Colin Jacas – backing vocals; Alfalpha – backing vocals; Chris Mercer – tenor sax; Bud Beadle – baritone sax. There is also a possibility that guitarist Gus Isadore also plays on the album, though he receives no particular song credits.

Recorded at MRI Studios, Los Angeles; Decibel Studios, London; Air Studios, London; Trident Studios, London.

Produced by Marc Bolan. Engineered by Gary Ulmer; Mike Stavrou and others.

Following the return of a more measured critical response, the album peaked at 26 in the charts.

"I saw T. Rex for the first time in eight years last year ... up credibility gulch without a paddle and they were fantastic. On record my acquaintance is also patchy. In 1972 I came to acquire a copy of 'The Slider' and I was amazed to discover that T. Rex played like nobody else has ever played, either before or since. A weird wonderful fantasy that was quite unique ...

I caught up again with T. Rex on 'Futuristic Dragon', last year's messy Bolan produced come-back album. What had once been appealingly simplistic was now trite. The sound an unconventional mix of synthetic rock plus touches of disco and rampaging JCB orchestrations was a quagmire ... Still, it was ambitious and parts of it succeeded.

Ambitious 'Dandy In The Underworld' is not, but it does succeed. He's ditched Gloria Jones... All keyboards are now handled by Dino Dines. Steve Currie and Davey Lutton hung around on bass and drums for 'I Love To Boogie' ... 'Universe' and 'Visions Of Domino', but it's mostly Herbie Flowers and Tony Newman, the session vets now in the stage band. That's the basic line up with contributions from a few others ...

It's a very consistent album, very listenable, well arranged, immaculately played, but it lacks the weirdness and inspiration of 'The Slider', of which it sometimes sounds like a more sensible professional copy.

As his must hit single 'Soul Of My Suit' shows, Marc's voice is as good as ever and his guitar playing, though missing that strangulated spark of yore, is more assured than ever. You can have fun trying to guess who the dandy is – Dylan or Bowie? Bolan presumably ...

As usual there's the odd Bolan mixture of obscurantist philosophising and onomatopoetic gobbledegook, offset by those melodic, even more irrelevant choruses. But something's missing. The pseudo-innocence seems to have been replaced by pseudo-seriousness in places; the fey by the flippant.

Nevertheless, it's a return to form and it's got twelve tracks."

Phil McNeil, NME

Go Now / Drive Me Crazy (Disco Lady) (EMI 2570)

Release date for a second Bolan co-produced Gloria Jones single. (The previous Gloria Jones release had been entirely self-produced). It too failed to achieve any sort of success.

"Gloria, in tandem with her man Marc Bolan, who recently claimed to be the Godfather of Punk ... didn't do a lot to Phil Spector's 'To Know Him Is To Love Him' a couple of months back. Now she's done even less for the old Moody Blues hit ... It's taken slow and Gloria attempts to get soulful, but to no effect. Surely the Godfather of Punk can produce with a little more pizzazz than this?"

Steve Clarke, NME

Apollo Theatre, Manchester, Lancashire, England

Set list: 'Jeepster', 'Visions Of Domino', 'New York City', 'Soul Of My Suit', 'Groove A Little', 'Telegram Sam', 'Hang-Ups', 'Debora', 'I Love To Boogie', 'Teen Riot Structure', 'Dandy In The Underworld', 'Hot Love', 'Get It On'

Saturday 12th March

Apollo Theatre, Glasgow, Strathclyde, Scotland

The Glasgow concert was originally scheduled for this date. However, due to vital equipment being accidentally left behind in Manchester, the concert was rescheduled for the following night.

Sunday 13th March

Hanley Hall, Stoke On Trent,
Staffordshire, England

This concert was cancelled at the last minute so as to accommodate the rearranged Glasgow show.

Apollo Theatre, Glasgow, Strathclyde,
Scotland

Set list: 'Jeepster', 'Visions Of Domino', 'New York City', 'Soul Of My Suit', 'Groove A Little', 'Telegram Sam', 'Hang-Ups', 'Debora', 'I Love To Boogie', 'Teen Riot Structure', 'Dandy In The Underworld', 'Hot Love', 'Get It On'

Monday 14th March

Colston Hall, Bristol, Gloucestershire,
England

Set list: 'Jeepster', 'Visions Of Domino', 'New York City', 'Soul Of My Suit', 'Groove A Little', 'Telegram Sam', 'Hang-Ups', 'Debora', 'I Love To Boogie', 'Teen Riot Structure', 'Dandy In The Underworld', 'Hot Love', 'Get It On'

Tuesday 15th March

London Weekend Television Studios,
Kent House, Southbank, London,
England

Marc was present in the LWT studios while Gloria Jones was recording her performance of 'Go Now' for 'Supersonic'. Donovan visited Marc and Gloria during the recording of the show, though he was not an official programme guest. Two takes were done; the first one had to be stopped midway through the recording due to problems with the sound system. The backing track was a newly recorded one, which included stronger guitar work by Bolan. The performance was a solo one by Gloria. Neither Bolan nor Donovan joined her on stage. The final edit of the show included Marc introducing Gloria's slot, however the actual date of broadcast remains uncertain. It's even possible that the performance was not used.

Wednesday 16th March

Unconfirmed television studio, Paris, France

Marc and Gloria again went to Paris to record a television spot for another French programme. There are no further details. It's likely that they didn't return from Paris until the following day.

Harvey Goldsmith Entertainments Presents

T.REX
PLUS ★ THE DAMNED

STARTS AT 7·30pm

MARCH 10th	NEWCASTLE, City Hall
MARCH 11th	MANCHESTER, Apollo, Ardwick
MARCH 12th	GLASGOW, Opollo
MARCH 13th	HANLEY, Victoira Hall Stoke-on-Trent
MARCH 14th	BRISTOL, Colston Hall
MARCH 17th	BIRMINGHAM, Odeon
MARCH 18th	LONDON, Rainbow Theatre

flyer

Thursday 17th March

Odeon, Birmingham, Warwickshire, England

Set list: 'Jeepster', 'Visions Of Domino', 'New York City', 'Soul Of My Suit', 'Groove A Little', 'Telegram Sam', 'Hang-Ups', 'Debora', 'I Love To Boogie', 'Teen Riot Structure', 'Dandy In The Underworld', 'Hot Love', 'Get It On'

Friday 18th March

Soul Of My Suit / All Alone (EMI T. Rex MARC 16)

The single failed to match the success of its parent album reaching a high point of 42.

"A couple of halfway decent ideas which unfortunately have nothing much to do with each other and therefore don't even clash in an interesting manner ... he sounds as if he's having trouble singing while keeping his cheeks sucked in."

Charles Shaar Murray, NME

"Marc Bolan is causing a little stir with his very lifelike impersonation of a Muppet ... although a lot of cynics are giving Marc stick for joining in the punk fun, his stance is far more endearing than that of those who ... are passing down negative comments. Unfortunately Marc recorded this single before he had listened to the new wave sound, so though his heart is in the right place, his music has not yet benefited from association with his new found friends."

Caroline Coon, Melody Maker

Rainbow Theatre, Finsbury Park, London, England
Set list: 'Jeepster', 'Visions Of Domino', 'New York City', 'Soul Of My Suit', 'Groove A Little', 'Telegram Sam', 'Hang-Ups', 'Debora', 'I Love To Boogie', 'Teen Riot Structure', 'Dandy In The Underworld', 'Hot Love', 'Get It On'

Saturday 19th March
Pavilion, West Runton, Norfolk, England
Set list: 'Jeepster', 'Visions Of Domino', 'New York City', 'Soul Of My Suit', 'Groove A Little', 'Telegram Sam', 'Hang-Ups', 'Debora', 'I Love To Boogie', 'Teen Riot Structure', 'Dandy In The Underworld', 'Hot Love', 'Get It On'

Sunday 20th March
Locarno, Portsmouth, Hampshire, England
Set list: 'Jeepster', 'Visions Of Domino', 'New York City', 'Soul Of My Suit', 'Groove A Little', 'Telegram Sam', 'Hang-Ups', 'Debora', 'I Love To Boogie', 'Teen Riot Structure', 'Dandy In The Underworld', 'Hot Love', 'Get It On'
(The Damned joined in) for the encore of 'Get It On'.

Tuesday 22nd March
Advision Studios, 23 Gosfield St., London, England
Recording session which saw several versions of 'Young Girl Of Love' recorded.

Wednesday 23rd March
BBC Television Centre, Wood Lane, Shepherd's Bush, London, England
A performance of 'Soul Of My Suit' was recorded for what was to be Bolan's last appearance on BBC Television's 'Top Of The Pops'. The appearance was broadcast on 24th March.

Thursday 24th March
Marc did a photo session for the 'Daily Mirror' with The Damned.
Broadcast date for the performance of 'Soul Of My Suit' recorded for 'Top Of The Pops' (BBC 1). See entry for 23rd March.

Tuesday 29th March
London Weekend Television Studios, Kent House, Southbank, London, England
The final edition of 'Supersonic' featured T. Rex performing live in the studio. One song, 'Soul Of My Suit', was performed using the same arrangement that the band had been playing on tour. T. Rex were then joined by other studio guests including Dave Edmunds, Ray Davies, Alvin

Stardust, Elkie Brooks, Gloria Jones and John Lodge for a rendition of 'Sweet Little Rock 'n' Roller'. Midway through the song Marc disappeared from camera shot, allegedly because he wanted to direct the show himself and/or to get Mike Mansfield on stage to sing along. Marc also introduced the programme in the trademark Mike Mansfield style. The programme was transmitted on 2nd April.

Saturday 2nd April

Transmission date for 'Soul Of My Suit' and 'Sweet Little Rock 'n' Roller' filmed for 'Supersonic' (ITV). See entry for 29th March.

Tuesday 5th April

Decibel Studios, Stamford Hill, London, England

Studio session recording demos. Other sessions were held throughout April. Among the songs recorded were: 'Mellow Love', 'Foxy Boy', '20th Century Baby', 'Shy Boy' (two takes), 'Hot George' and 'Love Drunk'.

For this particular recording session, Bolan used none of the regular members of T. Rex, opting instead to use session musicians. Eric Allen, Stan Berrer, Frank Riccotti and Ray Cooper worked on the songs.

Wednesday 6th April

Unconfirmed television studio, Paris, France (?)

Marc was again in Paris, probably for yet another television slot. No further details are available.

Friday 8th April

Trident Studios, St. Anne's Court, Soho, London, England

Mixing of songs recorded three days earlier with Ray Cooper adding more percussion overdubs.

Saturday 9th April

Air Studios, 214 Oxford Street, London, England

Date for a studio session that produced 'Boogie With Ya'll Baby', a track co-written with Gloria Jones.

Saturday 16th April

CBS Studios, London, England

A string arrangement, written and conducted by David Katz, was recorded on this date. Though it's not certain what song this was for. Probable candidates, 'Mellow Love' or 'Write Me A Song' appear to have been recorded after this session.

Monday 18th April

Air Studios, 214 Oxford Street, London, England

The single version of 'Dandy In The Underworld' was recorded on this date. This involved re-recording some guitar parts and adding strings and a new vocal track.

Monday 25th April
Air Studios, 214 Oxford Street, London, England
Recording session which resulted in the basic tracks for 'Love Drunk', 'Write Me A Song' and 'Celebrate Summer'.

Tuesday 26th April
Granada Television Studios, Manchester, Lancashire, England
Another television performance to promote 'Soul Of My Suit' took place on the Granada produced show 'Get It Together', another one of that company's kids' tea-time music programmes. T. Rex performed a live version of 'Soul Of My Suit' in the studio. The programme was networked the following day.

Wednesday 27th April
Transmission date on ITV networks for the edition of 'Get It Together' featuring 'Soul Of My Suit'. See entry for 26th April.

Friday 29th April
Air Studios, 214 Oxford Street, London, England
Recording session which produced basic track for 'Mellow Love'.

April
Decibel Studios, Stamford Hill, London, England
A demo session was held at the above studio probably in April, though it's possible an EMI studio was used. Four songs were recorded: 'Shy Girl' (2 takes), 'Love And The Foxy Girl' (2 takes), 'Hot George' and '20th Century Baby'. The only people involved in the session were Marc (vocals, bass and guitar), Dino Dines (clavinet, strings and synthesisers) and Miller Anderson (guitar, bass and possibly drums). In addition a drum machine was used. 'Shy Girl' and 'Love And The Foxy Girl' later had their titles changed.

Thursday 5th May
Air Studios, 214 Oxford Street, London, England
Studio session which produced further work on the backing tracks for 'Celebrate Summer' and 'Write Me A Song'.

Saturday 14th May
Air Studios, 214 Oxford Street, London, England
Bolan attended an Alfalpha session, co-producing and playing guitar on 'If I Just Can Get Through Tonight', though only Jeff Dexter received an actual production credit when the album was released. The song 'Spinning Around' was also completed on that day and may also feature Marc on guitar. He was partly at the studio to see the string arranger at work for possible future use on T. Rex recordings.

Monday 16th May
Air Studios, 214 Oxford Street, London, England
Another tape containing the single version of 'Dandy In The Underworld' was produced on this date. This was probably a production master for the forthcoming single release.

TISDAG 24/5.

Tuesday 24th May

Grona Lund, Stockholm, Sweden

The final T. Rex live concert took place in this park in Stockholm. Originally another date in Sweden was scheduled, but this was cancelled.

May (?)

Utopia Village, Chalcot Road, London NW1, England

Studio session which saw the recording of 'Weird Strings', the mellotron string section for 'Celebrate Summer'.

A second (undated) tape from this studio containing 'Classic Rap' and 'Teenage Angel' was also produced. These are solo demos. It's possible they were recorded at the same session.

Friday 3rd June

Dandy In The Underworld / Groove A Little / Tame My Tiger (EMI T. Rex MARC 17)

The single was the first (excluding the two non-T. Rex discs) since Pewter Suitor to fail to reach the charts.

"The very lovely Marc "I was the first punk" Bolan slows it right down for a deathly dirge suitable enough for the gloomiest of occasions. 'Tame My Tiger' on the B side... is up tempo and, excluding the horrendous intrusion of a cheapo cheapo string machine, has much more singles appeal...".

Caroline Coon, Melody Maker

"The title track ... is the kind of over solemn dog spittle that Marc gets into when he feels important. But 'Groove A Little' and 'Tame My Tiger' are unpretentious little rock pieces that ride around the turntable more than happily."

Charles Shaar Murray, NME

Monday 6th June

The Roundhouse, Chalk Farm, London, England

Marc attends The Ramones concert at the above venue and is photographed with the band after the gig.

Saturday 18th June

Popfestival, Sports Park, Boxmeer, Netherlands

A festival was scheduled for this date at the above venue. Other acts on the bill were Mr. Big, Golden Earring and several Dutch bands. T. Rex were scheduled to headline. However, it's extremely unlikely that the performance took place.

Wednesday 22nd June

Granada Television Studios, Manchester, Lancashire, England

An excellent live in the studio performance of 'Dandy In The Underworld' was included/wasted in this edition of 'Get It Together' which was networked on 29th June. It was to be the last time that Miller Anderson's performed with the band.

Wednesday 29th June

Transmission date of the edition of 'Get It Together' featuring 'Dandy In The Underworld' on ITV networks. See entry for 22nd June.

Tuesday 26th July

Air Studios, 214 Oxford Street, London, England
Probable date for the Steve Harley session which produced 'Amerika The Brave'.

Friday 5th August

Celebrate Summer / Ride My Wheels (EMI T. Rex MARC 18)
The second single in succession to disappoint commercially. It too failed to reach the charts. Marc's handwritten and typed lyric sheets seem to indicate 'Celebrate Summer' was originally titled 'Summer Celebration'.

"For one golden instant I thought Marc had finally pulled off the unalloyed pop triumph that he needs as a convincing viable follow up to 'Get It On'. This isn't it, but it's certainly the most likeable single he's made in a very long time ...".

Charles Shaar Murray, NME

Saturday 6th August

London Weekend Television Studios, Kent House, Southbank, London, England
Marc appeared on 'Saturday Scene', the LWT children's show. He was interviewed by Sally James and appeared alongside Helen Shapiro. The show was broadcast live.

Sunday 7th August

Unconfirmed studio, London, England
Marc held a studio session either at Decibel Studios in Stamford Hill or at Air Studios in Central London. What material was recorded remains unknown.

Tuesday 9th August

Granada Television Studios, Manchester, Lancashire, England
Recording date of the first edition of Granada's 'Marc' show. It featured mimed, but specially recorded versions of 'Sing Me A Song', 'I Love To Boogie', 'Celebrate Summer' and 'Jeepster'. The show was transmitted 24th August. Music tracks were recorded in the morning, while filming took place in the afternoon. This pattern was repeated for all the subsequent shows.

Wednesday 10th August

Granada Television Studios, Manchester, Lancashire, England
Recording for the second episode of 'Marc', networked on 31st August. This show included versions of 'Celebrate Summer', 'Ride A White Swan' and 'Endless Sleep'.

Monday 15th August

Granada Television Studios, Manchester, Lancashire, England
Marc spends time at Granada Studios working on the 'Marc' shows.

Monday 22nd August

Granada Television Studios, Manchester, Lancashire, England

This edition of 'Marc', broadcast on 7th September, included performances of 'Groove A Little', 'Let's Dance' 'Celebrate Summer' and 'Hot Love'.

Tuesday 23rd August

Granada Television Studios, Manchester, Lancashire, England

The fourth episode of 'Marc', broadcast on 14th September featured performances of 'New York City', another take of 'Endless Sleep', this one slightly longer than that previously shown and 'Dandy In The Underworld' featuring a live vocal by Bolan.

Wednesday 24th August

Transmission date for the first edition of 'Marc' on ITV networks. Like all Granada pop shows it went out late in the afternoon.

Wednesday 31st August

Transmission of the second edition of 'Marc' on ITV networks.

Sunday 4th September

Capital Radio, Euston, London, England

Marc appeared on 'Hullabaloo'. The interview had been pre-recorded, whether that day or earlier in the week remains unconfirmed.

Monday 5th September

Granada Television Studios, Manchester, Lancashire, England

It's possible that some work on the fifth and sixth episodes of 'Marc' was done on this date.

Tuesday 6th September

Granada Television Studios, Manchester, Lancashire, England

The penultimate edition of 'Marc' was recorded on this date and broadcast on 21st September. It featured another performance of 'Sing Me A Song', a video of Marc filmed in a park in Manchester "performing" 'Celebrate Summer' and a version of 'Get It On'.

Wednesday 7th September

Transmission of the third edition of 'Marc' on ITV networks. See entry for 22nd August.

Granada Television Studios, Manchester, Lancashire, England

The final edition of 'Marc', broadcast on 28th September featured a special guest appearance from David Bowie. T. Rex performed 'Debora' and 'Sing Me A Song'. Also included was the version of 'Ride A White Swan', as recorded for the second show. Bolan and T. Rex then backed Bowie on a version of 'Heroes', though they were not included in camera shot. Finally Bowie joined T. Rex for a live studio of a new song entitled 'Standing Next To You', a joint composition between Bolan and Bowie. The jam came to an abrupt halt when Bolan slipped from the stage when attempting to grab the microphone stand leaving Bowie in fits of laughter. There was no studio time available for a second take.

Friday 9th September
Unknown office, Victoria, London, England
Marc was interviewed by Dave Rooney, a fan, at Keith Altham's office in the early part of the afternoon. This was probably the last interview Marc gave.

Wednesday 14th September
Transmission of the fourth edition of 'Marc' on ITV networks.

Friday 16th September
In the early hours of the morning, following an evening spent at Morton's Club in London, Bolan is fatally injured in a car accident on Barnes Common, South West London when the Mini driven by Gloria Jones goes out of control and hits a tree at a notorious black spot on the road. Bolan, in the front passenger seat, takes the full brunt of the impact. Gloria Jones is also seriously injured. Her brother Richard, following in another car with a companion alerts emergency services. Bolan is pronounced dead on arrival at hospital. Within two hours of the accident the news has gone nation-wide.

Wednesday 21st September
Posthumous transmission of the fifth edition of 'Marc' on ITV networks.

Wednesday 28th September
Posthumous transmission of the final edition of 'Marc' on ITV networks.

Afterword

Despite extensive research, there are a number of concerts which I know to have taken place, but for which I have been unable to locate information.

Among these are appearences in Munich, Vienna and Essen all between 1968 and 1970. Some of these may have been as support act.

There are also several provincial British dates for which I would like to obtain further information, e.g. a 1968 appearance at Manchester's Magic Village.

If anybody has information regarding these particular appearences or anything else missing from the chronology, please contact me by e-mail at *klif@hotmail.com*.

Please use "Bolan info" as the subject header.

Thanks in advance.

Appendix

Proposed 1972 North American tour schedule

9th September   – Place des Arts, Montreal, Quebec, Canada
10th September   – Massey Hall, Toronto, Ontario, Canada
11th September   – Kleinhams Music Hall, Buffalo, New York, USA
12th September   – Cornell University, Ithica, New York, USA
13th September   – The Orpheum / Aquarius Theatre, Boston, Massachusetts, USA
14th September   – ABC Television Studios, New York, New York, USA – 'Dick Cavett Show'
15th September   – Academy Of Music, New York, New York, USA
16th September   – Academy Of Music, New York, New York, USA
17th September   – Spectrum, Philadelphia, Pennsylvania, USA
20th September   – Constitution Hall, Washington DC, USA
22nd September   – Municipal Auditorium, Atlanta, Georgia, USA
23rd September   – Syria Mosque Theatre, Pittsburgh, Pennsylvania, USA
24th September   – Music Hall, Cleveland, Ohio, USA
26th September   – University Butler, Muncie, Indiana, USA
27th September   – Music Hall, Cincinnati, Ohio, USA
29th September   – Ford Theatre, Detroit, Michigan, USA
30th September   – Arie Crown Theatre, Chicago, Illinois, USA
2nd October   – Kiel Auditorium, St. Louis, Missouri, USA
5th October   – Municipal Auditorium, Austin, Texas, USA
6th October   – Music Hall, Houston, Texas, USA
7th October   – McFarland Auditorium, Dallas, Texas, USA
8th October   – Civic Centre Music Hall, Oklahoma City, Oklahoma, USA
9th October   – Dick Clark – 'American Bandstand', New York, New York, USA
10th October   – Civic Auditorium, Santa Monica, California, USA
12th October   – Winterland, San Francisco, California, USA
13th October   – Seattle Arena, Seattle
15th October   – Vancouver Gardens, Vancouver, British Columbia, Canada

Proposed 1972 Australian tour schedule

8th December   – Kuyong Tennis Courts, Melbourne, Australia
9th December   – Milton Tennis Courts, Brisbane, Australia
10th December   – Randwick Race Course, Sydney, Australia
12th December   – Weston Springs, Auckland, New Zealand

14th December   –   Memorial Drive, Adelaide, Australia

16th December   –   Subiaco Stadium, Perth, Australia (later changed to the Wacca Cricket Ground)

Proposed 1974 North American tour schedule

26th September   –   Tower Theatre, Upper Darby, Pennsylvania, USA

27th September   –   Worcester Auditorium, Worcester, Massachusetts, USA

28th September   –   Erie County Field House, Erie, Pennsylvania, USA

29th September   –   Veterans Memorial Auditorium, Columbus, Ohio, USA

5th October   –   Academy Of Music, New York, New York, USA

6th October   –   Capitol Theatre, Portchester, New York, USA

9th October   –   Celebrity Theatre, Phoenix, Arizona, USA

10th October   –   Colisseum, Denver, Colorado, USA

12th October   –   Long Beach Arena, Long Beach, California, USA

13th October   –   Golden Hall, San Diego, California, USA

14th October   –   College Of The Desert, Palm Desert, California, USA

16th October   –   Arena, Medford, Oregon, USA

19th October   –   Memorial Arena, Victoria, British Columbia, Canada

21st October   –   Pacific Coliseum, Vancouver, British Columbia, Canada

22nd October   –   Kinsmen Fieldhouse, Edmonton, Alberta, Canada

23rd October   –   Stampede Corral, Calgary, Alberta, Canada

24th October   –   The Gymnasium, University Of Manitoba, Winnipeg, Manitoba, Canada

26th October   –   Ambassador Theatre, St. Louis, Missouri, USA

27th October   –   Ambassador Theatre, St. Louis, Missouri, USA

1st November   –   Villa Park, Villa Park, Illinois, USA

2nd November   –   Villa Park, Villa Park, Illinois, USA

3rd November   –   Riverside Theatre, Milwaukee, Wisconsin, USA

6th November   –   Civic Theatre, Minneapolis, Minnesota, USA

9th November   –   RKO Theatre, Davenport, Iowa, USA

10th November   –   Morris Auditorium, South Bend, Indiana, USA

13th November   –   Parthenon Theatre, Hammond, Indiana, USA

14th November   –   Armory, Fort Wayne, Indiana, USA

15th November   –   Armory, Fort Wayne, Indiana, USA

18th November   –   Auditorium, Grand Rapids, Michigan, USA

19th November   –   Auditorium, Grand Rapids, Michigan, USA

22nd November   –   Michigan Palace, Detroit, Michigan, USA

23rd November   –   Michigan Palace, Detroit, Michigan, USA

24th November   –   Agora Ballroom, Columbus, Ohio, USA

25th November   –   Agora Ballroom, Cleveland, Ohio, USA

27th November   –   Albee Theatre, Cincinnati, Ohio, USA

29th November   –   Savannah Civic Theatre, Savannah, Georgia, USA

30th November   –   Savannah Civic Theatre, Savannah, Georgia, USA

Proposed 1976 British Isles dates

4th February   –   Town Hall, Yeovil, Somerset, England

13th February   –   Parr Hall, Warrington, Lancashire, England

22nd February   –   New Theatre, Cardiff, Glamorgan, Wales

23rd February	–	Ireland
24th February	–	Ireland
25th February	–	Ireland
26th February	–	Ireland
27th February	–	Ireland
29th February	–	Civic Hall, Barrow, Cumbria, England
5th March	–	Carnegie Hall, Dunfermline, Fife, Scotland
7th March	–	Unspecified venue, Dundee, Angus, Scotland

Proposed 1977 French Tour Schedule

3rd February	–	Nantes
4th February	–	Nantes
5th February	–	Toulouse
7th February	–	Paris
9th February	–	Lyon
10th February	–	Gien
11th February	–	Paris
12th February	–	Caen

Other Titles available from Helter Skelter

Coming Soon

Steve Marriott: The Definitive Biography
by Paolo Hewitt and John Hellier £18.99
Marriott was the prime mover behind 60s chart-toppers The Small Faces. Longing to be treated as a serious musician he formed Humble Pie with Peter Frampton, where his blistering rock 'n' blues guitar playing soon saw him take centre stage in the US live favourites. After years in seclusion, Marriott's plans for a comeback in 1991 were tragically cut short when he died in a housefire. He continues to be a key influence for generations of musicians from Paul Weller to Oasis and Blur.

Pink Floyd: A Saucerful of Secrets
by Nicholas Schaffner £12.99
Long overdue reissue of the authoritative and detailed account of one of the most important and popular bands in rock history. From the psychedelic explorations of the Syd Barrett-era to 70s superstardom with Dark Side of the Moon, and on to triumph of The Wall, before internecine strife tore the group apart. Schaffner's definitive history also covers the improbable return of Pink Floyd without Roger Waters, and the hugely successful Momentary Lapse of Reason album and tour.

The Dark Reign of Gothic Rock:
In The Reptile House with The Sisters of Mercy, Bauhaus and The Cure
by Dave Thompson £12.99
From Joy Division to Nine Inch Nails and from Siouxsie and the Banshees to Marilyn Manson, gothic rock has endured as the cult of choice for the disaffected and the alienated. The author traces the rise of 80s and 90s goth from influences such as Hammer House of Horror movies and schlock novels, through post-punk into the full blown drama of Bauhaus, The Cure and the Sisters of Mercy axis.

Psychedelic Furs: Beautiful Chaos
by Dave Thompson £12.99
Psychedelic Furs were the ultimate post-punk band – combining the chaos and vocal rasp of the Sex Pistols with a Bowie-esque glamour. The Furs hit the big time when John Hughes wrote a movie based on their early single "Pretty in Pink". Poised to join U2 and Simple Minds in the premier league, they withdrew behind their shades, remaining a cult act, but one with a hugely devoted following.

Bob Dylan: Like The Night (Revisited)
by CP Lee £9.99
Fully revised and updated B-format edition of the hugely acclaimed document of Dylan's pivotal 1966 show at the Manchester Free Trade Hall where fans called him Judas for turning his back on folk music in favour of rock 'n' roll.

The Nice: Hang On To A Dream
by Martyn Hanson
The Nice were Keith Emerson's band prior to superstardom with Emerson, Lake and Palmer. Formed as a backing band for soul singer PP Arnold, The Nice went on to lay the foundations for what would become progressive rock. Their debut LP mixed rock with jazz and classical music, but it was their hard rock reinvention of Leonard Bernstein's "America" that took them into the US and UK charts, and influenced their biggest fan Jimi Hendrix to reinterpret "The Star Spangled Banner."

Marc Bolan and T Rex: A Chronology
by Cliff McLenahan £13.99
Bolan was the ultimate glam-rock icon; beautiful, elfin, outrageously dressed and capable of hammering out impossibly catchy teen rock hits such as "Telegram Sam", and "Get It On". With their pounding guitars and three chord anthems T Rex paved the way for hard rock and punk rock.

The Sharper Word: A Mod Anthology
Ed Paolo Hewitt £9.99
Hard-to-find pieces by Tom Wolfe, novelist Tony Parsons, poet laureate Andrew Motion, disgraced Tory grandee Jonathan Aitken, Nik Cohn, Colin MacInnes, Mary Quant, et al, document the clothes, the music, the clubs, the drugs and the faces behind one of the most misunderstood and enduring cultural movements.

Back to the Beach: A Brian Wilson and the Beach Boys Reader
Ed Kingsley Abbott £12.99
Revised and expanded edition of the Beach Boys compendium Mojo magazine deemed an "essential purchase." This collection includes all of the best articles, interviews and reviews from the Beach Boys' four decades of music, including definitive pieces by Timothy White, Nick Kent and David Leaf. New material reflects on the tragic death of Carl Wilson and documents the rejuvenated Brian's return to the boards. "Rivetting!" **** Q "An essential purchase." Mojo

Harmony in My Head
The Original Buzzcock Steve Diggle's Rock 'n' Roll Odyssey
by Steve Diggle and Terry Rawlings £12.99
First-hand account of the punk wars from guitarist and one half of the songwriting duo that gave the world three chord punk-pop classics like "Ever Fallen In Love" and "Promises". Diggle dishes the dirt on punk contemporaries like The Sex Pistols, The Clash and The Jam, as well as sharing poignant memories of his friendship with Kurt Cobain, on

whose last ever tour, The Buzzcocks were support act.

Serge Gainsbourg: A Fistful of Gitanes
by Sylvie Simmons £9.99
Rock press legend Simmons' hugely acclaimed biography of the French genius.
"I would recommend A Fistful of Gitanes [as summer reading] which is a highly entertaining biography of the French singer-songwriter and all-round scallywag"- JG Ballard
"A wonderful introduction to one of the most overlooked songwriters of the 20th century" (Number 3, top music books of 2001) *The Times*
"The most intriguing music-biz biography of the year" *The Independent*
"Wonderful. Serge would have been so happy" – Jane Birkin

Marillion: Separated Out
by Jon Collins £14.99
From the chart hit days of Fish and "Kayleigh" to the Steve Hogarth incarnation, Marillion have continued to make groundbreaking rock music. Collins tells the full story, drawing on interviews with band members, associates, and the experiences of some of the band's most dedicated fans.

Blues: The British Connection
by Bob Brunning £12.99
Former Fleetwood Mac member Bob Brunning's classic account of the impact of Blues in Britain, from its beginnings as the underground music of 50s teenagers like Mick Jagger, Keith Richards and Eric Clapton, to the explosion in the 60s, right through to the vibrant scene of the present day.
'An invaluable reference book and an engaging personal memoir' – Charles Shaar Murray

On The Road With Bob Dylan
by Larry Sloman £12.99
In 1975, as Bob Dylan emerged from 8 years of seclusion, he dreamed of putting together a travelling music show that would trek across the country like a psychedelic carnival. The dream became a reality, and On The Road With Bob Dylan is the ultimate behind-the-scenes look at what happened. When Dylan and the Rolling Thunder Revue took to the streets of America, Larry "Ratso" Sloman was with them every step of the way.
"The War and Peace of Rock and Roll." – Bob Dylan

Currently Available from Helter Skelter

Gram Parsons: God's Own Singer
By Jason Walker £12.99
Brand new biography of the man who pushed The Byrds into country-rock territory on Sweethearts of The Rodeo, and quit to form the Flying Burrito Brothers. Gram lived hard, drank hard, took every drug going and somehow invented country rock, paving the way for Crosby, Stills & Nash, The Eagles and Neil Young. Parsons' second solo LP, Grievous Angel, is a haunting masterpiece of country soul. By the time it was released, he had been dead for 4 months. He was 26 years old.
"Walker has done an admirable job in taking us as close to the heart and soul of Gram Parsons as any author could." **** *Uncut* book of the month

Ashley Hutchings: The Guvnor and the Rise of Folk Rock – Fairport Convention, Steeleye Span and the Albion Band
by Geoff Wall and Brian Hinton £14.99
As founder of Fairport Convention and Steeleye Span, Ashley Hutchings is the pivotal figure in the history of folk rock. This book draws on hundreds of hours of interviews with Hutchings and other folk-rock artists and paints a vivid picture of the scene that also produced Sandy Denny, Richard Thompson, Nick Drake, John Martyn and Al Stewart.

Al Stewart: True Life Adventures of a Folk Troubadour
by Neville Judd £20.00
Authorised biography of the Scottish folk hero behind US Top Ten hit "Year of The Cat". This is a vivid insider's account of the pivotal 60s London coffee house scene that kickstarted the careers of a host of folkies including Paul Simon – with whom Al shared a flat in 1965 – as well as the wry memoir of a 60s folk star's tribulations as he becomes a chart-topping star in the US in the 70s. Highly limited hardcover edition!

Rainbow Rising: The Story of Ritchie Blackmore's Rainbow
by Roy Davies £14.99
Blackmore led rock behemoths Deep Purple to international, multi-platinum, mega-stardom. He quite in '75, to form Rainbow, one of the great live bands, with Ronnie James Dio and enjoyed a string of acclaimed albums and hit singles, including "All Night Long" and "Since You've Been Gone" before the egos of the key players caused the whole thing to implode. A great rock 'n' roll tale.

ISIS: A Bob Dylan Anthology
Ed Derek Barker £14.99
Expertly compiled selection of rare articles which trace the evolution of rock's greatest talent. From Bob's earliest days in New York City to the more recent legs of the Never Ending Tour, and his new highly acclaimed album, Love and Theft, the ISIS archive has exclusive interview material – often rare or previously unpublished – with many of the key players in Dylan's career: his parents, friends, musicians and other collaborators.

The Beach Boys' Pet Sounds: The Greatest Album of the Twentieth Century
by Kingsley Abbott £11.95
Pet Sounds is the 1966 album that saw The Beach Boys graduate from lightweight pop like "Surfin' USA", et al, into a vehicle for the mature compositional genius of Brian Wilson. The album was hugely influential, not least on The Beatles. This the full story of the album's background, its composition and recording, its contemporary reception and its enduring legacy.

King Crimson: In The Court of King Crimson
by Sid Smith £14.99
King Crimson's 1969 masterpiece In The Court Of The Crimson King, was a huge U.S. chart hit. The band followed it with 40 further albums of consistently challenging, distinctive and innovative music. Drawing on hours of new interviews, and encouraged by Crimson supremo Robert Fripp, the author traces the band's turbulent history year by year, track by track.

A Journey Through America with the Rolling Stones
by Robert Greenfield UK Price £9.99
Featuring a new foreword by Ian Rankin
This is the definitive account of their legendary '72 tour.
"Filled with finely-rendered detail ... a fascinating tale of times we shall never see again" Mojo

Razor Edge: Bob Dylan and The Never-ending Tour
by Andrew Muir £12.99
Respected Dylan expert Andrew Muir documents the ups and downs of this unprecedented trek, and finds time to tell the story of his own curious meeting with Dylan.
Muir also tries to get to grips with what exactly it all means – both for Dylan and for the Bobcats: dedicated Dylan followers, like himself, who trade tapes of every show and regularly cross the globe to catch up with the latest leg of The Never Ending Tour.

Calling Out Around the World: A Motown Reader
Edited by Kingsley Abbott £13.99
With a foreword by Martha Reeves, this is a unique collection of articles which tell the story of the rise of a black company in a white industry, and its talented stable of artists, musicians, writers and producers. Included are rare interviews with key figures such as Berry Gordy, Marvin Gaye, Smokey Robinson and Florence Ballard as well as reference sources for collectors and several specially commissioned pieces.

I've Been Everywhere: A Johnny Cash Chronicle
by Peter Lewry £12.99
A complete chronological illustrated diary of Johnny Cash's concerts, TV appearances, record releases, recording sessions and other milestones. From his early days with Sam Phillips in Memphis to international stardom, the wilderness years of the mid-sixties, and on to his legendary prison concerts and his recent creative resurgence with the hugely successful 2000 release, American Recording III: Solitary Man.

Sandy Denny: No More Sad Refrains
by Clinton Heylin £13.99
Paperback edition of the highly acclaimed biography of the greatest female singer-songwriter this country has ever produced.

Emerson Lake and Palmer: The Show That Never Ends
by George Forrester, Martin Hanson and Frank Askew £14.00
Drawing on years of research, the authors have produced a gripping and fascinating document of the prog-rock supergroup who remain one of the great rock bands of the seventies.

Animal Tracks: The Story of The Animals
by Sean Egan £12.99
Sean Egan has enjoyed full access to surviving Animals and associates and has produced a compelling portrait of a truly distinctive band of survivors.

Like a Bullet of Light: The Films of Bob Dylan
by CP Lee £12.99
In studying in-depth an often overlooked part of Dylan's oeuvre.

Rock's Wild Things: The Troggs Files
by Alan Clayson and Jacqueline Ryan £12.99
Respected rock writer Alan Clayson has had full access to the band and traces their history from 60s Andover rock roots to 90s covers, collaborations and corn circles. Also features the full transcript of the legendary "Troggs Tapes."

Waiting for the Man: The Story of Drugs and Popular Music
by Harry Shapiro UK Price £12.99
Fully revised edition of the classic story of two intertwining billion dollar industries.
"Wise and witty." The Guardian

Dylan's Daemon Lover: The Tangled Tale of a 450-Year Old Pop Ballad
by Clinton Heylin UK price £12.00
Written as a detective story, Heylin unearths the mystery of why Dylan knew enough to return "The House Carpenter" to its 16th century source.

Get Back: The Beatles' Let It Be Disaster
by Doug Sulpy & Ray Schweighardt UK price £12.99
No-holds barred account of the power struggles, the bickering, and the bitterness that led to the break-up of the greatest band in the history of rock 'n' roll.
"One of the most poignant Beatles books ever." Mojo

XTC: Song Stories – The Exclusive & Authorised Story
by XTC and Neville Farmer £12.99
"A cheerful celebration of the minutiae surrounding XTC's music with the band's musical passion intact ... high in setting-the-record-straight anecdotes. Superbright, funny, commanding." Mojo

Born in the USA: Bruce Springsteen and the American Tradition
by Jim Cullen £9.99
"Cullen has written an excellent treatise expressing exactly how and why Springsteen translated his uneducated hicktown American-ness into music and stories that touched hearts and souls around the world." Q****

Bob Dylan
by Anthony Scaduto £10.99
The first and best biography of Dylan. "The best book ever written on Dylan" Record Collector "Now in a welcome reprint it's a real treat to read the still-classic Bobography". Q*****

Mail Order

All Helter Skelter, Firefly and SAF titles are available by mail order from the world famous Helter Skelter bookshop.
You can either phone or fax your order to Helter Skelter on the following numbers:

Telephone: +44 (0)20 7836 1151 or Fax: +44 (0)20 7240 9880
Office hours: Mon-Fri 10:00am – 7:00pm,
Sat: 10:00am – 6:00pm, Sun: closed.

Postage prices per book worldwide are as follows:

UK & Channel Islands	£1.50
Europe & Eire (air)	£2.95
USA, Canada (air)	£7.50
Australasia, Far East (air)	£9.00
Overseas (surface)	£2.50

You can also write enclosing a cheque, International Money Order, or registered cash. Please include postage. DO NOT send cash. DO NOT send foreign currency, or cheques drawn on an overseas bank. Send to:

Helter Skelter Bookshop,
4 Denmark Street, London, WC2H 8LL, United Kingdom.
If you are in London come and visit us, and browse the titles in person!!

Email: helter@skelter.demon.co.uk
Website: http://www.skelter.demon.co.uk